The Originals

The Originals:
The New York Celtics
Invent Modern Basketball

Murry Nelson

Bowling Green State University Popular Press
Bowling Green, OH 43403

A Sports and Culture Publication

Series editors

Douglas Noverr
Larry Ziewacz

Copyright 1999 © Bowling Green State University Popular Press

Library of Congress Cataloging-in-Publication Data
Nelson, Murry.
    The Originals : the New York Celtics invent modern basketball /
Murry Nelson.
        p.   cm.
    Includes bibliographical references (p.   ).
    ISBN 0-87972-793-4 (cloth). -- ISBN 0-87972-794-2 (pbk.)
    1. Original Celtics (Basketball team)   I. Title.
GV885.52.073N45   1999
796.323'64'097471--dc21
                                                    99-22733
                                                        CIP

Cover design by Dumm Art

CONTENTS

ACKNOWLEDGMENTS

This book was first conceived in 1991 and I have been carrying out the research and writing on this volume since that time. Obviously, when one spends so much time on producing such a work, many people become instrumental in achieving the final result. I hope that I can remember all of them. Wayne Patterson of the James Naismith Memorial Basketball Hall of Fame Archives and library was of great assistance. He provided everything that I asked for and even more than I hoped for at the library's archives. Librarians at Penn State University's Pattee Library were also helpful, particularly those at Interlibrary Loan where I was able to receive many microfilms of newspapers from the 1920s.

I interviewed a number of people, but most helpful were the late Les Harrison, Harry Litwack, the late Shirley Povich, Hal Lebovitz, Norton Rose, Edward Reilly, Richard Triptow, and Richard Lapchick. Gus Alfieri provided information and understanding. Rob Edsall drew the maps that appear in the book. Ken Tuckey provided materials on Horse Haggerty from the *Reading Eagle*. David Trevaskis provided legal documents. In addition, Steve Correia of St. Norbert College, Ron Smith and Jack Selzer of Penn State, and Doug Noverr of Michigan State read early drafts of the manuscript. Doug was vital in his review of the manuscript and I sincerely appreciate his encouragement as well as his willingness to help me bring the book together. Many of my professional colleagues at the North American Society for Sport History and the Popular Culture Association encouraged me over the years and I thank them for their support.

In my trips to Springfield, my sister-in-law Susan Sagendorf and her husband, John, provided me with a place to stay, good food, and company. My wife, Elizabeth, was supportive despite the inconveniences of my traveling to examine materials or interview subjects, leaving her to walk the dogs and chauffeur the children.

The manuscript was prepared many times by a number of staff assistants in the Department of Curriculum and Instruction at Penn State. I thank all of them and the department for support and patience with this work.

I wish to thank Diane Knerr for her careful editing of the manuscript.

No one, of course, can take responsibility for any of the material that may appear here. That is mine alone. This book has been arduous to assemble but it was gratifying to know that the Original Celtics may now get some of the long-forgotten recognition that they richly deserve. If my book helps in that manner, I am honored, since my greatest debt is to this team that has provided me with so much pleasure more than a half century after they ceased to play competitive basketball.

Murry Nelson
July 1999

INTRODUCTION

APRIL 1921

In New York City in mid-April of 1921 the weather was still cool and damp. The headlines spoke of continual war reparations from Germany, starvation in Russia and the open-door policy in China. Of more concern to most New Yorkers was the opening of the baseball season. The Yankees, led by Babe Ruth, were hopeful of succeeding Cleveland as American League Champions. Basketball, specifically professional basketball, did not exist, judging by the coverage (or lack of it) in the New York City newspapers.

Nevertheless, more than 10,000 fans found their way on Saturday night, April 16, to the 71st Regiment Armory on New York's east side to watch the New York Whirlwinds of Tex Rickard meet the original Celtics owned by Jim and Tom Furey. A crowd of such size was startling for any indoor sporting event, but even more so for a basketball game being played long after the college season had ended.

This game, however, was of singular interest. It pitted two New York City squads, both claiming basketball supremacy, against one another. The Whirlwinds had been recently assembled by George Lewis "Tex" Rickard, a former gold miner in Alaska, saloon owner in the western United States and for the past ten years promoter of championship heavyweight boxing matches beginning with the Jack Johnson-Jim Jefferies bout in Reno in 1910. After relocating to New York City he had promoted boxing matches in Madison Square Garden leasing the arena for the Jess Willard-Frank Moran fight.

After World War I the Rickard-Madison Square Garden partnership became firmly established with enormous help by Rickard's "discovery" of Jack Dempsey whose bouts after 1919 were handled by Rickard. Having signed a ten-year lease with New York Life, the Garden's owners, in 1920, Rickard promoted horse shows, track meets, the circus, political conventions as well as boxing matches.[1] He formed the Whirlwinds with the intention of using them to showcase professional basketball in the Garden. However, after drawing only 1428 spectators to an opening season game against the Eastern League champion, Camden, Rickard moved his squad to armories around the city.[2]

Rickard assembled an impressive squad. The leading scorer was Barney Sedran, a 5-foot 4-inch forward who had played for the City College of New York from 1909 to 1911, had been a professional star for nearly ten years, and held the all-time record for field goals in a game. He scored 17 field goals in 1913-14 while playing for Utica in the New York State League. More impressive than the 17 field goals is that they were made with an open basket, since the New York State League was the last to add backboards in the 1921-22 season.

Sedran had teamed with Max (Marty) Friedman since playing in their New York City neighborhood as youngsters in the early 1900s. Though he began playing professionally at sixteen, Friedman "officially" turned professional in 1910 at the age of twenty-one when the Hudson River League was formed. He earned $5 per game. Teaming with Sedran in Utica in 1913-14, Carbondale of the Pennsylvania Intercounty League in 1914-15, Jasper of the Eastern League in 1915-17, and Albany of the New York State League in 1920-21, the two became known as the "Heavenly Twins" because of their skill and winning ways. The two were joined once again on the Whirlwinds.[3]

A third Whirlwind starter was Nat Holman, a graduate of Savage School of Physical Education and the coach of the City College of New York. Acknowledged as one of the two greatest players of the 1920s (Johnny Beckman was the other), Holman could shoot, pass, drive and play defense as well as any player in basketball. During the 1920-21 season Holman played for Germantown of the Eastern League, where he led the league in scoring and the Germs to the Eastern League title, as well as for Scranton, champions of The Pennsylvania State League.

Holman's running mate at guard was Harry Riconda, an experienced professional in both the Eastern and The Pennsylvania State League. He was also a teammate of Sedran and Friedman on the Albany Senators, champions of the New York State League.

The center of the Whirlwinds was Chris Leonard, a graduate of Manhattan College in 1912 and a former infantryman in World War I. Though only six feet tall, he was a good jumper. He began his professional career with Albany. He had also played for Germantown in the Eastern League and Pittston of The Pennsylvania State League, where in 1920-21 he finished fifth in the league in scoring.

The Whirlwind's foes were the original Celtics, a team first formed in 1914 and composed of young Irish lads affiliated with a settlement house on New York's west side. After World War I Jim and Tom Furey had reconstituted the team as the Original Celtics with only Pete Barry, a New York State League player, a holdover from the pre-World War I squad. Barry, a six-footer, began his professional career in 1915 and, at age twenty-four in 1921 was a seasoned professional who was an excellent all around player. He would remain a Celtic player until 1936 when he retired from the game.

The unquestioned star of the Celtics was the aforementioned Johnny Beckman, a five-foot, nine-inch forward who was known as the Babe Ruth of basketball because of his spectacular shooting. As early as 1914 Beckman was known as a prolific scorer with Kingston in the New York State League. In both 1920 and 1921 while playing for Nanticoke he led The Pennsylvania State League in scoring. In 1918 and 1920 while playing for DeNeri he had also led the Eastern League in scoring.

Henry G. (Dutch) Dehnert was a barrel-chested six-footer who had played with Beckman at Nanticoke in 1920, then with Beckman at Thompsonville in the Interstate League and with Scranton in The Pennsylvania State League. Dehnert is often credited with inventing the give and go in the pivot; though that is unlikely, he and the Celtics perfected it.

Oscar (Swede) Grimstead had played professional basketball for many years, starting with various independent teams, then with Utica of the New York State League in 1913. He switched to DeNeri of the Eastern League the next year. In 1920 and 1921 he played for Pittston in The Pennsylvania State League as well as Trenton in the Eastern League.

Ernie Reich, a New York City native, was the Celtic captain who began his career as a professional with White Plains of the Hudson River League. He was a veteran of the Interstate, Eastern and The Pennsylvania State Leagues, captaining Scranton in 1919 when they were The Pennsylvania State League champions in the first half of the season. He averaged almost seven points per game for Reading in 1921 as well as for Scranton in 1920. Within a year he was dead.

These players had been playing with/or against each other for years. They had perfected their games and both teams laid claim to the title of world champion. Most of the players were from New York City yet the professional game had never been successful in that city. The few franchises that tried to succeed there soon folded as fans stayed away in droves because of lack of interest. Thus, this contest, and the following one that drew 8,000 to the 69th Regiment Armory, were seen as possible signs of future financial success for a professional team playing in a league and representing New York City.

The teams were to meet in a best of three series, first at the 71st Regiment Armory where international or amateur rules would be followed at the choice of the Whirlwinds. This meant that there would be one designated free-throw shooter for all fouls shot by each team. Also, the discontinued (double) dribble was not allowed, there would be two referees rather than one (actually a referee and an umpire) as well as a few other less vital rule differences.

The court itself differed in amateur and professional rules in terms of court size and the use of a cage, though the latter point was not enforced and a cage was used by most professional teams. Either made of wire mesh or fish net, the cage surrounded the court to a height of no less than eleven feet. The cage kept the ball in continuous play, which meant the games were finished in about one hour with twenty-minute halves and a brief half-time break. It also served to protect the players from unruly fans who would throw items at the players, jab them when they came near the cage "walls" and even burned them with lit cigarettes. Play was "live" off the net so the ball could be passed off it or even shot into the basket using the net![4]

The size of the court was to be 65 feet long and 35 feet wide. The rules stated that "under no circumstances can a floor be more than five feet short in either length or width, and then only by two-thirds vote of the managers."[5] Official balls were between 30 and 32 inches in circumference and between 21 and 24 ounces in weight, which are heavier and larger than today's official basketballs.

The game was one of fast ball movement, patience before shooting, and tough defense. Games were extremely rough and it was common to have players knocked out in the course of a contest. Because there was no center court line, no ten-second rule, and no backcourt violation, teams often stayed in their end passing the ball and moving slowly up court in search of an opening before shooting. Shooting and rebounding were usually done on the floor; few players "took to the air." It was not that players did not see the advantages to such plays; they did, but they also saw the disadvantages.

The games then were short, very rough and low scoring with fouls called for offenses such as holding, tripping, blocking, charging, and others but all at the discretion of the referee. Players could be disqualified at any time for unnecessary roughness, profanity, slugging, etc., but most referees would not do this without repeated warnings. There was no certain number of fouls that eliminated a player (college rules allowed four before disqualification in the early 1920s).

The appeal of the game seemed to be reflective of the players—few went to college and most were from working-class families and minority ethnic groups. The most prominent ethnic groups were the Irish and the Jews, with a smattering of Germans, Poles, Czechs and Scandinavians. Most had learned the game in eastern cities, often at settlement houses, ethnic athletic clubs or churches affiliated with these sites. The fans would often be limited in appreciation of technique, but were highly impressed by the rough play that characterized the game, similar to the hard checking in today's hockey games. The ball movement would have been appreciated by soccer followers, of whom there were many at that time, though the subtlety of passing and dribbling may have been lost to fans of a game they may have never played. The newness of the game itself meant that it was often being reshaped by its young, devoted practitioners.

Game one of the series was played on a Saturday night in mid April, though the date is in dispute. Media coverage of professional basketball, particularly in April, was not simply poor; it was nonexistent. In New York, the *Times* which Peterson called, "even then the paper of record," did not carry a line of type on the games. The *Herald* with a much more extensive sports section matched the *Times*' lack of coverage as did the *Philadelphia Inquirer,* the paper of unofficial Eastern League reporting. The *Cleveland Plain Dealer,* the *Chicago Tribune,* and the *New York Tribune* all ignored these contests. A week later the *Wilkes Barre Record,* the chronicle of The Pennsylvania State League, carried a long paragraph account of the first game that was played on the previous Saturday, April 16.

The lack of media coverage for the Celtic-Whirlwind contests was not just a result of the overwhelming popularity of baseball and its dominance of the sport pages as the new season began. Rather it was reflective of the disdain with which the media held the sport of professional basketball. To the media the game was dirty, rough and played by uneducated ruffians unlike the college game which was widely covered by the newspapers and seen as a cleaner, purer sport. Likewise, there were those who saw *all* professional sports as tainted, with the Black Sox Scandal of the 1919 World Series just coming to trial at that time. Newspapers, of course, would have covered the sport if their customers would have demanded it. However, there seemed less concern in a city the size of New York than in the smaller cities like Scranton, Trenton, and Reading where professional basketball was the only "big league" activity.

This situation was not replicated in Philadelphia where the Eastern League was well covered by the *Inquirer.* New York, however, was not much for professional basketball even though most of the players were from there. In the 1921-22 season the Celtics drew large crowds, but these began to dwindle in the next season. In 1926 when the Celtics joined the American Basketball League, New York papers, even the *Times,* finally gave them regular, though not extensive coverage.

Despite the lack of newspaper coverage, the fans showed up at the 71st Regiment Armory. Since Furey was always promoting his Celtics and Rickard's "life" was promotions, it would be safe to assume that they devised some network to communicate news of the contests to potential spectators.

Approximately 10,000-11,000 spectators viewed game one. Two referees, Alex Turner and long time Eastern League official Ward Brennan, refereed the clash. They called 53 fouls, 28 on the Whirlwinds, 25 on the Celts. The Whirlwinds, "wormed the ball up under the basket repeatedly and tried no more than four long shots, each of which tallied,"[6] while the Celtics "resorted to heaving and fell down lamentably in these tactics."[7]

The game was won by the Whirlwinds, 40-29 (or 40-27).[8] During the game Holman had 22 points all on team foul shots. Sedran was reported to have made five of the Whirlwind's total nine field goals. Beckman had 25 points, 23 free throws and a basket. Grimsted and Barry picked up the other two baskets.

Later that week, probably on Wednesday April 20, the teams met again, this time in the 69th Regiment Armory where 8,000 more fans jammed the arena to see the Celts win 26-24. In that game, professional rules were used and each player shot his own foul shots. Again Beckman led the Celtics in scoring with 17 of the 26 points and all three Celtic field goals. The Whirlwinds had more field goals with six, but fewer free throws with twelve. Sedran and Leonard each had two baskets.

After these two games, there was certainly a great deal of anticipation for game three of the series. It never took place and probable reasons were fear of rioting fans, lack of agreement on money and Furey's offer to Holman and Leonard to join the Celtics.

What is true is that Furey did sign the two Whirlwinds for the Celtics shortly afterward. Sedran credits this for the Whirlwinds being disbanded. And the acquisition of Holman and Leonard would be the two pieces that would complete the Celtics. Beginning in the 1921-22 season, the Celtics with Holman, Leonard, Barry, Beckman and Dehnert as the core began their dominance of professional basketball, a dominance that only ended with the dissolution of the Celtics in the spring of 1928. At that time Holman, Leonard, Barry and Dehnert were still the core of the team with Beckman having been traded in mid-season the year before.

No team compared to the Celtics in the 1920s in innovation, intelligence, skill, and winning percentage. The Celtic Era of Professional Basketball has faded in the memory of those who follow the game. It is a fate undeserving of their greatness and one that this volume hopes to alter.

1

NEW IMMIGRANTS, NEW SPORT—
THE CULTURAL SYMBIOSIS
OF BASKETBALL AND ETHNIC GROUPS

Post-war America is often depicted as a happy-go-lucky boom time—the Roaring 20s with its carefree flappers and all the bathtub gin one could want. To a certain extent that was true, but to a large extent that period was one of struggle and competing ideas of America. Geoffrey Perret notes that the 1920s were "The first decade of the twentieth century . . . (though) still large areas of American life (were) in the grip of the Victorian/Puritan/Frontier past. It was the struggle between these two worlds that gave tension and shape (to the decade). . . ."[1]

Some data may help to illustrate these tensions brought on by sharp dichotomies moving toward reconciliation. In 1920, 81 percent of the U.S. population was native born whites, but only 3/4 of those whites were the children of native born parents. Over 20 percent of the population had foreign parents with nearly 14 percent of the white population foreign born. The remaining ten percent of the population were American Negroes with almost all of them living in squalor in the South.[2] Thus, the figurative and occasionally literal clash of new immigrants, second-generation Americans, and blacks leaving the South to settle in Northern cities resulted in tension in many urban areas.

American immigration had peaked during the twenty years prior to World War I and most of those immigrants remained in the city of arrival, usually New York. Despite the sharp reduction in immigration because of the Great War, the nation retained strong xenophobic attitudes. These culminated in the passage of restrictive immigration laws in 1921 and 1924.

Economically, the "boom" times affected the wealthy much more than the middle and lower classes. In 1920, the top 1 percent of the population (financially) earned 15 percent of all earned income. By 1929, one-third of all personal income was earned by the top 5 percent and approximately 5 percent of all stockholders held 77 percent of all stock.[3] The U.S. economy "was very largely unregulated and in consequence its overall benefits were very unevenly distributed."[4] The economic and political isolationism of the decade meant few foreign markets were

7

available for American products. Thus, there was an increasing demand for absorption on the domestic markets which became glutted within the decade, an early foreshadowing of the economic turmoil to come in the 1930s. Yet undeniably the decade was one of tremendous change, excitement, and accomplishment."[5]

America was undergoing large social changes throughout the 1920s which exacerbated underlying tensions between various groups (the wealthy and the working class, between generations, rural-urban conflicts). Regarding the latter conflict, for the first time, in 1920, more Americans were living in towns than in the country.[6]

Thus America was far from a homogeneous, stable, and universally prosperous society and tensions sometimes bubbled to the surface. Immigration laws were one institutional equilibrator to reduce the stresses and strains within society. Another such device was the development of spectator sports and team loyalties which served to channel aggression into socially acceptable directions.[7] "It was in the twenties that sport became the all-consuming interest that we know so well."[8] As both Allen[9] and Carter[10] observed, athletic competitions had become national mass entertainment and "Freed from the exhausting work disciplines of the nineteenth century, Americans were, in fact, discovering sports directly."[11]

"In 1928 it was estimated that almost one-fourth of the national income was spent for leisure activities" and, of that, approximately $200 million was spent on sports in some manner.[12] The reasons why sport became so popular at that time were summarized by Noverr and Ziewacz. These included the following:

1. a weariness of war;
2. army experiences which introduced millions of Americans to many sports such as football, baseball, basketball, soccer, boxing and track and field;
3. an outlet for exaltation of the human spirit and individual achievement in a nation undergoing monumental changes;
4. a technological revolution e.g. more leisure time, a shorter work week, greater mobility thanks to the automobile;
5. support from organized religion, i.e., Christian virtues and a healthy body were viewed as mutualistic; and
6. expansion of sports publicity through both newspapers and, the new media phenomenon, radio.

Rader claims that the modern sports page which had originated in many papers as early as the 1880s or 1890s, "did not become a standard feature in all major daily newspapers until the 1920s." In addition the

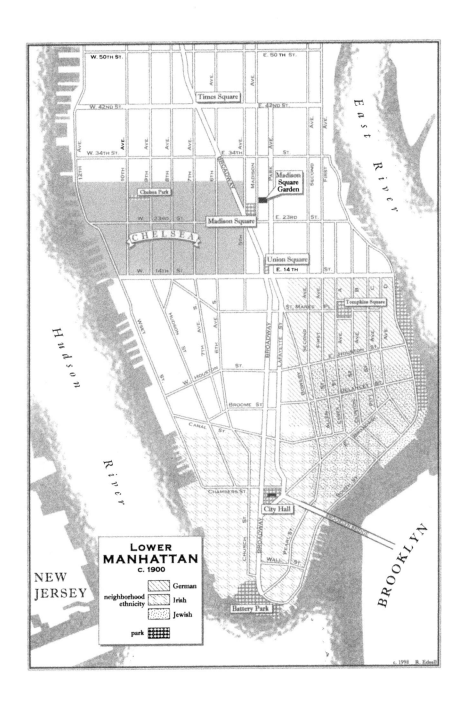

LOWER
MANHATTAN
c. 1900

neighborhood
ethnicity

German

Irish

Jewish

park

NEW
JERSEY

Jack Dempsey, heavyweight boxing champion (c) flanked by Johnny Beckman (1) and Nat Holman (r) taken around 1927.

twentieth century, particularly the 1920s, "brought to the fore a new generation of writers specializing in sports."[14] These included Grantland Rice, Paul Gallico, Westbrook Pegler, Ed Sullivan, Quentin Reynolds, and Tom Meany among others. Of course the impact of newspapers was also enhanced by decreasing illiteracy. As literacy increased, so did newspaper demand for sports news increase, resulting in an increase of the pages in daily newspapers dedicated to sports.[15]

There were some who saw the rise in sport interest directly attributable to legendary sports heroes that peopled the age. Grantland Rice, for example, asked and answered the question, "Just why was this period from 1919 to 1930 called the Golden Age of Sport?" The answer is a simple one. It is because this postwar period gave the game the greatest collection of stars, involving both skill and color, that sport has ever known. . . ."[16] Rice's view was echoed by John Kieran who said, "Never before had there been so many outsanding attractions in so many different fields in such a limited period of time."[17] Almost overnight, heroes sprang up, thanks to the media, especially radio. Ruth, Dempsey, Jones, Tilden, and Grange all had power and crowd appeal.

Danzig and Brandwein asked the following:

"What names are bigger in football than Grange and Rockne, than Nurmi and Paddock in distance and sprint running, than Weissmuller and Ederle in swimming, than Shore in hockey, than the Celtics in basketball?"[18]

The playing of sport, of course, is usually a conscious decision initially entered into for reasons of pleasure. At first that pleasure is physical—the exhilaration of play—then there is the added dimension of mental acuity which fuels the competitive drive. Later, in professional sport, comes the economic pleasure—the acquisition of economic capital to make the play a vocation and to make the pleasure of sport pay for one's well-being and family.

Embedded within this framework, particularly for immigrants or the children of immigrants, is the establishment and retention of cultural capital. Since the term was popularized in the 1970s by Pierre Bourdieu, cultural capital has most often referred to education. However, cultural capital can be established in a variety of ways. Harker explains, "Just as our dominant economic institutions are structured to favor those who already possess economic capital, so our educational institutions are structured to favor those who already possess cultural capital, in the form of the habitus (i.e., disposition) of the dominant cultural faction."[19] The acquisition of cultural capital, then, acts as a screen—a filter in the reproductive scheme of a hierarchical society. The challenge for members of the nondominant classes such as immigrant groups, is to determine what appropriate cultural capital is and how to acceptably obtain it since *how* one acquires such capital is as important as the acquisition itself.

In addition to education, Bourdieu explores this proposition in relation to language and linguistic exchanges in art, French society, and sport.

The last area, addressed in Bourdieu's work, *Sport and Social Class,* discusses the role of sport among the various social classes and how people acquire a taste for such sport. In doing this, Bourdieu describes sporting activities "as a supply intended to meet a social demand."[20]

Bourdieu specifically addresses radically new sporting activities such as volleyball and basketball which almost immediately moved from amateur game to professional, spectator sport. Usually, this transition took place in the "educational establishments reserved for the elites of bourgeois society" where folk art in fields like dance and music were gradually transformed into high art forms.[21] Basketball, however, did not follow this institutional path. The time between basketball's invention and its practice as a game or amateur sport was relatively short—less than ten years before the establishment of professional teams and a professional league (The National Basketball League was located around Philadelphia in 1898). Professional basketball was produced by "the people" and it "returned to the people in the form of spectacles produced for the people . . . as one branch among others of show business."[22] The professional basketball scene in the 1920s was performed in armories, small church gyms, or make-shift courts throughout the Northeast. The spectacle of sport became one "produced by professionals for consumption by the masses."[23] This aptly describes the state of professional basketball at the time.

Though sport was originally developed for the elite, it became useful to the dominant classes as a divertissement for the masses of immigrant youth. Institutions like schools, churches, and settlement houses were competing at the turn of the century in struggles "totally or partly organized with a view to the mobilization and symbolic conquest of the masses and therefore competing for the symbolic conquest of youth."[24]

To many immigrant groups, a sports career was a contradiction in terms, but to many poor youth from among these groups, it represented a potential for lifting them out of their impoverished existence. It was fortuitous that basketball's creation coincided with the beginning of the largest influx of new immigrants to the United States ever. The purpose and use of sport—in this case basketball—is viewed differently by different classes or groups.

Basketball, particularly professional basketball, was largely a working-class, ethnically based sport. Yet in many cases in the 1920s, the immigrant family was unfamiliar with new American sports, particularly basketball. Harry Litwack, longtime Temple basketball coach and a member of the South Philadelphia Hebrew Academy (SPHA) team in the 1930s, recalled that his parents were too busy to keep close tabs on him in the early 1920s. He worked setting up chairs around the basketball court receiving free admission to games. They were glad that his basketball interests kept him in the neighborhood though he would often be out late at basketball games when he was barely a teenager. Basketball was, in a sense, trusted by the immigrant family.

It was only a block. . . . It was a matter of about maybe three or four minutes, that's where the (team) originally played and that's how I got the job with a friend of mine setting up the chairs. My mother knew where I was. I'd come home and have something to eat and about 7:30 I'd go back.[25]

Families, then, were tolerant of "alternative" forms of education, culturally and intellectually. One may choose other forms of cultural capital than sport but the family as culture remains vital to the banking of such capital. Many families encouraged these sporting endeavors since they provided "the opportunity to add a well paid breadwinner to the family."[26]

The establishment of cultural capital may accrue in a variety of ways that produce consonance within the family and the ethnic group. One is economic capital as cultural capital, the acquisition of money. Many groups have seen this as the *ne plus ultra* of "acceptance" at least on one's own terms, if not necessarily that of the dominant class. How one acquires such money may be more or less important, depending upon the culture and family. At one extreme is the belief that acquisition (means) is inconsequential to possession (ends). At the other extreme, the ends are inconsequential unless means are appropriate. This often meant reflecting the state mores of the dominant classes, even if those mores are more mythological than actual when applied to the dominant classes themselves.

A way of judging the successful accumulation of cultural capital is through fame or notoriety. In some groups or families this may mean *negative* capital because this may imply hubris, bringing shame and derision to the family rather than admiration and fame. Still, fame in an appropriate forum may be deemed a successful form of cultural capital, especially among youth of the classes involved.

It is clear that professional sport can lead to fame, economic success, and respect. The examples of today are easy to behold and need not be discussed here. Of even greater concern is the way that sport was viewed in the 1920s through the accumulation of cultural capital, particularly among the Irish, Germans, and Jews of America, notably in New York City and the Northeast.

Germans, Irish, and Jews in Immigration and Sport

Between 1820 and 1930, over 15 million immigrants came from Germany. These immigrants represented the largest number of members of one nationality arriving in the United States. These Germans came in various waves—pre-Civil War, post Civil War (to 1900), pre-World War I, and post-World War I—though the latter number was significantly reduced for obvious reasons. The arriving Germans represented various religious affiliations. Many German Jews, who identified themselves as German as much as they identified themselves as Jews, were included in some of the earlier waves of German Protestants. The post-Civil War émigrés were largely German Catholics from Bavaria and Southern Germany. The large number of German Catholics rivaled the entrenched Irish Catholics for power in the American Catholic Church. "Constant agitation among the German clerics and a boiling sense of outrage among the Irish bishops" ensued.[27] Amelioration was achieved through the ascension of James Cardinal Gibbons to the position of Cardinal of New York City in 1887. Ultimately, the two groups were reconciled and the Germans and Irish "ruled the 'rooftop' [of the church] together to the notable exclusion of the Poles and the Italians."[28]

By the beginning of World War I, anti-German sentiment was common but there were some notable exceptions. The newly arrived Jews from Russia and Poland "were overwhelmingly pro-German. All of them had come to America to flee the pogroms."[29] Thus, they were pro-German if only because they were so violently anti-Russian. The seemingly unlikely alliance of Germans, Irish, and Jews seen on the Celtics basketball team was emblematic of these same alliances being played out on the larger stage of New York City.

The athletic fields and arenas, indeed, reflected these alliances in various ways. O'Connor noted this pattern and the effect it had on a number of ethnic groups, particularly Germans.

One way for a minority to win acceptance in the American scheme, among its generally sports-mad fellow citizens, is on the athletic field, baseball diamond, or in the boxing ring. Thus, the Irish, and later the Italians, were tremendously uplifted by the example of the prize fighting champions they produced. Germans, however, showed little aptitude for fighting with fists padded. But baseball, the 'American pastime' as it once was, with its geometric order, its requirement of technical skills as well as brute strength and quick reflexes, and its disciplined pattern, appealed to something in the German psyche.[30]

So, too, with basketball, though it was less "orderly" with court size not exactly standardized then. It was a rough, though appealing game in the manner which the Celtics performed. It didn't hurt that the Celtic success was inextricably linked to the Germans on the Celtic team—Leonard, Beckman, Dehnert, and Reich—all German Catholics.

Like their German Catholic counterparts, the Irish Catholics of New York viewed sport as a wise investiture of cultural capital. "Like religion and politics, sports offered possibilities to the Irish, who were excluded from business and professions by the Anglo Protestant establishment. And athletics provided the Irish community with badly needed heroes."[31]

Sport, however, also stigmatized the Irish, who were seen as strong but dumb—good for digging ditches, building railroads, pounding criminals, and playing athletics. As McCaffrey and others allude, strong backs indicated weak minds. "The association of Irish Americans with baseball, the great national game, indicates that they accepted the United States more than it did them."[32] Riess saw baseball as "a good source of vertical mobility for Irishmen, the ethnic group at the bottom of the job hierarchy in the late nineteenth century."[33] "The Irish role in sports expressed alienation as well as assimilation."[34]

The Irish were linked to the Jews in some obvious ways—through their prominence in show business and their associations with trade unionism. The lower-class status of both groups made them easy allies in labor, show business, and ultimately, in sport.

The Celtics had been founded originally as an Irish Settlement House team on Manhattan's West Side with players like Morrisey, McArdle, Barry, Whitty, Calhoun, McCormick, and Kennedy. The team had appeal among the local Irish populace before World War I. After the war, the Celtic name would initially attract Irish spectators. Whether they would stay to support basketball on a team with only two of the original Celtics was uncertain.

From 1921 to 1926, Nat Holman was the only Jewish member of the Celtics. In 1926 the Celts obtained Davey Banks, also Jewish, and a prolific scorer. He was from New York City and had performed for the SPHAS in Philadelphia and in the Metropolitan League for Brooklyn, among others.

As a Celtic player, Holman was aware of the esteem that Jews held for him. In a 1974 letter he stated:

During my career as a professional basketball player—especially when I was the only Jewish player on the Celtics—I was very much aware of the Jewish following that supported me in a number of cities on the circuit. While I always played at my very best, I tried even harder when I knew the Jewish community was rooting for me.[35]

In his thorough and insightful history of sports and the American Jewish experience, Peter Levine examines and explains this phenomenon in general as well as regarding basketball in particular. He questions the exclusive, scholarly stereotype by noting that immigrant Jews, by their actions, were obviously more adventurous and less tied to the stereotype of Jews as exclusively people of the book. To many Jews, embracing American opportunity and experience included a love of sport.

The growth and acceptance of sport as a new way of spending leisure time hinged on its promotion as an activity full of social purpose, one even capable of transforming immigrants into competent workers replete with new American values and character. Consciously emphasized as a mechanism of Americanization, especially for the children of Jewish immigrants and other outsiders, it was, from the outset, a critical melting point where majority and minority people intersected and, as such, a special place for illuminating the ongoing process of assimilation.[36]

Through sport, one could be more American and not any less Jewish. "Like Catholics and other ethnics, the Jews sought acceptance without the loss of traditional values."[37] This was especially noteworthy in New York City where, by 1920, almost half of all American Jews lived (constituting 30 percent of the population of 4.3 million New Yorkers).[38] The lower East Side held 75 percent of the Eastern European Jews in the city.

At about that same time, nearly 10 percent of the Germans in the U.S. and over 12 percent of the Irish lived in New York City's five boroughs. These groups lived in contiguous neighborhoods largely in South Manhattan from 14th Street south. Today, the East Village which abuts the Lower East Side was largely German at the turn of the century. The lower East Side which bordered that area held 75 percent of the Eastern European Jews in the city. Though the bulk of Irish lived uptown and in Brooklyn, 40 percent of the population of the wards below Canal Street were Irish.

A large segment of the Jewish media encouraged Jews to take part in athletics to be more American and because "athletics and morality go hand in hand."[39] It was recognized that athletics were a powerful opportunity to overcome the bookish stereotype mentioned earlier, the belief that Jews neglected physical development because of their deep devotion to intellectual and spiritual development.

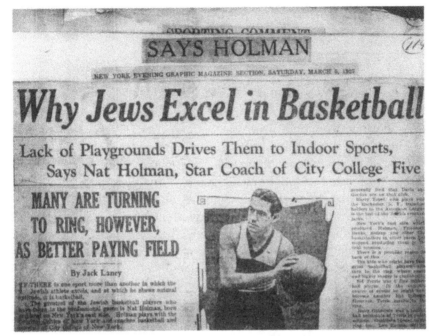

This headline from 1927 appeared in one of the many daily papers of New York City.

Of the athletics entered into, none was received with more enthusiasm than basketball. An early University Settlement House team (1903-1905)—with members known as the "busy izzies"—won the New York Settlement House Championship. This provided early role models for Jewish youth such as Barney Sedran, Marty Friedman, Lou Sugarman, Harry Brill, and others.[40] Nat Holman noted that "Thanks to the Settlement Houses, we always had a place to play basketball . . . It was not a new game on the Lower EastSide (in 1905). It was very popular."[41] Levine claimed, "Jewish children flocked to the sport making it a significant part of everyday community life."[42]

Basketball's "newness," being invented in 1891, made it a continually evolving sport into and beyond the 1920s. This had distinct advantages and disadvantages. A clear disadvantage was a lack of tradition—parents had usually not played basketball nor were they very familiar with its nuances so it was not a game "handed down" from father to son. Of course, most immigrant parents had no time for games, particularly one non existent in their country of origin.

Nevertheless, basketball's freshness attracted young people. The fact that it was a game that their parents hadn't played was appealing to many young adolescents seeking venues to establish their own identities.

Harry Litwack recalled that a number of Jews who came to the SPHA games did not really understand the game but they cheered loudly for their Jewish boys.[43]

Many teams evolved from settlement house teams or grew from participation and sponsorship of some ethnically based institutions. "Sponsoring a pro basketball team like the all Polish Detroit Pulaskis was a means of rallying the group." The SPHA team originally hired only Jews, the Brooklyn Visitation team only Irish.[44] Many games were followed by a community dance, a way to entertain and bond the community. This was one of the reasons that games were played in ballrooms. It allowed people to attend games who might not have done so but for the dance afterward. This continued at least into the 1930s.

As Jewish players excelled, the Jewish community became greater fans of basketball and, by doing so, they "became more 'American' in turn, by watching their own kind transform it into a Jewish majority sport . . . encouraging ethnic pride and identification."[45]

The investment in basketball by Jews was seen as not just an American experience, but one consonant with Jewish culture, a suitable and respected source of cultural capital. Thus, "long before basketball became a national entertainment vehicle, it was a local sport operating on amateur and professional levels that provided a cheap and available form of amusement totally integrated into the local community's social fabric."[46]

Levine's assertion is complemented by that of Nat Holman, the original Jewish player on the Celtics. In a letter to Buddy Silverman in 1974, Holman stated:

Excellence in sports helps Jews to be even prouder of their great heritage so they can keep their heads high without feeling inferior to any other group. It helps non-Jews to understand that Jews are not only "people of the book"; they also share in the wholesome activities and interests of all their fellows.[47]

This understanding by non-Jews was not always apparent, even to "sympathizers" of this issue. Paul Gallico, the famed sports essayist, felt that basketball was a natural sport in which Jews would excel because "it is a game that above all others seems to appeal to the temperament of Jews. . . . I suspect, that it appeals to the Hebrew with his Oriental background (because) the game places a premium on an alert, scheming mind and flashy trickiness, artful dodgery, and general smart aleckness."[48]

Ed Sullivan also thought Jews were ideally suited to basketball. Using Holman, Chick Passon of the SPHAs, Banks, and Benny Borgeman as examples of Jewish youngsters who are "crackerjacks," Sullivan noted:

Jewish players seem to take naturally to the game. Perhaps this is because the Jew is a natural gambler and will take chances. Perhaps it is because he devotes himself more closely to a problem than others will.[49]

The Celtic Composition

The original Celtics had begun as a settlement house team in the Chelsea district located on the West side of Manhattan, an area north of today's Greenwich Village to the south of Penn Station—a distance of roughly two miles. At the turn of the century this neighborhood was already one of transition, a characteristic still prevalent in the 1990s. The neighborhood had been Irish and held other recent immigrants in the mid to late 1800s, but was changing as native New Yorkers and later immigrants moved out of the city to Brooklyn, which did not become incorporated into New York City until 1898. The growth in New York City in 1870 and 1880 was largely the result of "large scale immigration from Germany and Ireland."[50]

The Chelsea neighborhood, acknowledged as a "tough" area,[51] was still a neighborhood with a large number of Irish families. These young Irish lads constituted the Celtic teams during 1914-17, but the reconstituted Original Celtics after World War I retained only two of these Irish Americans, John (Pete) Barry and Johnny Whitty. Whitty never played very much, serving as seventh man on seven-man clubs. He also doubled as club manager, unofficial road manager, and sometimes coach. These latter functions allowed him to retain his position on the Celtics through 1928 (though he did work as the manager of the Ft. Wayne team in the American Basketball League from 1925-28 before returning to the Celtics). Though there is no explicit evidence to support this, it is not unlikely that Whitty also served as a kind of community liaison promoting the Celtics and preserving ties with the Irish American community.

Pete Barry probably served this latter function also, and he stayed with the Celtics until 1928. Barry's assets, however, were more noticeable on the court where his six-foot frame and versatility allowed him to play all positions well.

In 1921, Barry and Whitty were joined by a third Irishman, George Haggerty—the only non-native New Yorker to log significant time (more than one year) with the Celtic squad. Haggerty was a native of Springfield, Massachusetts. When he traveled to Reading, Pennsylvania to play for the Reading Bears at the behest of former Springfield resident and Reading star, Andy Sears, Haggerty felt at home in the city. In fact, after playing for more than 100 teams in twenty years, Haggerty returned to Reading and resided there from his basketball retirement until his death in 1961 at the age of sixty. Haggerty was less comfortable in New York City despite the large Irish population and his popularity every place he played. His presence certainly was an asset to the Celtics' appeal in the Irish communities of New York City and other cities of northern New Jersey and southern New York.

Eddie Burke, a Metropolitan League star, played on the Celtics from 1922-25. Though never one of their starters or stars, his Irish good looks and native New York City roots could not have hurt the Celtics' appeal to the Irish community. Thus, the Celtics maintained a "presence" in the Irish communities of the New York City region during the entire existence of the team.

Czechs were the final ethnic group represented by a Celtic regular. Joe Lapchick, a native of Long Island, did not have significant effect on ethnic support of Celtic games, since Czechs constituted a much smaller number of people in the city and the region compared to Germans, Irish, and Jews. Nevertheless, his excellence as a player and his contribution to the team's success overall not only improved the team's performance but also exemplified possibilities for other eastern European immigrants to successfully assimilate and acquire cultural capital.

The Media and Ethnicity

The newspapers made much of the backgrounds of professional basketball players in an apparent effort to exploit interest along ethnic lines and, ultimately, to sell basketball along with newspapers. The newspaper articles were often inaccurate in their information. One example occurs in Hugh Bradley's 1927 *New York* article which states that Dave Banks "is not a native New Yorker. He comes from Philadelphia," which was absolutely incorrect.[52] Another New York City writer, "Lank" Leonard, referred to Lapchick and Banks as the "tall Pole and the little Jew." In his story, he notes that Banks is also known as "Rabbi."[53] Lapchick was, of course, not Polish, and though Banks was Jewish, the constant religious referencing would not have been tolerated today. Banks was commonly referred to as the "young Hebrew" or the "Hebrew star" by the *Philadelphia Inquirer*'s Gordon MacKay in 1926-27, but this may have also been in reference to his previous employment in 1924-25 and 1925-26 with the SPHA squad. In a March 15, 1928, account in which Banks was battered in a Philadelphia/Celtics game, the *Inquirer* noted that "Banks got a deep gash in his forehead and the blood spurted out and his face crimsoned." After being attended by a physician, "The young Hebrew, dizzy but courageous, returned to the battle."[54] Lapchick was often referred to as Polish although he was Czech. Leonard was called Irish, though he was German. Dehnert was called a

Dutchman because of his nickname which was probably anglicized from "Deutsch" as in "Pennsylvania Dutch."

These labels were not done in malice, but to identify the players as representatives of ethnic groups, to break or to extend stereotypes of such groups. The reporters reflected the feelings of the times rather than attempting to set ethnic groups against one another. After all, it was the teams themselves that chose such appellations as sources of pride and identity. Names of teams reflected vocations and symbols (Shoe Pegs, Electrics, Potters, Glassblowers, Miners) as well as ethnicity (Buffalo Germans, Hebrews, Celtics, Jew(el)s, Busy Izzies, Knights of St. Anthony) so being referred to as a Hebrew, a Catholic, a German, etc., followed rather naturally.

The Celtics became successful by drawing on diverse ethnic groups for their players and fans. This led to success on the court because of the quality of the players and success at the box office because of the cultural capital that different groups "invested" in the basketball successes of their young ethnic group members. Levine noted that "For both adults and children, appreciation of and connection to Jewish basketball encouraged assimilation to unfold within the rich fabric of the ethnic, Jewish world in which they lived."[55] He also notes in a postscript the parallels between the Jewish experience of sporting success/assimilation and that of American blacks. Though the success he chronicles is less dramatic because of historically embedded racism, the analogy of establishing cultural capital through the investiture of basketball or sport generally is validated to a large degree.[56]

Summarizing the Era

The 1920s was a period of transition, truly the beginning of the 20th century, rather than that which the calendar indicated as 1901. The end of World War I signaled the end of one era and the onset of a new, modern one. Not everyone wanted this transition and the 1920s was a period of dichotomous tension rather than an unabashed plunge into modernity. A decrease in immigration allowed for the massive influx of immigrants that had flooded America's shores in the twenty years prior to the Great War to build ethnic communities while moving toward greater assimilation and acceptance into the societal mainstream. The end of the war and the increase in both time and money for many American workers abetted a growing interest in sport in the United States. Both the number of participants in sport and the number of fans attending sport events increased dramatically through the 1920s. The greater interest was reflected in more media coverage of sporting events. Sportswriters like Grantland Rice, Westbrook Pegler, and Paul Gallico made sports coverage more respected and more interesting. The onset of radio coverage of sports events piqued the nation's interest even more.

Basketball was a sport being shaped and developed in the 1920s, particularly in the professional ranks. The top regional professional teams attracted varying numbers of fans in the early 1920s. The best players often played for two, three or more leagues, which helped them financially, but hurt the establishment of a team concept within professional basketball.

"Professional basketball was essentially an activity put on by community groups and for community groups," notes Ted Vincent.[57] A basketball game was usually followed by a dance in some local hall or armory which served to cement community and/or ethnic elations. The ethnic connection for pro basketball was established in a period of great effort among minority groups "to build a community solidarity to alleviate the conditions . . . (of) rampant alcoholism, the disorganization of the marriage group . . . delinquency of boys and sexual immorality of girls."[58] Basketball served as cultural capital for a number of immigrant groups, particularly the Irish, the Germans, and the Jews (who constituted most of the emigrees from Russia and Romania in the early 1900s). The game was an investment in both American culture and a modified re-investment in these immigrant cultures.

The Celtics' greatest successes came when they went against popular practice by composing a squad of men from more than one ethnic group. The rationale was that these were the best players in the game; but, coincidentally, they also brought along the support of ethnic groups which they represented. Diverse support brought cultural and economic success to the team members both individually and collectively. As a result, basketball was seen as an appropriate venue for the growth of cultural capital.

2

CONTRACTS AND CONVEYANCES

From the time of its invention in 1891 basketball spread throughout amateur athletic circles largely, at first, through the network of YMCAs and YMHAs which swiftly adopted the sport for winter indoor fitness. Settlement houses also spread the "gospel" of basketball, indoors and out, to entice youth, to participate in the the sport because it allowed for great flexibility and innovation. Still, the game was largely low scoring, often confusing in its rules, and very rough.

Local rules often varied within different regions in terms of both rules and style of play. Within ten years of basketball's invention professional leagues had begun in parts of the northeastern United States. A continuing desire arose for more standardized rules in order to enhance the popularity of the professional game (and lead to greater profit).

Until 1921 the professional basketball game remained largely in flux regarding teams, leagues, and rules. Despite that degree of fluidity, the game also remained largely regionalized. Until regionalization was outstripped by national teams and leagues, the professional game remained underattended and underappreciated. The Celtics, more than any other team or players, were largely responsible for the reversal of fortunes of professional basketball in the 1920s. They became the most widely known basketball team in the United States, a 1920s version of "America's team."

The success of the Celtics and subsequent league teams of professional basketball was coincidental with two advances in technology and law that allowed each of the individual Celtic stars and, ultimately, the Celtic team to achieve the dominance, and professional rewards commensurate with such dominance. These advances which occurred in two areas—dependable rail travel and contract law—will be the focus of this chapter. The effects of the rail system will be examined in the context of player mobility, communication, fan interest, and team travel. The successful growth of professional basketball from 1910 to the 1930s is linked to the nation's rail system, as well as the intercity advancement in trolleys and the development of the New York City subway system.

The contractual latitude that players originally enjoyed, and that owners seemed helpless to change, ended in the early 1920s with the implementation of the exclusive contract. Though the insertion of such a clause was relatively simple and straightforward, the effects were dramatic and felt almost immediately, accelerating the demise of a number of teams and leagues. The clause of exclusivity was offset by skyrocketing salaries which will be examined and put into the economic frames of the period.

The Railroad & Early Professional Leagues

The golden age of passenger rail in the United States was from about 1897 to 1920.[1] That coincided with the largest wave of immigrants to arrive in America and helped to increase the number of passenger-miles on the various railways of the country. By 1916 the average citizen was riding the train ten times a year.[2] Those citizens were often changing railroad lines as well as trains as they traveled. A number of small railroads had tried to join together in the 1880s, but they were "disunited" by the Sherman Antitrust Act of 1890.

During the period of 1915 to 1920 "the importance of the railroad passenger services of that day could be seen in the ubiquitous station or depot found in almost every village, town and city in the nation."[3] And that linkage allowed many small cities and towns to sponsor a professional basketball team and, thereby, to make their case as being "big league" cities. Thus, it was the railroad that made this possible.

In the period between 1915 and 1919 there were no fewer than four top professional leagues operating in relatively close proximity in the northeastern United States. One of the earliest professional leagues was the Eastern League which had been founded by William J. Scheffer in 1909. Scheffer, a sportswriter, printer and referee, had originally founded the Philadelphia Basketball League in 1902, but it folded in 1909. His new Eastern League had three franchises in or around Philadelphia, then added three franchises in New Jersey (Trenton, Elizabeth, and Paterson) and one in Reading, Pennsylvania.

By 1915 the Eastern League was in its seventh year, equaling Scheffer's Philadelphia League for most consecutive years in operation. The 1915-1916 teams were located in Camden and Trenton, New Jersey, Reading, Pa. and around Philadelphia (Jasper, Greystock, and DeNeri). The teams played twice a week and rail travel made the contests easy to schedule and play. Reading was the farthest from the others but was linked to and through Philadelphia by both the Reading Railroad Company and the Pennsylvania Railroad. Trenton and Camden connected to Philadelphia via the Pennsylvania Railroad and the Jersey Central.

The New York State League, begun in 1911 with six teams, had overcome a year of suspended operations by 1915 and fielded, once again, six franchises all located in, or in close proximity to, the Hudson River Valley which was served by the New York Central Railroad. The franchise cities were Schenectady, Mohawk, Hudson, Utica, Cohoes, and Saratoga. As with the Eastern League, no city was more than two hours by rail from any other city.

The Pennsylvania State League had been founded in 1914 by the coal barons of Pennsylvania's anthracite coal region located around the Scranton Wilkes-Barre area. Besides those two cities, there were six other coal town teams—Freeland, Carbondale, Nanticoke, Pittston, Hazelton, and Plymouth. These cities were served by the Jersey Central Railroad which ran from Jersey City to Scranton through Wilkes-Barre and Nanticoke, and connected with the Pennsylvania Railroad just south of Wilkes-Barre at Buttonwood. In addition, the Delaware and Hudson Railroad ran north from Scranton through Carbondale, Oneonta, New York, and north into Albany and Troy. Finally the Lackawanna and Wyoming Valley Railroad connected the whole valley from Scranton south to Pittston.

The last league at the time was the Interstate League founded in 1915; it ran until 1921. This league, more than the other three, relied on the punctuality of the railroads since the six franchises were more spread out within three states—New York, New Jersey, and Connecticut. In New York were Brooklyn and Kingston, the latter a refugee from the New York State League which returned to that league for the 1921-22 and 1922-23 seasons. The three teams in New Jersey were Paterson, Elizabeth, and Jersey City, all near New York. The Connecticut team was Stamford. The cities were all linked through the Jersey Central Railroad, the Pennsylvania Railroad and the Delaware and Hudson, all of which linked the New Jersey cities with Brooklyn. The New York Central ran to Kingston from New York City and the New Haven ran from New York City to Hartford through Stamford. From Stamford to Kingston, the greatest distance, a team might need three to four hours if they did not make swift transfer in New York at Grand Central Station.

Thanks to the railroads, the leagues could incorporate and flourish.[4] Of additional assistance were the intercity trolleys of the various regions, which allowed fans and players to move from one city in a region to another on a more timely basis. In some cases extra trolleys were provided for special occasions, for example in the Pennsylvania State League Championships special trolleys between the competing cities (Scranton and Nanticoke in 1920, Pittston and Scranton in 1921).[5]

Within the New York City area, the Interborough Rapid Transit Company and the Brooklyn Rapid Transit Company had lines connecting Brooklyn, Queens, Manhattan, and the Bronx. This helped fans and players get to games in Brooklyn and to Grand Central.[6]

Rail passenger traffic peaked in 1916, but in 1917 Congress began to provide financial grants in aid for highways, eventually causing a loss of rail passengers and a deterioration in service.[7] Thus, by the 1920s rail traffic had stopped growing and began a slow decline that only reversed in the early 1940s. Nevertheless passenger service remained profitable in the 1920s, though barely so.[8] "Timetables or schedule books were still fat, and all towns and cities in the late thirties still had very adequte railroad passenger service."[9]

The railroads had been brought under the Federal Possession and Control Act of December 1917 to assist in the control and coordination needed for the war effort. "It should be noted that the United States was the first of the warring nations to take such action."[10]

The control of the railroads and the need for men in the armed forces caused the suspension of all professional basketball leagues. Stover notes that all unnecessary civilian passenger travel was discouraged and timetables were consolidated.[11] All four of the major leagues returned after war's end to find continued Federal coordination of the railroads. Once control was returned to the various independent railroad companies in 1921,[12] most railroads "embarked upon multi-million dollar improvement programs"—including new roadways, track, locomotives, and passenger cars.[13] This included the advent and swift integration of diesel electric locomotives on many lines. Originally built for Army use in 1918, the diesels quickly began to replace the steam engines which were already the subject of new city smoke ordinances.[14] The new diesels sped freight and passengers across most northeastern routes, most prominently the Pennsylvania Railroad—the busiest system in the world in the 1920s. With the extension of that line into New York City by underwater tunnels and the building of Penn Station in 1910, the Pennsylvania Railroad became the leading freight and passenger carrier.[15] The Celtic players were among the thousands of passengers served each day.

The railroad abetted the development of professional sport leagues of all types, but none rivaled basketball in the number of "major" leagues. This allowed small cities throughout the northeast to claim major professional league status and possibly, a league or "world" championship.

In addition, the basketball venues were usually located in the city centers not far from the railroad stations. "Without the railroad and its centralizing tendency, it is doubtful that the concept of the city as a center of material and cultural activities would have developed so fully."[16]

As the railroads helped to create leagues, they also aided the players' efforts to advance themselves economically. The players, without agents or formal contracts, operated as independent contractors. Joe Lapchick recalled the following:

The good players were well known, and they were all after the good high dollar. We would meet at the information booth in Grand Central Station on our way to games to talk basketball . . . Some of the players we met in Grand Central were Benny Borgemann, Honey Russell, Elmer Ripley . . . Ray Kennedy, Dutch Dehnert, Dave Wassmer, Marty Friedman, Barney Sedran, and Eddie White.[17]

Additionally, Nat Holman recalled that:

It was common practice for all outstanding professional players to carry a railroad time-table as part of his equipment so he'd know at what hour the last train left and how he might make his best connections to get home. It was not unusual for a good player to perform in the Pennsylvania State League each Tuesday and Thursday, and in the Eastern League on Monday and Wednesday—then fill in the other evenings as often as he could. A good player hired himself out for $10 or $15 per game; an outstanding fellow might get as much as $35. Traveling was largely by train.[18]

The Celtic players, like most of the top professionals, soon found that the railroad could make them much richer using the practices described briefly by Holman. By playing on more than one squad, the players would be able to play one owner's offer against another. They could also assure themselves of games almost every night in the week. Since they were paid by the game, this practice would clearly enhance their incomes.

Though some of the player's professional careers began earlier, starting in 1915 allows one to view the peripatetic nature of the outstanding Celtic players in the years 1915 to 1921 when the team inaugurated a "simple" practice that anchored players to one team. In 1915 Beckman, Reich, Haggerty, and Leonard were already playing professional basketball.

Haggerty only seemed to play regularly for two squads—Reading of the Eastern League and Troy of the New York State League. Eastern League connections with Albany–Troy were relatively simple via Philadelphia and New York on the Pennsylvania Railroad and the New York Central, or through Scranton to Albany on the Delaware and Hudson.

Ernie Reich appeared in contests for DeNeri of the Eastern League, Jersey City of the Interstate League and Norwalk, which played as an independent squad. His connections would have paralleled Haggerty's with the addition of trips to Norwalk on the New Haven Railroad. John Beckman played for both DeNeri and Paterson (New Jersey of the Interstate League). His travel patterns would have been largely on the New York Central and the Pennsylvania or Reading Railroads. Chris Leonard was not always the busiest player, appearing with Paterson and unnamed independent teams. The next year, however (1916-17), Leonard appeared for Hazelton of the Pennsylvania State League, Glens Falls of the New York State League, Danbury of the Interstate League and later, Newark, after Danbury dropped out of the league.

That same year, 1916-17, Beckman played for Reading (Eastern) and Bridgeport and Newark of the Interstate league, while Reich was in the lineup for DeNeri (Eastern) and Jersey City (Interstate). In addition, these three players were maintaining residences in New York and were spending as many nights as possible at home. The Pennsylvania, the New York Central, the Delaware and Hudson, and the Jersey Central made all this physically possible and many other players "took to the rails" to increase their incomes.

During World War I all of the major leagues suspended operations, the Interstate League for 1917-18 and 1918-19; the Pennsylvania State League halfway through 1917-18 and for all of the 1918-19 season; the New York State League for 1917-18 and 1918-19; the Eastern League shortly after the 1917-18 season began and through 1918-19. This was not to say that professional basketball and its players suspended play, however.

Most of the Celtic players were playing on war industry teams while working for the various war plants. Beckman worked and played for the Standard Shipyard Team headquartered in the Brooklyn Naval Yards. He also played for the Newark Turners, an independent squad that won the New Jersey State championships, and the Troy (New York) Trojans, also playing as an independent team when league action was suspended. Beckman could commute to the former games by subway and rail, while riding the New York Central to Troy for games. Because there were fewer trains for independent civilian use during the war, independent teams played closer to home allowing Beckman to spend no more than a night or two per week away from home.

Reich also played with a shipyard team—Downey Shipyard and for a rival Newark team—the Whirlwinds Athletic Association Squad. Reich's need for interstate rail travel was greatly curtailed. This was true for other professionals working in shipyards and playing for teams like Dehnert (playing for Downey), though some players, like Leonard, served in the army (infantry) in 1918.

One of the Shipyard teams that existed during World War I.

The end of the war brought a boom in many sectors of the American economy and, with the release of government controls of many industries, a marked increase in entrepeneurship. All four of the major basketball leagues resumed operations with some changes in the franchises. The Eastern League continued with six teams in approximately the same locales. The Pennsylvania State League was down to five teams (from seven) while two of these leagues grew. The Interstate League added two franchises which totalled eight in the league, and the New York State League expanded from six to ten.

More teams meant more jobs and the players could capitalize on that, which most did. The Celtic players were a good example. Beckman played on at least three teams in 1919-20, Leonard appeared on four rosters, Holman on four, Haggerty two, Dehnert three, Barry four, Lapchick three. The next year (1920-21) Beckman was again on at least three rosters, Leonard five, Holman four, Haggerty two, Reich three, Lapchick four, and Dehnert five.

To be sure none of them played regularly with no more than three teams; being on more rosters gave the players the leverage to constantly raise their salaries as they negotiated on a game-by-game basis with the various club owners. As long as the railroads offered multiple trains daily to every small to mid-sized city (as well as the major metropolises, of course), the better players would be economic successes.

There was a cost to players who chose to perform in multiple leagues and that was the obvious wear and tear the body had to endure playing six nights (or more) a week and riding trains on a seemingly incessant basis. For example, Johnny Beckman began his peregrinations at the age of twenty and continued that life for more than 25 years.

Starting his first game, October 8, 1915, and up to and including his last game on April 30, 1916, 195 days (including Sundays) elapsed. During this time the well known forward played 174 games. He played with fifteen different quintets and in three different leagues, besides taking part in every series of any account in this section (of the Northeast).[19]

To illustrate the endurance the players needed, one week in the basketball life of Chris Leonard will be presented. The week chosen will not be unusual, only one of which data can be found. During 1920-21 Leonard played for the following teams—The Prospect Big Five Team, an independent team that played as the home team on Sunday and Wednesday nights at Prospect Hall in Brooklyn; the New York Whirlwinds, an independent team in Manhattan that played at the 22nd regiment armory; Hartford of the Interstate League (though he only appeared in three games in the first half of the year); Pittston of the Pennsylvania State League (who normally played home games on Fridays, but switched to Saturdays during Lent); and Coatesville of the Eastern League who played Monday night home games.

Thus Leonard had league games twice a week in each league, games with the Big Five team twice a week, and a game once a week with the Whirlwinds for a total of seven games during some weeks.

The week of February 19-27, 1921, was typical. It was the middle of the second half for both the Eastern and Pennsylvania State Leagues. Mid-February was also a popular time for New York basketball fans, so both the Prospect Big Five and the Whirlwinds had games. Leonard's week, then looked like this:

Saturday, February 19	Nanticoke at Pittston
Sunday, February 20	Prospect Big Five, Brooklyn
Monday, February 21	Germantown at Coatesville
Tuesday, February 22	Pittston at Wilkes Barre
Wednesday, February 23	Coatesville at Camden
Thursday, February 24	Whirlwind Contest
Saturday, February 25	Scranton at Pittston
Sunday, February 27	Prospect Big Five at home

On Saturday night after the Pittston game, which ran about an hour, Leonard could have caught a night train to Jersey City and arrived by 1

a.m., then taken the train or the ferry to Manhattan, the subway to his home, and been there by 2:30. However, it is likely he caught an early morning train on Sunday and was back in the city before noon.

The game in Brooklyn was part of a regular doubleheader each week. Depending on the game, Leonard could leave as early as 5 p.m. or as late as 11 p.m. The last train to Philadelphia left at midnight and Leonard could have taken it. Again, it is more likely that he took a morning train to Philadelphia after spending the night in his own bed. He would be in the city by noon, change trains and be in Coatesville in the afternoon. The games in the Eastern and Pennsylvania State Leagues usually started at 9 p.m., ran an hour, and were over by 10:15 p.m. He scored six points in the Coatesville victory over Germantown and his Whirlwind teammate Nat Holman scored 17 of the 20 points in the 24-20 game. Leonard then spent the night at his Coatesville "home," probably a local hotel, and took the morning train to Philadelphia where he changed to a train to the Wyoming Valley.

Again Leonard would arrive in the afternoon, a couple of hours later, and would probably eat in Scranton or Wilkes Barre, before heading to the arena.

The next morning, Wednesday, Leonard traveled back to Philadelphia and took the ferry across the Delaware River to Camden. That evening he failed to score as Camden won 36-29 over Coatesville. He then likely took a late train home to New York.

Chris Leonard could sleep in on Thursday, but likely had a Whirlwind contest scheduled that evening at the 22nd regiment armory. No conclusive record is readily available to indicate that the Whirlwinds played that night but the odds are good that they did. Holman's Germantown team played on many Fridays as did Sedran and Leonard, Whirlwind players in the New York State League. As members of the Whirlwinds, Thursdays and Sunday afternoons were most likely game time for them.

Again Leonard got to spend a night at home, possibly two nights since there is no record of a Friday night game and if one was played, it was likely for a local team. After these nights at home, Leonard would have headed out on Saturday back to Pittston on the Jersey Central, or on the Delaware and Hudson. That evening he scored three in a 35-28 loss to Scranton that dropped Pittston to 5-5 in the second half league standings. On Sunday, Leonard headed back to New York for a Prospect Big Five game in Brooklyn and the travel merry-go-round continued.

As noted earlier, this endless traveling was not unusual. The better the player, the more in demand he was and, usually, the more he traveled. Regarding Beckman's travels, S. O. Grauley wrote:

Beckman probably plays more basketball and makes more money than any two cage game stars in the business. He is never idle and chases the dollar all over. He plays in three leagues plus in double headers with the Celtics on Sunday and he is in great shape. Fans love the great shooter.[20]

The players were travelers and the railroad system abetted this practice. The players' independence and economic well being was a direct result of the mobility the railroad accorded them. Not everyone, however, found this to his liking. The various owners found it maddening to recruit a player for their roster, only to have him not show up for a crucial game because of a better offer from another owner. "No manager could count on his starting team from one game to the next."[21] The only agreement among league owners was that a player could only be on one team's roster in a league.

Peterson observed that "players were drawn from the National League to the New England League by higher salaries as early as 1901."[22] The early owners could not solve that problem nor could their brethren in successive league endeavors.

By 1909 some players were carrying the colors of five or more teams each season. William Scheffer wrote in the *Reach Guide* that year that he had been told by a manager in New Jersey that just twenty men represented the ten teams he had booked for home games the previous season.[23]

From the owners' point of view things only got worse. Joe Lapchick recalled that he was getting $10 a game in 1919, but soon was able to play one manager against another and get as much as $15 per game.

The standard rate of pay was a dollar a minute, but the rates gradually increased until I got up to $90 to $100 a game no matter how many minutes I played. When there was a clash of dates I took the best offer. There was no income tax at the time, and I began to really live it up.[24]

Just by way of contextualizing what Lapchick says there was little inflation in the 1920s. Average income was about $2,000 per year with the price of a new home running on average, $350-$700. Thus, Lapchick's pay from a "modest" 100 games a year, might be $10,000—five times the national average.

The most expensive basketball ticket was just over a dollar, but venue capacity was often 2,000 or less. Thus, it was clear that the battle for players among owners foreshadowed disastrous results.

In an effort to gain more control, the owners in three of the leagues agreed to allow their presidents to find a mutually agreeable and economically feasible solution. That was the formation of a National Basketball Commission whereby Thomas Brislin, president of the Pennsylvania State League; William Scheffer, president of the Eastern League; and M. J. B. McDonagh, president of the New York State League, agreed to restrict players to one league, to fine teams that play against a team with ineligible players, and to not permit league teams to play exhibition games with independent teams in any city or town where a member of the commission has jurisdiction. They also agreed to terminate all league schedules the third week in March to allow for a World Series among the league winners.[25]

A number of players were suspended for violating the agreement. Holman was banned from Scranton in January for playing with Germantown of the Eastern League, and Beckman and Grimstead were threatened with suspension by the Eastern League for not showing up for a Trenton game. Grimstead was subsequently suspended.

Despite these actions, the agreement was not working. Players thumbed their noses at it and many owners ignored it. The *Wilkes Barre Record* noted in February 1921 that "about 80 percent of the men playing on Eastern League teams are also regulars on State League Clubs" (State League Cage Notes). The co-owner of the Trenton Tigers of the Eastern League, Joey Manze, was kicked out of the league and formed a new Trenton franchise which was accepted into the Pennsylvania State League.

In addition to the agreement not holding, the leagues were often burdened by owners' poor business practices. S. O. Grauley constantly railed against this in the *Philadelphia Inquirer*. In November 1920 he marveled that:

The absolute unbusinesslike method in which the league exists makes any one familiar with professional sports wonder how the league exists.[26]

Grauley was not just a newspaper reporter; he was also the vice president of the Eastern League and the former owner of the DeNeri franchise in the league.

In January 1921, Grauley noted that the agreement (adopted as an Eastern League rule) against Eastern League players playing in another league when their Eastern League team was playing would be enforced in the league's second half of the season.

Still, the players continued to maintain the upper hand until the confrontation came to a head in April. Following the completion of the Eastern League season, Germantown, the league champion, agreed to play a contest against the new Trenton franchise in the Pennsylvania State League. William Scheffer, who prized loyalty and responsibility, was irate and threatened heavy fines if the game was played. The players replied that the season was over, the league had no jurisdiction and they played the game with the support of the Germantown owners.

Meeting the next day the Eastern League owners took more oblique action than direct fines. Surmising that the players would not pay the fines and might leave the league, the owners disbanded the league and, within a week, formed a new league with Harrisburg admitted in place of Germantown.

The owners of the various league franchises could not survive all these machinations, amidst steady financial drain. At the end of the 1920-21 season, both the Interstate League and the Pennsylvania State League ceased operations. There were now only two major leagues in the East, but Jim Furey, the Celtic owner, created a new, but simple way of threatening both these leagues.

Furey had faced the same problems as the league owners and in 1921 he began signing his players to exclusive contracts. This meant that in return for a considerably higher guaranteed wage, each Celtic player agreed to play basketball for no other team. This hurt the leagues in two ways. First, Furey had now placed under exclusive contract the biggest stars in the game. Neither the Eastern nor the New York State League would be able to trumpet the presence of Beckman, Dehnert, Holman, Haggerty, Barry, Reich, or Leonard. That, in itself, was crippling. What proved fatal to the leagues, however, was the amount of money that Furey guaranteed his stars. Beckman and Holman received approximately $10,000 each with the others receiving almost that much. The high pay made other players demand more money from their owners, which ultimately was a death knell for the leagues.

At first the Celtics were locked out of playing against Eastern League teams. Neither the Celtics nor the Eastern League crowds were drawing the necessary crowds to cover costs and in December 1921 the Celtics entered the Eastern League. This only served to delay the ultimate collapse of the league. Across new leagues such as the Metropolitan, players' salaries had increased dramatically. John Murray noted the following:

While it is true that many of the leading professional players received over $7,000 for last season's work, it is also true that a more conservative policy must take place during the coming season in order to insure a successful year for the management, promoters, and players alike. The development of quite a number of youngsters who will be placed on many of the leading clubs will not only add new faces to the line ups of the various teams, but will also lessen the big expenses of former years. The cost of renting the armories, auditoriums and halls, together with the enormous price of publicity without counting the cost of the home players, visiting attractions and music, have oftentimes amounted to over a thousand dollars for the staging of a single game.[27]

The Eastern League experienced financial crises in 1921-22 as both Scranton and Wilkes-Barre, franchises added after the Pennsylvania State League folded, followed that lead, leaving the league at the halfway point and at season's end, respectively. The Harrisburg franchise changed hands three times before the Celtics acquired it. Philadelphia dropped out halfway through the season. According to Grauley, expenses had doubled in one year and attendance had not risen. The owners, he noted, had signed players to too much money on contracts. To save the league, players must be asked to take a cut. Salaries are "staggering high."[28]

The salaries remained high, fueled by Furey's Celtic contracts. In December 1922, Grauley repeated the admonition that Eastern League teams must cut player salaries to survive. The players refused and in January 1923, the Eastern League died. At the end of the 1923 season, the New York State League followed suit.

The Railroad Resurrects Pro Basketball

Though the Metropolitan League was alive and did reasonably well through the decade, player salaries were reduced in the league. The Celtics had started 1922 in the Metropolitan League, but "One week prior to the closing of the first half, they withdrew from the league at the request of the Furey brothers . . . because of financial reasons."[29] All of the noted Eastern professionals were playing in the Metropolitan or the New York State League in 1923. Many were also playing in local leagues in Brooklyn, Philadephia, or other cities to supplement their income. Only the Celtics were able to continue as full-time professionals on one team and, again, this was due to the railroad.

When the Eastern League folded in 1923, the Celtics had already left the league and made a living for themselves through barnstorming, i.e., traveling around the country playing local teams. Though they were not the first professional basketball team to travel exclusively, they were the best at this also. Peterson observed that:

Barnstorming trips by major teams were fairly common during the early years, especially when a league died in mid-season or when a team found it could make more money in independent play . . . . In 1914-15 a team called the New York Nationals (made up of players from the Rockaways on Long Island), went all the way to the West Coast and claimed 44 victories in 45 games.[30]

The most successful and "long running" team of barnstormers before the Celtics was a squad put together by an early basketball pioneer named Frank Basloe of Herkimer, New York. In his autobiography, *I Grew Up with Basketball,*[31] Basloe chronicled his career as a player, vaudevillian, and promoter and the teams he created.

In 1903, from the age of 16, Basloe played and promoted basketball games in northern New York and New England. His various 31st Separate Co. teams and subsequent Oswego Indians and Giants teams won league and regional championships. As they became more "well traveled," they were known also as Basloe's Globe Trotters. Beginning in 1913, they extended their realm to the Midwest traveling by train to Ohio, Illinois, Indiana, and Wisconsin. One of the players on Basloe's 1912-13 squad was Oscar (Swede) Grimstead who played for the original Celtics from 1919-21.

Basloe's Globe Trotters extended their play to encompass the East and Upper Midwest, but not until 1919-20 did they play as many as 100 games in a season. By then Basloe's teams were good and well traveled, but not the acknowledged world champions that the Celtics were.

So the Celtics took to the road, or rather to the rails. In the 1922-23 season, they played 205 games, winning 193 and appearing before more than 1.5 million fans, including 23,000 on Washington's birthday in Cleveland. They crisscrossed the northeastern quadrant of the United States from Maine to Indiana and east to Washington, D.C.

The next year (1923-24) featured the Metropolitan League and a Philadelphia League with a number of outstanding independent teams throughout the East and Midwest. Thanks to the outstanding rail connections provided by the Baltimore and Ohio (Philadelphia to St. Louis and Chicago, south from Buffalo and Rochester), the Pennsylvania (New York to Chicago, Buffalo, Rochester, Detroit), the New York Central (New York to Montreal and Boston) (New York and Montreal to Rochester and on to Cleveland, Chicago and St. Louis), the New Haven (New York to Hartford and Boston), the Chicago, Milwaukee, and St. Paul (Chicago to Wisconsin cities), the Celtics played throughout Massachusetts, New York, Wisconsin, Pennsylvania, Ohio, and more than eighty cities in nineteen states. They were both financially and competitively successful.

The Celtic success at extending their territory was so impressive that a number of owners of professional football teams (including

George Halas and George Marshall) felt that a new, professional basket-ball league linked via rail from Boston to Washington to Chicago could be successful. Thanks to the Celtics' groundbreaking tour and the rail-road connections, the American Basketball League (ABL) debuted in the fall of 1925.

The Celtics plied the northeastern quadrant again in 1924-25, but the next year extended their play all the way to Florida via lines like the Southern Railway System, the Seaboard Coast Line and others. The longer trips and the existence of the ABL caused the number of Celtic contests to fall to only 102 in a year.

By 1926-27, the ABL succeeded in obtaining the Celtics, and the Metropolitan League was near death. Just as the rails had allowed play-ers to engage in five regional leagues, it now led to the success of a true, national league with eight teams and fewer than 100 slots for profes-sional basketball players. The independent teams that survived returned to largely regional play and most of the players held "real" jobs rather than made their living by playing basketball. Harry Litwack recalled that by 1930 his great SPHA team had two teachers, a luggage salesman, a sporting goods dealer and only one full-time professional athlete, Chicky Passon, who also played professional baseball.[32]

The Railroad and the Exclusive Contract: A Summative Assessment

Within five years of the invention of basketball, players were receiving pay for their play, though none were making a living at basket-ball. The first professional leagues, begun as early as 1898, were essen-tially within the same metropolitan region with travel by trolley or train. The rail system in America began consolidating as early as the 1830s and by the 1900s most of the track in the nation was already in place. The sport of basketball, however, was still too new and dynamic to attract many fans beyond the local regions.

In order to truly institutionalize professional basketball, three things had to come together: (1) the game had to become more standardized; (2) individual "stars" needed to become known; and (3) the newspaper media had to take to the game, publicize it and create rivalries. All of these things began to occur in the mid 1910s and four professional leagues were able to establish themselves in four Northeastern regions—Philadelphia, the Wyoming Valley of Pennsylvania, the Hudson River Valley, and the New York City area stretching to Connecticut.

The local media took to the game and its new heroes, many of whom were playing in more than one league thanks to the rail service that effectively linked the northeast together. In 1916, passenger rail ser-vice peaked in the United States and the professional basketball leagues of the northeast were frequent beneficiaries of that service. World War I caused a shutdown of the leagues because of costs, players being drafted or working in war industries, and the takeover of the rail system by the federal government.

By 1919, the leagues and the players were back and the railroads were able to serve them even better after upgrades were made to various roadbeds as part of the war effort. The economy boomed and the players took great advantage of it by playing on three or four teams regularly. The league owners were economically sound, but foresaw problems if player salaries escalated. The owners valued stability, controlled costs and team loyalty. The players, as independent contractors, valued economic compensation and competitive success. They recognized early on that they were a scarce commodity since college basketball players seldom went on to professional basketball and few new, outstanding players were coming out of the settlement houses and YMCAs of the cities.

Thus, the players pushed their advantage by exploiting the rail system to the limit. Though these were not unions, the owners sought to break the multiple team practices of the players by instituting league agreements, fines, and supervisors. None were effective and many professional teams and leagues fell into financial disarray.

The death knell for many leagues and teams tolled when the Celtic owners began signing players to extremely high salaries, some in excess of $10,000. In order to compete, many owners overextended themselves financially and by 1923, the four top leagues had all folded.

The Celtics made the best of the situation they had created by, once again, relying on the railroads for a solution. Emulating the Basloe Globetrotters of the 1910s, the Celtics became a barnstorming team from 1923-26 spreading professional basketball prowess throughout the East, Midwest, and the South.

In 1925, the success of the Celtics enlivened interest in professional basketball and led to the creation of a new national professional league, the American Basketball League. This league, which stretched from Chicago to Boston and South to Washington, D.C., built on the foundation the Celtics had laid in both basketball expertise and railroad scheduling.

Thus, the nature of professional basketball was dramatically shaped in the period 1915-30 by two factors outside the game itself—the American rail system and the exclusive contract. The decline of the economy during the Depression made professional basketball a "gypsy sport" once again until World War II set the stage for a new era in professional basketball.

3

HOW THEY PLAYED THE GAME

The Celtics were the dominant team in basketball in the 1920s, and the introduction showed the importance the games between the Whirlwinds and the Celtics had in marking a watershed for the progress of the game, both in play and fan appeal. A legitimate question to ask, however, is "What was basketball like at this time, that is, what was the actual nature of the play and the equipment involved in that play?" This chapter will detail some of the differences that characterized basketball in the early part of this century and contrast it with how the game has been played in the latter part of this century.

First, the court was not standardized. Professional basketball in the early 1920s was played, for the most part, in a cage which surrounded the court. The cage had been introduced in the early 1900s in the New York State league by Lew and Ed Wachter, stalwarts of professional basketball in New York, particularly in the Albany-Troy region from the early 1900s into the 1930s. All the best professional leagues in the 1920s (New York State, Penn State, Eastern, and Interstate Leagues) used it until the ABL eschewed its use when it began play in 1925. With a cage, the ball was in play at all times, since there were no sidelines or end lines. Though floor sizes were not always standard, championship games were required to be "played in a hall sufficiently large to allow the placing of a cage satisfactory to the league."[1]

The cage was specified at 65 feet long and 35 feet wide, a much shorter and narrower court than today's 94- by 50-foot size. The court had no half court marking other than a center circle. There was no ten-second rule on crossing half-court, no back-court violation, no shot clocks, and no three-second rule in the lane under the basket (which at that time was much narrower, allowing for the true "keyhole" shape which still lends itself to the vocabulary of the game).

There was no ruling regarding surface although wood predominated, particularly in the various armories. The surface could get dusty quickly and, occasionally "sweat," especially when laid over concrete, so players tried to find shoes that would grip various surfaces. Shirley Povich, longtime sports writer and editor for the *Washington Post,* recalled when he first saw the Celtics play in Bangor, Maine, when he was still in high school. Their play, he recalled, was dazzling, not only the best in the world, but far better than he could have even imagined. Interestingly, however, what also stood out in his mind, seventy-five years later, were the Celtics' shoes. He noted that he and his friends had never seen shoes with suction grips for better stability and control. "They didn't even sell shoes like that in Maine,"[2] he remembered. Such shoes would have been like the More Shu product pictured here.

The baskets were either twelve inches from the backboard, or, in some leagues, were open without any backboard at all. In those instances, the basket was hung from a long, steel ceiling support. With baskets like this, scoring was more challenging—particularly from a longer distance—so it was logical to work the ball inside for an easier shot. Time was not a factor—nor was getting in the lane—so patience was rewarded.

The basketball was bigger in circumference and had raised laces made from rawhide. The basketballs were 30 to 33 inches in circumference, with three inches of "leeway" compared to one-half inch for today's 29 1/2- to 30-inch basketball circumference. The weight of a basketball in the 1920s was 21 to 24 ounces. Today's basketball is standardized at 20 to 22 ounces. So, the 1920s basketball often could have been 20 percent heavier and as much as 12 percent bigger, and much harder to handle than today's basketball. Joe Lapchick described the ball as "oversized and lopsided and blackened by dirt and old age. The big bulky

Basketball shoe about 1920.

pumpkin was laced and one end of the leather thong always protruded. The rubber inflation valve was pushed down and laced over, but a lump was always present. . . ."[3] Because the size of the basketball was less consistent, shooting was much more difficult in the 1920s, particularly when no backboard was present. The lack of a backboard also made tapping the ball into the basket more problematic.

Referees and Rough Play

With lenient national rules, basketball play was extremely rough and it was not uncommon to have players knocked unconscious during the course of the contest. When the ABL began in 1925, the league chose to adopt amateur rules, which limited the number of personal fouls a player could amass in one game. Under the former rules, there was little accountability for personal fouls. National rules did not recognize personal fouls caused by the actions of players—such offenses called for a warning against repetition or disqualification to return to the game. Amateur rules mandated penalization or disqualification after the fourth offense. Clearly, the professional policy left much to the discretion of referees who seemed loath to disqualify players and bring on the ire of crowds. Both professionals and amateurs saw the other's fouling policies as leading to a rougher game. The professional rationale was described by William Scheffer in the basketball guide as follows:

The four personal fouls in the college rules that disqualifies a man is really a bad one. Players that just brush by their opponents, because there has been personal contact disqualifies a man. . . . The college men say they want to eliminate rough play which is positively true as all rough play should be eliminated. But which class of men play the roughest? You will not have to go very far to find that the college games have been the roughest. Is it the fault of the rules, as they certainly have tried to legislate to stop roughness? It is not the fault of the rules that a game is rough, it is the fault of selecting officials who do not know the game. There were more players injured in the college game than in the professional game, just because the proper officials were not selected. . . . The colleges selected two officials and between the pair the roughness is not eliminated because those officials do not know just when to use the whistle. . . . All the legislation in the world cannot eliminate rough play if the officials do not stop it. And unless proper officials who know the game are selected, the roughness will still go on in spite of new rules.[4]

He then went on to extol the use of professional referees as the professional teams used. It should be noted that William Scheffer was also the president of the Eastern Basketball League, so he was not entirely objective in his pronouncements. Nevertheless, the problem of fouling plagued basketball, particularly professional basketball in the 1920s. The same basic problem still exists today; that is, does a referee call a tight game and possibly lose high-caliber players early (and anger the paying customers), or does one allow more slack regarding such players and risk letting the game get out of hand (and anger the paying customers)?

The 1922 official rules stated, "Such offenses call for warning against repetition or disqualification without permission to return to the game." It took truly outrageous conduct for a player to be expelled from a contest and referees were commonly bumped, slugged, or threatened in games, which encouraged them to change their calls. Joe Lapchick explained the following:

Once the official tossed the ball up between the centers, he was chiefly concerned with keeping out of the way and staying alive. There was only one referee, and he had about as much authority as an ant in a herd of elephants. There were no lines on most of the courts, and the ref would have to chalk out the center jump and free-throw areas. When you lined up for a jump, the poor guy would get a stiff neck trying to keep the wise guys from creeping over the chalk lines and erasing them off with the toes of their shoes.

When you were fouled it was a *real* one! With only one referee, the guy who did the fouling usually got away with it. So you belted him back.[5]

As players and spectators let their disputations get the best of them, the referees were frequently abused. Again, Lapchick provides the following details:

When a referee gave the home team more than a fair advantage, the visiting team players would put on the "press." When the referee tossed the ball up at center, the forward and guard on the same side of the court would come head-on and right at the arbiter. When the two players met, the referee would be caught in the middle. After one such "press" the official usually got the message.[6]

But referees were not completely without respect. In 1995, Harry Litwack recalled that the typical 1920s referee "missed a lot of calls, couldn't see a lot, but what he saw he called. What he didn't see, he didn't call, *but the players had a lot of confidence in (men like) Herman Baetzel*" (my emphasis). Baetzel was the dean of professional basketball refereeing particularly in the Philadelphia area from about 1910-30. Like many of the referees of the time, Baetzel began as a player—in his case with Jasper of the Philadelphia League in the early 1900s. When the

Eastern League began in 1909, he was the first referee; he also refereed the last Eastern League game in 1923. Baetzel also refereed in the Pennsylvania State League, the Metropolitan League, and the ABL. When teams from two leagues met for a "world championship," Baetzel was the referee of choice—as in 1921 when he handled the Scranton (Pennsylvania State League Champions)–Albany (New York State League Champions) series. In 1922, Baetzel refereed the three-game league championship series that pitted Trenton against the Celtics. In a rugged series in which 154 free throws were shot in three games, Baetzel was highly praised for his performance. "Referee Baetzel," noted the *Reach Guide*, "did fine work in all the games."[7]

In 1924, Bill Scheffer wrote this of Baetzel:

While speaking of one of the best, all-around players in the country it is appropriate to mention an official whose reputation is known wherever basketball is played in the East. No matter what important contest is scheduled, if Herman Baetzel is suggested there is never an objection. Baetzel was a former player and has been officiating for fully fifteen years.[8]

The next year, Maurice Rosenwald, in discussing a Celtics–Kingston game, referred to Baetzel as "perhaps the best basketball referee in the country."[9]

The only referee to approach Baetzel in stature during that time was Ward Brennan of New York, who, from before World War I was officiating in the Interstate, New York State, and other leagues. Despite his army assignment as physical director at Camp Mills during World War I, Brennan was still able to continue some of his officiating. In 1918, he handled the Bridgeport-Ansonia (Connecticut) state professional championship. In describing that series, Raymond Curtis stated that Brennan was "considered one of the best referees in the country."[10] In that same guide, Brennan is pictured in his army uniform and identified as a "prominent referee."[11] Four years later, the *Reach Guide* pictured Brennan again and called him "one of basketball's best referees."[12] The *Wilkes-Barre Record* also referred to Brennan as "the best basketball referee in the East."[13]

Brennan was a "big manly man," according to the *Wilkes-Barre Record*. Referees needed that strength to both protect themselves and to fight for a good position to see the plays. One rule which presented a great challenge to the referees in professional basketball pertained to dribbling the basketball. The national rules permitted dribbling with two hands as well as stopping and starting at will. Thus, if a player was double-teamed and "trapped" after dribbling, he could step out of the

Ward Brennan, one of the outstanding referees of the 1920s pictured in his army uniform in 1918.

double-team by essentially busting through a defender and dribbling again. This necessitated rough, bodily contact, which was not illegal. A *New York Post* article by Stanley Frank in 1935 addressed the effect of rough play on referees as follows:

Then there was [referee] Lou "Doc" Sugarman, who had every front tooth in his head knocked out before he became a dentist and, as the outstanding exponent of the two-hand dribble, was sent flying on many short notice trips. Sugarman played through entire seasons without a shred of skin on his knees and elbows.

The Celtics' Style of Play

The Celtics perfected pass and cut basketball—referred to by some as Eastern Style. In a 1995 interview, Harry Litwack, long-time Temple coach and a professional with the SPHAs in the early 1930s, described the style in more detail as follows:

> Pass the ball to the forward, go to him. Pass to a forward, cut away from him. Pass to the center man, cut off. Pass, take a false step and go for the basket, get a bounce pass from a teammate. Give and go. That was all started originally by the New York Celtics.[14]

Litwack noted that the Celtics' tenure together, plus their outstanding talent as a team, allowed them to perfect their play.

The Celtic players described their individual play similarly. Bounce passes were not frequently used "because there was too much bounce, or, in some instances, no bounce at all."[15] The offense was a situation offense, as Litwack described—"free-wheeling, fast-passing pressure offense by the greatest ball handling team I ever saw." Lapchick noted that "(E)very pass and every move had a purpose, and the technique broke the backs of practically every team we met."[16]

Shirley Povich, longtime *Washington Post* sportswriter, first saw the Celtics in 1921 and many times after that. He recalled that, "They passed the ball to distraction. Dribbling was minimal because the ball was not dependable."[17]

The Celtics were credited with perfecting the pivot play. Dutch Dehnert would hand off the ball while his teammates would cut by him. In the nomination of Dehnert to the Naismith Memorial Basketball Hall of Fame in 1964, Lapchick noted that Dehnert's "pivot play could not be stopped." The ball came into the pivot fast and the Celtics knew that it would be passed off just as quickly with no lost motion."[18] Povich noted that Dehnert had a "big rump and knew how to use it to get himself and his teammates open."[19]

Haggerty noted that Beckman and Banks did most of the cutting for the basket and Beckman was also "a master of the fast break."[20] Possession of the ball was the keynote of play.[21] The Celtics were the first team to use set plays, but if necessary, they "could 'sit on the ball' for minutes on end."[22]

The Celtics' philosophy was simple—get the ball moving and hit a green shirt; the ball was whipped around quickly to "make it sing." Only one videotape of the Celtics is known to have been made. It runs less than ten minutes. Filmed on a rooftop court somewhere in New York, one sees the incredible deceptiveness of Dehnert and the swift, sure passing and cutting of Banks, Lapchick, and Barry.

In a 1922 article, the *Philadelphia Inquirer* described Dehnert's pivot play as beautiful. "Dehnert rushed up the floor and with Campbell on his back, took a pass and cleverly pivoted the ball to Holman and back to Dehnert and then to Holman on the foul line for a dead shot."[23] Later accounts refer to the Celtics' "dazzling passing attack,"[24] their "fine demonstration of passing,"[25] and their ability to "pass the leather with a speed that dazzled the visitors."[26] Another account had them "playing a clever passing game which kept the ball from their opponents during most of the play."[27]

The question could be raised, "How much did the Celtics control the ball in a game?" That is not easy to say since few accounts detail such data. There are some which do, however. In an important game in February of 1928, the Celtics faced the Philadelphia Warriors in Philadelphia. The Warriors had already defeated the Celtics three times of six games—so the contest was crucial to establishing "supremacy." With what was termed phenomenal passing and floor work, the Celtics embarrassed the Warriors in the first half, leading 19-3. "The accuracy of their bullet-like shots from one another was such that in the opening stanza they had complete control of the ball *17 times out of a possible 20*" (my emphasis).[28] This would also indicate not just control of the tap and subsequent passing, but excellent shooting and rebounding. In a 1926-27 ABL contest played in Boston against the Whirlwinds, each jump ball was noted. There were a total of thirty-eight with the Celtics winning 21 against a team credited with its finest performance of the year by one Boston writer, with 12 of the 19 first half jumps won by the Celtics. The Celtics usually worked hard in the first half to put an opponent away early so they could "coast" in the second half, relying on passing the time away, literally.

Shooting was not always excellent. It was barely good by today's standards as a result of all of the exigencies mentioned earlier. In February 1928, the *Cleveland Plain Dealer* included shooting percentages in the box scores of two Celtic-Cleveland Rosenblum games. In the first game, Cleveland was 10 of 47 for 21 percent while the Celtics were 8 of 46 for 17 percent shooting. The next night, the Rosenblums sunk to 7 of 56 for 12.5 percent and the Celtics improved to 13 of 36 for 35 percent—which was probably more typical for a Celtic performance.[29]

All of these accounts allow the Celtics' play to be presented in summary. The Celtics perfected a style of play known as Eastern Style basketball. It consisted of swift, accurate chest passes and hand offs to constantly cutting teammates. Play could be in the back court or in the forecourt near the basket for minutes. As the first team to have plays, the Celtics used the pivot play regularly, taking the ball from Dehnert, whose wide frame kept the defenders at bay.

The give-and-go play usually involved the forwards, most often Beckman or Holman, as scorers. One guard, the standing guard, usually Reich or, later, Barry, frequently did not go much into the forecourt, but instead laid back on defense and directed the ball in and out on offense.

The Celtics' shots were most often layups (which came from a tangle of arms and legs as picks were thrown) or long shots (which the swift Celtics ran down if the shots were unsuccessful). Cutting through the middle often resulted in body-jarring fouls which sent the Celtics to the free-throw line, where they commonly hit 70 percent (*very* high for the time) of their free throws.

Rebounding statistics were not compiled until the 1930s, which indicates the lack of importance placed on rebounding in contrast to the emphasis on ability to pass the ball. With a tap off after each score, control of the tap was a key to controlling the tempo of the game. Haggerty and Lapchick were great at the tap, while the other Celtics were great at anticipating where the ball was going to go—especially when the Celtics were outsized on the tap against someone like 6-foot 7-inch "Stretch" Meehan.

On defense, there was no team as aggressive as the Celtics. They were the first to play a switching man to man defense, and they took tremendous pride in their team defense. All of the former Celtics mention the effort that was put into defense. No one ever let up on defense. The result was that Celtic teams never felt likely to lose—even when they were down. Constant defensive Celtic pressure would lead to opposition breakdowns, and the Celtics almost always took advantage of the opponent's weaknesses.

Though the Celtics were the most skilled team in the game, they could play as rough as necessary to win or to convince their opponents that the Celtics were anyone's equal in aggressive play. Games commonly had players knocked unconscious or suffering bloody wounds. Holman was great at faking fouls, but Dehnert, Haggerty, Lapchick, and Barry were big and rough.

Big, of course, is a relative term. At only 5 feet 8 inches tall, it is difficult to imagine John Beckman being referred to as rough or rugged; but he was considered both—a man who would not quit. Leonard's tenacious defense earned him the nickname "Leech" or "Dog." At 6 feet, he could guard centers, forwards, or guards.

The great stars of the period scarcely left their feet in games on offense or defense; it was considered dangerous to do so since a player didn't know if his feet would be knocked out while he was in the air. Barney Sedran recalled the following:

Don't imagine that, in my time, we didn't think of the jump shot, the bread and butter shot of today. But it was suicide to shoot for the basket with your feet off the ground because you'd be lucky to come down alive. So for self-preservation, we had to keep our feet on the floor while making a shot. That way, it was much safer to take the belt you knew you were going to get.[30]

Thus, the game was a floor game. Great shooters like Beckman at 5 feet 8 inches, Holman at 5 feet 11 inches, Benny Borgmann at 5 feet 8 inches, and Barney Sedran at 5 feet 4 inches (and only 118 pounds) could score because of their quickness, accuracy, and ability to avoid or deflect severe pounding.

The Celtics also had to be in great physical shape since they played up to 200 games some seasons. Because of doubleheaders—most often against two different squads—they averaged better than a game per day. The running clock (not including the last three minutes of the game and extra periods) meant games frequently were completed in about one hour with two twenty-minute halves and a ten-minute intermission between halves. The cage, which prevented balls from going out of bounds, also sped up play. Still, the Celtic stamina had to have been exceptional since their second games were most often against the better of two opponents challenged in a doubleheader, and later games were played before larger evening crowds. Additionally, the Celtic style was to run, cut, and pass, and eventually tire their opponents out.

The Role of the Big Man

The big man's role in the early years of basketball was much different from today. Part of this difference was the nature of the agility and skill of the big players, but much was due to the physical, technical differences in the game as well. In basketball, it is a simple axiom that the taller one is, the closer one is to the basket. Thus, it would seem to make sense to seek out taller individuals to play on one's team. Size, however, does not assure agility, good ball-handling, shooting accuracy, ability to gain rebounding positions, or intelligence—all of which are necessary to defeat one's opponents. If all other traits are equal, height is a distinct advantage. It has often been said, "You can't teach height," but you can teach these other, valuable athletic skills. How much does height actually matter? Did it matter to the Celtics and their opponents?

The 1921-22 Celtics put the following players on the floor—Ernie Reich and Dutch Dehnert as guards, both 5 feet 11 inches or 6 feet—

though Dehnert weighed about 210 pounds; Nat Holman, 5 feet 11 inches, and Johnny Beckman, 5 feet 8 inches, as forwards; and George "Horse" Haggerty, 6 feet 4 inches and husky, at center. Pete Barry and Chris Leonard were the two men off the bench; these two were each about six feet tall. The Celtics were above average in height, but not decidedly so. For example, the 1922 Trenton team had Francis "Stretch" Meehan at center at 6 feet 7 inches with Maury Tome and Tom Barlow at guards at 6 feet 2 inches and 6 feet 1 inch, respectively. The forwards, Bernie Dunn and Frankie Boyle, were just under six feet. In all, this was a bigger squad than the Celtics and one of the biggest around.

By 1927-28, Joe Lapchick, 6 feet 5 inches, had replaced Haggerty, Davey Banks, 5 feet 5 inches, had replaced Beckman, and Holman, Dehnert, Leonard, and Barry were still on the squad. The Celtics' chief rival, the Warriors, had Al Kellet, a burly 6-foot 4-inch center; George Artus, another burly player, and 6 feet 2 inches; Tom Barlow; George Glasco, 5 feet 11 inches; and Jimmy "Soup" Campbell at 5 feet 8 inches." This was a big, rough team, which averaged more in height than the Celtics—so the Celtic team did not dominate in regard to its height.

From its inception in 1891, basketball had been more of a game of average size participants. Peterson explained what that meant in a short chapter on "Big Men" in *Cages to Jump Shots,* his examination of pro basketball's early years. Peterson notes that there are no reliable statistics on average heights of early professionals, but that until 1930, a six-footer was considered a big man. Peterson then examined the players selected in 1931 for an all-time, all-star team by Frank Morgenweck and Ed Wachter for a similar team in 1940.

Both Wachter and Morgenweck are members of the Naismith Memorial Basketball Hall of Fame, and both spent most of their careers in and around the New York State League, the Interstate League, and independent teams in the Northeastern United States, starting in about 1900. Without television or radio, and with minimal newspaper coverage, most of their choices for all time greats were players from the Northeast, particularly performers from the New York State League. The players on Morgenweck's first two teams averaged about 5 feet 10 inches—as did the first team selected by Wachter. My own research indicates that this was about average for professionals of the period from 1900-30.

Were Americans noticeably smaller seventy-five years ago? Why did so few big men play professional basketball? The answer to the first question is yes and no, which needs further explanation. Again, Peterson, using data from a 1912 study made for insurance companies that examined male policy holders from 1885 to 1908, found that the average man's height was 5 feet 8 1/2 inches, that only one man in 222,000 was 6 feet 11 inches tall, and that just four-tenths of a percent were 6 feet 6 inches or taller. Though using data which leaves out people who could not afford or chose not to buy insurance, there seems to be no relationship between height and income, so it is easy to accept Peterson's presentation of the data.[31]

He then went on to examine 1959 actuarial data which showed about an inch of growth, on average over almost fifty years. The percentage of men 6 feet 5 inches tall or above remained constant. He then concludes, "There is no reason to believe that the heel curve of height distribution has changed, and so there should have been plenty of tall prospects for basketball in the 1920s and before."[32]

If these tall men existed in equal numbers at that time, why were they not playing basketball? First, tall people were considered by many to be freakish and were not eager to expose themselves to ridicule because of their height. Peterson quotes Joe Lapchick as saying how embarrassing this was. "Wherever we went people stared at me and pointed to me like something in a sideshow, where you often found the 'giant' or the 'tallest man alive.'" Not surprisingly, tall men shrank from the limelight.[33]

Second, the game was a fast-paced, pass-oriented game in which tall men were viewed as ungainly—too clumsy and uncoordinated to play basketball. Lapchick noted that when he began to play basketball, most centers "were awkward and couldn't run."[34] They would get the tap off the rebound and then get out of the way. Smaller men could often outjump or outreach them. With little coaching and player development, the asset of height was overwhelmed by the debit of inability to run well or more quickly.

Big Men

A few talented big men did emerge from the years 1910-30. Three of the earliest big men in the pro game were Oscar (Swede) Grimstead at 6 feet 1 1/2 inches tall; Maurice Tome, 6 feet 2 inches; and George (Horse) Haggerty, 6 feet 4 inches. All were about the same age—born in the early 1890s—and became pros in about 1911. Grimstead, a native of New York City, began his career playing with various teams, including Frank Basloe's famous Oswego Indians team during 1912-13. Basloe referred to Grimstead as "tall, lanky, and fast," but photos of the period show a broad-shouldered (rather than lanky) man with obvious upper-arm strength. Grimstead was a center who relied on ball-handling and, as such, was the greatest ball-handler in basketball, according to Basloe.[35]

This was important as most offensive play involved the center and forwards—and only occasionally the guards. The center distributed the ball to the forwards who took most of the shots. The center had to be a good passer and defender, and Grimstead was both.

In 1913, Grimstead began playing with Utica in the New York State League on one of the finest teams of the era—which included Barney Sedran and Marty Friedman. Grimstead's career lasted until the late 1920s, by which time he had become a guard. This indicates both Grimstead's versatility and the fact that there was minimal difference between centers and guards in the 1910s in regard to height.

Since most play was done via swift ball-handling and cutting forwards, the size advantage for a center was the ability to block off defenders following or anticipating passes, or cutting off offensive players. This also carried over to defense where guards, in particular, excelled. Grimstead was the quintessential ball-handling center—quick, fast, and broad-shouldered with great passing instincts.

Grimstead had been preceded as an acclaimed center by Ed Wachter of the Troy Trojans, a team on which he began to play in 1909 after six years of professional play. Wachter was about ten years older than Grimstead, but wasn't a dominating center figure as Swede seemed to be. Wachter's Trojans included two of his brothers, one was Lew, Troy's business manager and captain. Ed, however, was the leader and is credited with devising the fast-passing game that was perfected by the future Celtics. The Trojans are credited by Basloe with the bounce pass, the short pass, the fast break, the legal block, and the long pass with all the players doing a lot of scoring—centers and guards as well as forwards.[36] The Wachter brothers, as noted earlier, also introduced the cage to professional play in upstate New York where it became popular.[37]

In the 1913-14 New York State League, Wachter and his Troy Trojans, four-time league champions, were edged by Utica for the championship. Utica, as noted, had Grimstead at center and Troy had Ed Wachter who was no longer playing center, but forward, as George Haggerty, a young man from Springfield, Massachusetts, had established himself as the big man's "big man."

George Haggerty began his professional career in Gloversville, New York, in about 1912. In 1913 he joined Reading, the defending Eastern League Champs led by Andy Sears, in addition to playing with Troy. Haggerty, who was nicknamed "Horse" by Bill Brandt of the old Philadelphia Record, was one of the biggest men in basketball with 230 pounds on his 6-foot 4-inch body. In 1913-14 he lived up to his nickname, playing in all sixty-three of his Troy teams' games and scoring 265 points on the well-balanced team which led the league in scoring.

Though Haggerty became an offensive liability in his later playing years, his early career found him in the top twenty in league scoring.

Haggerty was considered a giant, but his most unique trait might have been his ability to "palm" the ball, that is, to hold the ball with one hand—a feat almost unheard of in the 1920s when the basketball was as much as two and one-half inches larger in circumference than it is today. In fact, it may have been even larger when one considers the inaccuracy of measurement and the "lumpy" nature of the ball itself with its raised laces. In a *Washington Herald* article of January 1923, Haggerty is pictured holding the ball with a headline above his photo stating, "This giant can grip a ball with one hand." Another article noted "Celtic Giant Handles Ball Like Pitcher" with a photo caption calling Haggerty "the wonder of basketball." In the late 1920s, when Haggerty coached and played for Washington in the ABL, the team letterhead pictured Haggerty palming the ball.[38]

Haggerty was described as "light on his feet, able to time the ball well, . . . a superb rebounder, and . . . at his best on defense."[39] Haggerty's forte was, indeed, defense. "He was so big then, when human skyscrapers were not in vogue in basketball, that he usually got in the way of the opponents, and therein lay his chief value on defense."[40]

Maurice Tome was another young center in the New York State League in 1913-14, scoring 280 points while performing for Kingston in all sixty-four of their games. Johnny Beckman was a young teammate that year. Tome was 6 feet 2 inches and good enough to be included in Morgenweck's all-time second team selected in 1931.

Tome was referred to as a "close-guarding, arm-waving defensive specialist" by Bole and Lawrence,[41] though there were times that he was an offensive hero as well. Bole and Lawrence recount one such game when Tome was on Trenton, a team he played for in the late 1910s through the end of the Eastern League in 1923.[42] A Trenton native, Tome later coached at Trenton's Cathedral High School but also played for Metropolitan League teams which included Trenton's Bengals; Kingston (once again); and in 1925-26, Perth Amboy/Passaic managed by Frank Morgenweck, his manager at Kingston in the early part of his career.

The tallest man in basketball for many years was Francis P. (Stretch) Meehan, an unusual professional because he was a college graduate. Meehan was a lawyer trained at Seton Hall. But he was also 6 feet 7 inches tall and spent more time playing basketball than practicing law in his early career. Basketball paid much better—particularly for someone as tall and talented as Meehan, who made as much as $100 per game.

Meehan was an excellent foul shooter, though not a great shooter from the field. Playing with Scranton in the Pennsylvania State League,

Germantown and Trenton in the Eastern League, and with other independent teams like the SPHAs, Meehan also played for the Cleveland Rosenblums before they joined the ABL and the Warriors in the ABL. Meehan even played for a Celtics team that Jim Furey tried to resurrect in 1929 upon his release from prison for theft.

Meehan was masterful at getting the tap, the key to ball control in the 1920s when there was a tap-off after each score. In addition, whenever there was a tie-up on the floor, there was a jump ball from the spot of the tie-up. Meehan became adroit at tapping the ball through the hoop for a score when the jump ball was near his offensive basket.[43]

Meehan had one other skill which was a great asset to his team—his positioning on the pivot play at a time when it was first being developed. Bole and Lawrence quote a Philadelphia Bulletin article (likely from the 1920-21 season) describing this play:

Meehan's favorite trick, bending over and keeping the apex of the angle pointed into his opponents [sic] stomach, worked to perfection. Whenever Big Stretch got the ball and assumed the angular position, with his back to the basket and Skeets Wright (Philly center) trying to climb up his back, Holman would appear out of nowhere, dash full speed across Meehan's bow, collecting the ball in passing, and generally getting a chance to shoot before Willie Miller or the unfortunate Chick Passon could catch him.[44]

Despite not being known for his shooting prowess, Meehan did finish tenth in the Pennsylvania State League in scoring in 1919-20, sixth in the Eastern League in the first half of 1921-22, fourth in the Metropolitan League in 1922-23, and ninth in that same league in 1923-24. Meehan was not quick, but he was an excellent center for the time. He played good defense, worked the ball around, made free throws, and rebounded. He was one of the top two or three centers in the 1920s.

Undoubtedly, the finest center of that era was Joe Lapchick of the Celtics. He became the prototypical all-around center—a good shooter, rebounder, passer, and defender, though he had to develop his team play to fit into the Celtics' scheme of things.

After playing with a variety of leagues and independent teams, Lapchick became a Celtic in 1923 and helped bring the Celtics some of their greatest successes. Lapchick followed "in the shoes of Horse Haggerty, a real legend."[45] Lapchick also became a showman (a la Grimstead) in the post, perfecting his play when the Celtics returned to barnstorming in the 1930s.

When the Celtics entered the ABL in 1926, the Philadelphia Warriors were also in their first year in the league. Dissatisfied with the play of Stretch Meehan, the Warriors signed a muscular center, Al Kellet, from Youngstown, Ohio. in February 1927. Kellet was described as 6 feet 2 1/2 inches to 6 feet 4 1/2 inches tall and 200 to 225 pounds. He was mobile, agile, and rugged. His signing was made too late to affect Warrior play that year, but the next year he was a significant member of the 1927-28 Warrior squad, or "Cavemen." The intention of the Warriors was to outmuscle the Celtics, to slow them down, since the Celtics seemed to have perfected the speedy, ball movement manner of play. Kellet was an instrumental part of this plan, which as will be shown later, was not successful in the long run. Kellet continued a movement toward big, strong centers who could also score—a movement first started by Lapchick. Not until George Mikan in the 1940s would a truly big man dominate the game, but by then the game itself had changed.

Summarizing the Play of the Era

The Celtic style of play was adopted and adapted by hundreds of teams from high school to the pros. Playing on a shorter floor with rules and equipment that allowed for a game characterized by swift ball movement, the Celtics became the masters of basketball and subsequent dominant squads emulated or sought to emulate their style of play. The New York Renaissance squad, for example, first formed in the early 1920s, copied Celtic play. By the 1930s they were acknowledged as the finest team in basketball. They were anchored by a 6-foot 6-inch center, but had players as short as 5 feet 5 inches on the team as well. The key to all this was ball handling, speed, and agility. But, having those skills *plus* size was a marked asset.

4

THE CELTICS—A BRIEF HISTORY

In late 1918, following the end of World War I, a young man named Jim Furey, then twenty-five and a cashier in a department store, decided to reorganize what had been originally a settlement house basketball team on New York's west side. Composed entirely of young Irishmen, reflecting the ethnic composition of the neighborhood and the settlement house, the team began play in 1914, managed by Frank McCormack. According to Joe Williams, a sports writer for the *Brooklyn Eagle* in the early 1900s,

Around 1916 the New York Celtics were a third-rate light team from the west side of New York City, in the neighborhood of Hudson Guild and "Hell's Kitchen." The team was managed by Frank McCormack and among some of the players were Barry, Witty, Nally, Hart, "Specks" McCormack, Calhoun and Gargan—all local neighborhood boys.[1]

In 1911-12, the New York City Bureau of Recreation held its first inter park-playground basketball league, with two divisions—juniors (under 100 pounds) and seniors. At the same time, most settlement houses had representative basketball teams and the formation of the Celtics was timely and hardly unique.[2] The Celtics enjoyed modest success playing other New York City teams, but with the outbreak of the war in 1917 the team broke up.

In 1917, Frank McCormack entered the army and turned the team over to the Furey brothers. James Furey, along with his brother Thomas, a night club owner, saw professional basketball as an opportunity to make money and get some small degree of fame. Thus, they decided to capitalize on the Celtics' name for a fan base and promote the new Celtics, retaining some of the former Celtic players, notably James (Pete) Barry and Johnny Whitty. An early snag in this play was McCormack's refusal to sell the rights to the name to the Furey brothers.

Since a team at that time had almost no real assets except for players, uniforms, and equipment, the right to the name was a key to identity, assuring the fan recognition, and possibly, aiding in lining up opponents and places to play. Rather than negotiate with McCormack, Furey named the squad the Original Celtics and proceeded to sign new players for his team.

During the 1918-19 season, the Celtics compiled a good win/loss record while playing nearly all their games at the Central Opera House in Manhattan, and two Celtics, Barry and Kennedy, were named to a New York City All Star Team.[3]

John Peter Barry served the longest on the Celtic team from 1915 until World War I, then after the war from 1918 until 1936 when he retired from the game at the age of thirty-nine. Barry was born in 1897 and joined the Celtics soon after they were formed as a Chelsea neighborhood team on Manhattan's west side in 1914 by McCormack.

In 1913, Barry appeared in 55 games for Paterson of the New York State League and then played for various New York City teams. He played in the New York State League teams until finally playing exclusively for the Celtics and the Furey brothers beginning in 1921. In 1919-20, Barry was the second-leading scorer for the Knights of St. Anthony team of Brooklyn which included Celtic teammates Trippe, Kennedy, and Witte as well as Pete's brother, Tom. This team defeated many powerful squads including the Pennsylvania State League All-Stars, twice.

Joe Lapchick recalled that Barry ". . . was a good play maker, a good shooter, a fine rebounder, and he was tough, a very fine defensive player."[4] At six feet tall he could play inside or outside and could score quickly as he was often asked to do.

In 1919, Furey signed Ernie Reich, Joe Trippe, Eddie White and Mike Smolick, all excellent players who joined Barry and Whitty in the lineup. This team won 65 of 69 games[5] and "continually drew 4,000 people to home games. The record attendance for the season was 5,600 at the Edison Indians game."[6] The Celtics defeated every quality squad in the New York City region and spoke of themselves as world champions.

Celtic success was linked to the stability of their lineup. Most teams had a core of players who normally showed up for games, but could not be counted upon for each and every game because they sold their basketball skills on a game-by-game or week-by-week basis. Williams felt that "Tripp (sic) furnished the team with the First Spark of glory . . . with the great Tripp in the lineup plus much assistance from the improving Barry and John Witty the team started to go places, meeting and beating a much better grade of teams than previously."[7] Many of the Celtics players originally played in a Brooklyn professional league with Trippe, Barry, Smolick, White, and Whitty all competing for the Knights of St. Anthony squad.[8] Reich was a regular for Scranton of the Pennsylvania State League. Smolick and Barry also played in the New York State

League. Because the Celtics played almost all their games on Saturday or Sunday nights and leagues played on week nights, the squad was almost always intact.

After most games there was a dance on the court. The combination of rough, tough professional basketball and dancing, which appealed to both genders, was popular in New York City and throughout the Northeast. In addition, at least one observer, Sam Murphy of the *New York Evening Mail,* felt the imposition of prohibition also helped popularize basketball. "With prohibition now a certainty, many halls will be held at the disposal of the teams that ordinarily would have been given over to drinking fests. Owners of such places find that basketball and dancing go hand-in-hand and are encouraging this sport."[9]

Despite the outstanding record compiled by the Celtics, it was still questionable whether they were even the best in the city, let alone in the world. Thus, Furey continued to pursue better and better talent. For the 1920 season, the Fureys signed Henry "Dutch" Dehnert, Johnny Beckman, and Oscar Grimstead—all outstanding players and all New York City Natives.

Oscar "Swede" Grimsted

"Swede" Grimstead was a veteran center of various teams and leagues before Jim Furey signed him to a Celtic contract for the 1920-21 season. As early as the 1912-13 season, he was performing for Frank Basloe's Oswego (New York) Indians. Grimstead was from New York City and had played amateur ball there as well as with professional teams in White Plains of the Hudson River League in 1911-12 and with Hudson in 1911. He also had played in the New York State League in 1912-13 with Troy and Cohoes. Despite being a center, Grimstead was feted by Basloe as "the greatest ball handler in basketball. His style was that later used by the famous Harlem Globetrotters."[10]

After leaving the Oswego Indians, Grimstead played for teams in the Eastern, New York State and Pennsylvania State Leagues appearing for DeNeri, Paterson, Trenton, Utica, Pittston, Nanticoke, and Scranton. In 1920, Jim Furey added Grimstead to the Celtics, but by 1921 he had been replaced by George (Horse) Haggerty in what was probably a move dictated by both economics and Haggerty's size. Grimstead went on to play through at least the 1927-28 season when he was in his late thirties. In the 1921-22 season, Grimstead played for the Dodgers of the Metro League who went 12-8 to tie for the League's best record. His teammates were Marty Friedman, Barney Sedran, Elmer Ripley, Brennan, Gelb, and Norman. This was a powerful squad, but there is no record of them playing the Celtics, though that occurrence was highly likely.

Henry "Dutch" Dehnert

Henry George Dehnert was born in New York City in April of 1898. Little information is available on his early years even in Dehnert's own summary of his life for the Hall of Fame nomination. Dehnert did not play basketball in high school (and may not have even attended). Like most early professionals, he first played around the city for the YMCA, settlement house, and other amateur teams. He gained a reputation as a rugged, deft, ball-handling player from 1912-17.

His first, prominent professional team was the Ansonia (Connecticut) squad which also featured Ernie Reich, Dehnert's future Celtic teammate. Dehnert is supposed to have appeared for DeNeri in 1915 and Scranton in 1916, but the *Reach Guides* do not list him in league scoring lists. Ansonia went 14-9 in the Connecticut State League in 1917-18, edging the Blue Ribbons of Bridgeport by one-half game for the league title. A seven-game series between the two squads was arranged for March after the season had ended. In that series, Ansonia triumphed four games to two with Dehnert scoring 26 points—the third highest team total—and he led the team with fourteen field goals.[11]

Dehnert joined another future Celtic teammate, Chris Leonard, in 1917-18 on the Newark Turners, one of the New Jersey professional teams. In thirty-six contests against other New Jersey professional squads, Dehnert scored 198 points—good for third in the federation as the Turners went 25-11 and tied two games.

Dehnert also was a regular for the Downey Shipyard team of Staten Island during World War II. In February, March, and April, Downey and Standard, the other dominant shipyard team, met in a seven-game series held at the Sacred Heart Hall and the New Downey Club House, both on Staten Island. Led by Johnny Beckman, Standard won six games. The team rosters were rather "dynamic" for the series. Dehnert, for example, played the first two contests for Downey, scoring three and seven points respectively and the teams split the two games. Dehnert missed the next two games held in mid to late March, but reappeared for the games of April 2 and 9, scoring six and ten points, respectively. An unusual aspect of these games was that Dehnert played for Standard in these latter contests and was instrumental in their victory over Downey, four games to two.

It can be reasonably assumed that Dehnert's rapid change of allegiance could be traced to one source—money. Dehnert's actions were typical of most of the young professionals who followed the money. Before signing an exclusive contract with the Celtics in 1921, Dehnert played for Nanticoke and Scranton of the Pennsylvania State League,

Henry "Dutch" Dehnert about 1920.

Bridgeport and Thompsonville of the Interstate League, Philadelphia of the Eastern League, Utica of the New York State League, and St. James Crowns of the Brooklyn professional teams, among others.

Dehnert was an adequate scorer with four to eight points per game—a respectable count at that time. In 1920-21, he was seventh in scoring in the Pennsylvania State League with 198 points in 33 games. That same year, Dehnert scored 138 points in 15 games for Thompsonville. The previous year Dehnert had teamed with Beckman on Nanticoke to bring them a Pennsylvania State League Championship defeating Scranton three games to one.

Dehnert was not usually a big scorer. On the Celtics, the forwards, Beckman and Holman, scored the majority of the points. Instead, Dehnert excelled at passing, defense, and magnificent ball-handling. These attributes were so outstanding that in 1942, George "Horse" Haggerty, Dehnert's teammate on the Celtics for two years and a foe for at least eight other seasons, declared that Dehnert was "the greatest all-around player of all time."[13]

Dehnert's play was impressive enough to warrant selection in 1931 by Frank Morgenweck, veteran authority and Basketball Hall of Fame coach and contributor to the second five of his all-time great team along with Beckman and Holman. Dehnert's greatest skill was his pivot play, which he perfected while a member of the Celtics. Almost every mention of Dehnert describes the "invention" of the play and the subsequent paradigmatic change it had on the playing of the game. In Dehnert's Hall of Fame nomination, he claims *not* to have invented the play, but to have been "instrumental in creating the pivot play in about 1925-26 in Chattanooga."[14] Nat Holman noted that in 1920 his Germantown team occasionally used the play. Additionally, there are other instances of its use prior to Dehnert and the Celtics' use of it in 1925 on their "Southern tour."[15]

Despite this lack of "creation," there is no question that Dehnert and his Celtics made the play nearly unstoppable, necessitating a change in the rules of basketball. Dehnert asserted, "During 1928-29, the pivot play could not be stopped."[16] This might seem a bit self-serving, but other observers echo this assertion. In Neil Isaacs' book, *All The Moves* (his history of college basketball), he notes that, while where and when the Celtics began exploiting the pivot play was immaterial, certain constants do emerge:

A big standing guard was making trouble for the Celtics' attack. Dehnert backed inside, took a pass from Holman or Johnny Beckman, and passed off to one or the other as they cut past—picking off the defender, or, if the standing guard committed to one side, Dehnert would turn to the basket the other way. The play was so successful that it became the backbone of most offenses, enriched by a basic, double-post variation and it remains a staple of modern basketball.[17]

Zander Hollander tells a similar tale of the pivot play with Dehnert concluding, "This was the pivot play but we didn't even know it at the time."[18]

Is it really possible that a single maneuver could be so important in the perception, promotion, and history of the game of basketball? The evidence seems to indicate an affirmative answer. In Eber's advertising flyer promoting a game in the 1920s between the Celtics and the Western New York Champions, there is a teaser prominently displayed on the ad. It reads, "See the original pivot play starring the one and only "Dutch" Dehnert."[19] In 1942, when Dehnert coached the Harrisburg Senators in the American Professional Basketball Association, the first story on the team noted that the squad would be coached by "Henry (Dutch) Dehnert, credited with originating the pivot play."[20]

As Dehnert and the Celtics perfected the play over time, it *did* become virtually unstoppable, resulting in various changes to try to offset the decided Celtic advantage. In 1925 the newly formed American Basketball League instituted the three-second call that required a player with the ball to leave the lane, albeit briefly, before spending three seconds there, or risk a violation being called with the ball being awarded to the defensive team. When this failed to prevent the play from working consistently, "the league ruled 2.5 seconds in the foul lane with or without the ball on offense was a violation.[21] It should be remembered that at that time, the lane was only five feet across—making exiting the lane easier than today. According to Dehnert, the Celtics adjusted to the rule changes, cutting the pivot man's time in the lane to two seconds to execute the play successfully, and they again won the championship.

Unlike baseball, there are very few films of games from the 1920s and early 1930s. Descriptions of the play must be ascertained from second-hand sources such as newspaper accounts or interviews of those who attended games at that time. One exception, however, is a brief, early 1930s Celtics instructional film which features Banks, Lapchick, Hickey, Dehnert, Deighan, and Barry. In this film, there are a number of demonstrations of the pivot play and variations on it. Most impressive is the ball-handling of Dehnert with his deft hands manipulating the ball with amazing swiftness and guile. That, combined with his girth (6 feet, 210 pounds) and strength, would have made the play as unstoppable as advertised.

The St. Gabriel's middleweight team that won the New York City Championship and included three future Celtics—Reich, Beckman, and Leonard.

Johnny Beckman

Johnny Beckman is commonly acknowledged as one of the two greatest players (along with Nat Holman) of the 1920s. Though only 5 feet 8 1/2 inches and 156 pounds, Beckman was one of the fastest, toughest, smartest players in the game. He was also one of the finest rebounders and the best shooter of his day. Known as the "Babe Ruth of Basketball" for his scoring prowess, Beckman was born approximately 1892-95 and raised in New York City in the neighborhood of 36th Street and 8th and 9th Avenues, just north of the Chelsea district. His first organized team was the Christ Church Five, but his lightweight (or middleweight[22]) squad, St. Gabriels, was National Champion in 1910 Beckman's teammates on the St. Gabriels included Chris Leonard and Ernie Reich, future Celtic teammates, and Jack Murray, a future professional and later, a basketball writer.

As a professional, Beckman's career began as a member of the Opals of the Hudson County League. "Later he played with West Hoboken. He hooked up with the Troys of Union Hill, New Jersey, and with Sheepshead Bay."[23] Beckman's sketch in the *Biographical Dictionary of American Sports* indicates that his first professional action was with Kingston in 1914-15. However, Frank Basloe notes that Beckman, Leonard, Reich, and their Metropolitan Five teammates played Basloe's

Johnny Beckman about 1920.

Oswego Indians in 1913 and the *Reach Guide* for 1914-15 lists Beckman in 41 games in 1913-14 as a member of Kingston. He scored 292 points, third on the team, and had the highest per-game average on the squad.

By 1915-16, Beckman had established himself as one of the top shooters and scorers in the professional ranks. He played that season for

Paterson of the Interstate League, DeNeri of the Eastern League, the Newark Turners, and other occasional squads. In the spring of 1916, Beckman's Paterson squad, the Interstate League champions met Greystock the Eastern League champions in a three-game series. After two games played under two different sets of rules, neither team was willing to accept the other's rules and game three was never played. Beckman led Paterson with 12 points in game one and added 12 more in game two.

In another series that spring, Paterson played the Pennsylvania State League champions, Wilkes-Barre, with Wilkes-Barre winning twice, 31-22 and 22-17. Beckman scored 12 points and made eight of 17 free throws in game one while shooting all of his team's charity tosses. The Pennsylvania State League rule mandated one designated free-throw shooter per squad. In game two he scored six points. Beckman continued to play for multiple squads in a number of leagues until World War I when most of the professional teams suspended operations. Beckman then played on a number of independent teams in the New York City region as well as the Standard Shipyard team of Staten Island.

Beckman was an uncanny shooter who honed his skills in the New York State League, where backboards were not used until 1922. Beckman could take a lot of physical punishment in a game and not have it affect him. Joe Lapchick noted that Beckman " . . . had more moxie in his little finger than most athletes have in their whole bodies."[24] Lapchick also characterized Beckman as "a fighter, a leader, a great scorer and a perfect back-court operator."[25]

From his first year in a professional league (1913-14), Beckman was a top scorer and he led the Eastern League in 1918-19 before play was suspended for the war. In both the 1919-20 and 1920-21 seasons, Beckman led the Pennsylvania State League in scoring, the latter time by over 100 points. He led the New Jersey professional teams in scoring with 310 points in 33 games, was the leading scorer in the Shipyard series championship in 1918, had the top average in the Eastern League in 1919-20 (9.4) and his Nanticoke team won the 1920 Pennsylvania State League title, three games to one over Scranton. Thus, before joining the Celtics in 1920, Beckman was a recognized superstar, a leading scorer, and a consistent winner. Johnny Beckman was, at twenty-seven, one of the game's top players. He had been a professional for eight years and played in every league in the Northeast. In 1919-20 alone, he competed at various times for Bridgeport (Connecticut), Adams in the New York State League, DeNeri of the Eastern League, the St. James Triangles of Brooklyn, and occasionally jumped in with the Parsons Big Five team of New York City.

With a lineup of Beckman, Dehnert, Grimstead, Barry, Smolick, and Ernie Reich, who joined them after the season began, the Celtics over-powered most teams until they laid legitimate claim to the title of World's Professional Basketball Champions. The team was fast, tough, handled the ball well, and, with Beckman, shot well. Beckman, Dehnert, Grimstead, and Barry were all excellent rebounders and rugged defenders.

Jim Furey arranged to play the other claimant to the title, the New York Whirlwinds, who were owned and promoted by Tex Rickard, in a three-game series in April 1921. Rickard's promotional acumen could only be admired by Furey, but Furey knew basketball and its fans better. Rickard controlled the events for Madison Square Garden, but after failing to draw enough fans to Whirlwind games, he took to scheduling them at armories around the city. Every city had armories for military storage and training—New York City had more armories than any other city.

The Celtics played regularly at the 69th Regiment Armory where game two of the series was held. (Game one was played at the 71st Regiment Armory.) Both games drew more than 8,000 fans, probably more a reflection of Furey's promotional skills than Rickard's. A third game wasn't played for reasons that still remain unclear, but it most likely had to do with money.

The players played for the love of the game, the desire to win, *and* for money. There are numerous accounts of players negotiating at short notice with teams that wanted those players to play with their squad. The best players were used to "controlling their own destinies" and the flow of cash to them. Nearly the entire Whirlwind squad was involved in a series pitting the Pennsylvania State League champion Scranton team against the New York State League champion for "professional supremacy." That five-game series was interrupted after three games and game four deferred for nearly two weeks in order to play the Celtic-Whirlwind series.

Clearly, money was the central focus. Exactly how it impacted on the series was unclear. Beckman, the game's highest paid and most peripatetic player, may have demanded more. Sedran, the record holder for most points in a game, may have been a "sticking point," though he claimed that Furey's signing of Holman and Leonard of the Whirlwinds to the Celtics' contract for 1921-22 caused the series to founder. Yet, some assert that the signing took place two weeks later.

It was evident that the loss of Holman and Leonard removed all claims of the superiority of the Whirlwinds and the team folded soon afterward. It was also clear that the addition of two of the game's top players made the Celtics the undisputed kings of professional basketball.

Chris Leonard

Chris Leonard, one of the most versatile of the Celtics, was born in New York in 1890. He began playing basketball in various settlement houses and joined the St. Gabriels Saints in about 1906. His teammates on this squad included Johnny Beckman and Ernie Reich, future Celtic teammates. Unlike them, Leonard enrolled in 1909 at Manhattan College and played basketball there before graduating in 1912. He then turned to professional basketball. He was a teammate of Beckman and Reich once again on the Metropolitan Big Five squad in 1913-14. He was also offered a big contract by Frank Morgenweck to play on the Cohoes New York team in the New York State League, but felt he could make more money playing independently in New York City and refused the Cohoes' offer. He began playing for the Paterson Crescents in 1914-15 and in 1915-16.

That year (1915-16) Leonard had 163 points in 35 games as Paterson won the Interstate League title. Paterson then played in a series of contests against the Eastern League Champions (the Greystock Greys), the Pennsylvania State League Champions (Wilkes-Barre), and Kingston of the former New York State League.

In 1916-17, Leonard began playing on two teams regularly and two infrequently. The former two were the Danbury Hatters of the Interstate League and the Newark Turners (of that same league), for whom Leonard had been playing since the beginning of the season. When Danbury dropped out of the league at mid-season, the Turners took their place in the six-team league.

After the leagues all suspended operations during the 1917-18 season, Leonard entered the army as an infantryman in World War I. Following the war, he resumed his career in 1919 with Bridgeport of the Eastern League and the Newark Turners. In 1919, he also played with Pittston of the Pennsylvania State League (where he finished seventh in the league in scoring) and the New York franchise of the Interstate League until it was tossed from the league. Next, Leonard was signed by Jersey City of that league. Leonard also appeared in seven games for Troy near the end of the season, and "Troy, strengthened by the addition of Chief Muller and Chris Leonard, took the laurels in the second half."[26]

In 1920, Leonard played with Pittston (PSL), Coatesville (EL), the Prospect Big Five team of Brooklyn, and the New York Whirlwinds. In most of these games, six-foot-tall Leonard was the center. When he and Holman jumped to the Celts following the Celtic-Whirlwind series, Leonard became a guard—though on occasion he filled in as forward or center when Haggerty and (later) Lapchick were out of the lineup.

From 1922 to 1928, Leonard played exclusively for the Celtics, though his playing time diminished in his later years with the club. As a Celtic, Leonard was known for his tenacity on defense. This trait led to two nicknames that teammates bestowed upon him, "Leech" and "the Dog" (Unrelatedly, he was also called ".Archie" and "Chic" for unknown reasons.)

Nat Holman

Nat Holman was born on New York's lower east side in October of 1896.[27] He learned basketball in the small school playgrounds, the settlement house gyms and the streets of his neighborhood. In 1988, when recalling those early years, Holman said that in 1905, at the age of nine, he was playing basketball for Public School 75 on an under-95 pound team. He then played at Public School 62 as well as at Commerce High School.

It was at the Settlement Houses that I really got my start. Saturday night was like a big night out. We would schedule a game and there would be a dance before the game, between halves, and after the game. The players were very popular at the dance![28]

Holman had excelled at four sports in high school and his six brothers also were outstanding at various sports. He was all scholastic in both soccer and basketball. He liked baseball, but decided against it as a career after being offered a contract as a pitcher with the Cincinnati Reds in 1919. Instead, he broadened his work with basketball and physical education for youngsters, a decision he never regretted.[29]

The basketball that Holman first learned at the Henry Street Settlement House, the Educational Alliance, and the Seward Park playground was a fast-moving game necessitated by very close quarters. "They knew how to move the ball," Mr. Holman once explained. "These men played in small gymnasiums where you had to move fast. You couldn't stand around. Everything was free, voluntary movement."[30] Holman claimed that the lack of playgrounds was a factor leading to the success of Jews in basketball.[31] While still in high school, Holman played for the "Busy Izzies," an all-Jewish team with Barney Sedran, Marty Friedman, Woody Cohen, Jack and Alex Fuller.[32]

Following high school, Holman enrolled at Savage School for Physical Education. While still a student, he launched his professional career with the Knickerbocker Big Five from whom he received $5 a game. From then on Holman was constantly busy with various aspects of basketball—coaching, teaching, playing—as well as studying for his bachelor's degree, which he received in 1917. That same year he was appointed professor of physical education and basketball coach at CCNY. Within two years he had also begun a children's summer camp in New York State, assuring himself year-round employment and a year-round hectic schedule.

Holman, like most early professionals, played with many teams on a short-term contractual basis. Besides the Big Five Squad, he appeared briefly for Hoboken of the Interstate League in Greenville (NY) and with Norwalk of the Connecticut League all in 1916-17. Though he only played in 15 games with Hoboken, Holman scored 79 points with 23 in one contest.[33] Holman's teammates on Hoboken included Mike Smolick, Elmer Ripley, and Jack Murray, the former two, future Celtics and the latter, a former St. Gabriels Middleweight squad teammate of Chris Leonard, John Beckman, and Ernie Reich. With Norwalk, Holman teamed with Smolick once again, Ernie Reich and Chris Leonard.

Beginning in 1917, Holman was a full-time CCNY instructor and coach and a part-time professional player. Holman coached soccer and freshman basketball while teaching courses in hygiene. He played for a number of independent teams since all of the top leagues suspended operations during World War I. Holman enlisted in the Navy where he served "a year or so"[34] and then returned to be head coach of CCNY at the age of twenty-three, the youngest college coach in the country.

After returning from the Navy, Holman also resumed his professional playing career with the Bridgeport Blue Ribbons of Connecticut and the Whirlwind Athletic Association team of Newark, a squad which went 23 and 9 with two ties in 1918-19. On the Blue Ribbons, he teamed again with Elmer Ripley as well as John Beckman and Barney Sedran, the phenomenal scorer. Beckman also enrolled in graduate school at NYU from which he received a master's degree in physical education in 1920.

Beginning in the 1919-20 season, Holman led a busy double life as a player and coach. The CCNY Lavender were 13-3 that year playing mostly on Saturday nights. Holman played for Jersey City of the Interstate League, Albany of the New York State League, Scranton of the Pennsylvania State League, Germantown of the Eastern League, and with independent, New York based squads. Most of his playing was for Germantown where, in 28 games, he scored 199 points for a 7.1 points per game average. He appeared in three games for Albany, three for Scranton, and for some games with Jersey City of the Interstate League.

At the end of the league season, Scranton had finished as one of two winners of the split season. They used Holman in the league championship against Nanticoke, led by Beckman and Dehnert. The Nans won the best of five series, three games to one, with Holman the leading scorer in the series with 32 points in four games. He also had the most field goals with 13.

The next year Holman's club at CCNY was 11-4 but the squads he played for had even better seasons. Germantown won the Eastern League title led by Holman who had 285 points (an 8.4 average) to lead the league in scoring. He finished second in assists with 48. Holman appeared in eight games for Westfield of the Interstate League, two in the first half and six in the second half of the season, scoring 93 points for an 11.6 ppg average. Holman was also on Scranton's roster during the year, but like the year before, joined them for the playoffs. Holman joined Elmer Ripley, Stretch Meehan, and Dutch Dehnert to help the Miners to a two-game sweep of the playoff series with Pittston.

In April 1921, Holman and Scranton played a five-game series against the Albany Senators, champions of the New York State League. In a drawn out series that was played over seventeen days, the Miners won three games to two. In the middle of that series, Holman joined his New York Whirlwind teammates, some of whom were his Albany foes, to play an attendance-setting series against the Celtics in New York City (described earlier in the Introduction and in chapter nine of this volume). By the end of the 1921 season, Holman had become a Celtic, which he would remain until the team broke up in 1928.

As a player Holman was a good shooter, a great passer, and a tremendous coach on the floor. He saw the whole game at once, as well as each individual battle, and knew at a glance how to exploit an uneven match-up on offense or defense. A 1921 promotional brochure for the "Moreshu" basketball shoe had sketches of eleven players of the time; Holman's sketch referred to him as, "The cleverest man with a basketball playing the game today." That "cleverness" was often exhibited in the many exaggerated falls he took to the hardwood which usually resulted in foul calls against his opponents.

Holman was a man in motion, on and off the court. Before "settling down" on the Celtics, he played "six and seven nights a week finishing up with two on Sundays."[35] To accomplish this, "we fellows carried 'time-tables' around with us in those days, railroading from one city to another."[36]

After becoming a Celtic exclusively, he still had to deal with his coaching and making Celtic games. In the 1988 interview, Holman explained how he was able to be "two places at once."

The boys would practice from 3 to 5 p.m. On certain days I would turn the practice over to my assistant. That way I could make a game, say in Germantown,

PA. I was always around for the first half of every game. We would go to the locker room at half-time where I would talk with the team. Then as they went back for the second half I would find the back door where an automobile picked me up to go to the next game.[37]

Despite the hectic schedule, Holman made most Celtics games from 1921 to 1928 and during that time the Celtics rarely lost. In 1921-22, Holman's first year under exclusive contract with the Celtics, he helped the team win the championship of the Eastern League. After joining the league near the end of the first half of the season, the Celtics went 16-4 to capture the title of the second half. Holman was second on the team (to Beckman) and sixth in the league in second-half scoring. In 19 games he scored 124 points for an average of 6.5 per game. His 25 assists led the team and they finished second in the league.

The next year Holman averaged 8 points as the Celts went undefeated in the Metropolitan League (12-0) before returning to the Eastern League for 6 games, in which Holman had 42 points. Following the withdrawal of the Celtics, the Eastern League collapsed and for the next three and a half years the team played throughout the East, Midwest and in parts of the South. It is nearly impossible to find accurate records of that time so Holman's averages are not known. The outstanding record of the team was known because they won over 90 percent of their games. These were the Celtics that shaped a saga of real greatness.

The Great Celtics

Just before the opening of the 1921-22 season, Jim Furey signed George (Horse) Haggerty. Haggerty had come to Reading in 1913 from Springfield, Massachusetts, at the encouragement of the great Andy Sears, who had finished second in the Eastern League in scoring while leading the Reading Bears to the league and "world" championship. Haggerty played with Reading until joining the Celtics in 1921, and also performed with teams in the Penn State, New York State, and Interstate leagues. A 6-foot, 4-inch, 230-pounder at the height of his career, Haggerty was acclaimed for his rebounding and defensive ability and, at twenty-seven, was at his peak when he joined the Celtics. George Haggerty joined the Celtics for the 1921-22 season and played two full seasons as the center. In 1923, Haggerty was replaced by Joe Lapchick, a younger, more mobile player and a better scorer. Haggerty went to the Ft. Wayne Knights of Columbus squad where he tore a tendon in his ankle but stayed another year with them before signing with the Washington Palace team of the new ABL in 1925-26 as a player coach. He was with the Palace team until 1928 when he retired at thirty-five.

Haggerty is possibly most famous in Celtic lore for an apocryphal story first told by Nat Holman and repeated in innumerable secondary sources. The tale concerned Haggerty inbounding the ball in a tightly contested game for the Palace squad against the Celtics. In *Holman on Basketball*,[38] Holman noted that he suddenly yelled, "Horse, here," and Haggerty responded to the stimulus of his old teammate's cry by passing him the ball which Holman converted for a basket for the Celtics. A true story? Possibly, but even if it isn't, just its *possibility* illustrates the closeness of the Celtics squad.

Haggerty's size, defense, and deft ball handling fit exquisitely with the skills of Holman, Beckman, Leonard, Reich, Dehnert, and Barry. Tom Meany, the legendary sportswriter for a number of New York newspapers summarized the Celtics this way.[39]

They were faster by far than any of the teams they played, for basketball had not yet become the swift game it is today. Shooting skill was everything with the ability to take a physical pounding the second qualification. . . . (Their) speed allowed them to get more shots and to avoid punishment from the plodding players of the era.

Furey was confident of the superior abilities of his team and sought to maximize the money that he could make through their games by keeping them out of a league. Thus, they could play independent and league teams of any league and retain their flexibility. Up until this time, teams had played non-league teams on a relatively regular basis and players performed for two, three, or even four teams simultaneously, playing sometimes six nights per week.

To ensure a stable team, Furey had introduced a new concept to professional basketball—the exclusive contract. None of the Celtics could play for any professional basketball teams except for the Celtics. In return for this "loyalty," Furey provided lucrative contracts, thus ensuring that "They could concentrate their skill with the one team."[40] This was the beginning of the end of what Meany referred to as wildcat basketball, as well as the many regional professional leagues that flourished in the Northeast.

Furey's plans were thrown off a bit by the 1920 agreement that the Penn State, New York State, Interstate, and Eastern Leagues had signed to prevent players from playing off one team against the other for a player's services. One aspect of that agreement was that "No league team will be permitted to play exhibition games with any independent team in a city or town where a member of the commission has jurisdiction."[41] Though the Penn State and Interstate Leagues had failed after the

1921 season and the New York State League had abrogated the agreement early on, President Scheffer of the Eastern League pressed his league's owners to enforce the agreement, though it had been routinely violated the previous year.

The Celtics, then, lost eight of the best teams in the East with whom to compete. Initially, Furey and the Eastern League owners thought they did not need each other. The Celtics played the best teams in the Metropolitan New York Association of Teams and defeated, among others, the Armory Big Five of Mt. Vernon, New York, with Joe Lapchick; the Jersey Stars, in a game where Pete Barry scored seven field goals in the 37-34 victory; and Metropolitan League teams like Paterson, Brooklyn, and the Visitation Triangles. However, it was not enough for Furey and his high contracts.

At the same time, the Eastern League was witnessing financial ruin with its new Harrisburg entry. That franchise was purchased by another New York team, which also had financial problems. In mid-December, both the Celtics and the Eastern League looked for significant financial improvement when the Celtics purchased the New York Eastern League franchise and entered the league. Because most Celtic players had signed earlier Eastern League contracts which they had ignored, Furey had to compensate various Eastern League teams who had claims to his players. Haggerty was dealt from the Celtics back to the Reading Bears who were unable to meet his salary demands, so they sold him back to the Celtics within a week.

Once the managerial concerns were ironed out, the Celtics proceeded to win consistently after a 2-2 start which ended the first half of the season, one dominated by Trenton with its 24-3 won/lost record. In the second half, Trenton and Camden tied with 15 and 5 records, but the Celtics edged them for the second-half title with a 16-4 record. The Celtics and the Trenton Tigers, each winners of half a season, were to meet for the Eastern League title in a three-game series.

Near season's end Haggerty played in a few games for Visitation in the Metropolitan League, but generally, the exclusive contracts held fast. The next year the six regulars were all back to play, along with Johnny Whitty, who was really a manager, and only played on rare occasions. In addition, Furey had signed Eddie Burke, a handsome young New Yorker, to fill Reich's spot on the roster.

Burke had finished third in the Metro League in scoring the previous year, averaging nearly 10 points per game for the Visitation Triangles Squad. Burke either signed a non-exclusive contract or violated it without penalty during the next year as he continued to appear in the Visitation line-up during the 1922-23 season.

Having the squad return intact for another season was highly unusual, as Tom Meany noted. "The Celtics were the first team, in the true sense of the term, in basketball; because, for the first time, five men played together, night after night, from the start of the season until its finish."[42]

Before the beginning of the 1922-23 season, the Metropolitan League voted to add two teams to the league—one in Elizabeth, New Jersey, and the other the Original Celtics. The Furey brothers felt that being in the Metropolitan League would mean greater profits—travel was minimal, lodging and meals not an issue, and arenas had large capacities. The six teams in the Metropolitan League had done well financially in 1921-22, when other Eastern leagues had struggled or ceased to exist. The Celtics had not done as well financially in the Eastern League as Jim Furey had hoped, but no other team had the burden of exclusive, high paying contracts.

The Celtics competed in the Metropolitan League from October 8 to November 12, 1922, when they left the league "because of financial reasons."[43] Despite the presence of great opponents like Frank Bruggy, Marty Friedman, Barney Sedran, Tom Barlow, Davey Banks, Joe Lapchick, Honey Russell, and Benny Borgeman, the Celtics had little difficulty in going 12-0 before abandoning the league. Beckman and Holman were in the top five in scoring but, apparently, success on the court was not sufficient to produce financial satisfaction for the Furey brothers.

As soon as the Celtics withdrew from the Metropolitan League, the Fureys began negotiating to re-enter the Eastern League and on November 22, 1922, their return was announced. The league needed the Celtics' drawing power and the Celtics needed a bigger payoff, which was guaranteed by the league of $900 per week.

The Celtics took over the Atlantic City Sandpiper franchise and played their home games at the Steel Pier Armory. The previous holders of the franchise had compiled a two-win, six-loss record and, as in the previous year, the Celtics took over that losing record. The Celtics proceeded to win five of their first six games, losing only to Trenton's Tigers after leading at halftime.

Three weeks later the Atlantic City franchise was sold to Marvin Riley, who immediately initiated cost cutting measures to save the franchise and the Eastern League which was hemorrhaging financially. Unlike the previous year when they owned the franchise, the Celtics and Furey had entered the league as contractual employees with the $900 weekly guarantee divided among the players ($600) and their promoters/managers, Jim and Tom Furey ($300). Of course, the Atlantic City owner had assumed that profits would largely exceed that $900, but the more the Celtics won, the less the fans attended.

The new franchise owner, Riley, announced that *his* contract with the Celtics would only be for $400 a week. When the Celtics announced to Riley that they would not accept the financial cut, they were fired and replacement players were swiftly hired for the Sandpiper franchise.

League attendance continued to decline and both Reading and Atlantic City withdrew. The four team Eastern League tried to go on, but on January 19, 1923, the league succumbed.

At that point the Celtics again took to the road, becoming almost exclusively a barnstorming team, winning nearly 200 games in the season. John J. Murray stated, "The marvelous record made during the past season by the famous Original Celtic team of New York City is perhaps the greatest record ever made during one season by any professional team."[44] Murray was not unbiased. "Jack" Murray had been a member of the famous St. Gabriel's team in 1910, the middle-weight champions of the Metropolitan district. His teammates included Ernie Reich, Johnny Beckman, and Chris Leonard. The four also played together for Norwalk, Connecticut, in 1918-19 and Murray was Dehnert and Reich's teammate on Ansonia (Connecticut) in 1917-18 and Beckman's teammate on the Newark Turners.

Murray could have just been "tooting the New York City horn," but in his claims he had ample evidence to back it up. For the season, the Celtics played 205 games, winning 193, losing 11 and tying one. They were 17-1 in two leagues and they played in 114 cities before 1.5 million basketball fans. In February, the Celts played a doubleheader in Cleveland that drew 23,000 people. The Celtics, Murray concluded, "are truly the wonder team of basketball."[45]

The Lapchick Addition

At the end of the 1922-23 season, Haggerty was not resigned by the Fureys and "the Horse" went to Fort Wayne, Indiana to play for the Knights of Columbus team for $100-per game.[46] Haggerty had slowed considerably and his shooting, never good, had become abysmal. In his stead, the Celtics signed Joe Lapchick, a 6-foot 5-inch center from Yonkers who could jump, run and score. Lapchick was twenty-three, the son of Czech immigrants and he had been playing semi pro since he was fifteen, and professionally from the time he was eighteen.

Unlike most of the original Celtics, Joseph Bohomiel Lapchick was *not* born and raised in New York City, but rather he was a native of Yonkers, New York, and began playing basketball on organized squads before he was a teenager. Lapchick was born in 1900 in Yonkers. His father was a policeman and later a trolley motorman, which were not high-paying jobs, and young Joe had various odd jobs to earn money as early as nine when he was a caddie at a local golf course. Later he was a water boy for a local baseball team. These led to Lapchick's first sports interests—golf and baseball. He also played basketball in parks and corner lots, though the "equipment" was crude—a cap stuffed into an old discarded soccer ball.[47] Joe's son, Richard, embellished the accounts of Joe's early "career," obviously from conversations with his father. After Joe's mother, Frances, found her son playing a version of street basketball that involved passing the ball under the bellies of teams of ice wagon horses to teammates in order to score, his parents forbade him from playing this street game. The boys often had telltale odors from stepping in the "gifts" the horses left in the street and young Joe could not play again since his "smell" would give him away. In order to fool his parents, he kept the following at a friend's apartment,

. . . a separate set of playing clothes . . . Joe never had the telltale odor and Frances thought he had reformed. This arrangement worked well until the day Joe went to his friend's house and discovered that his mother had found Joe's clothes and burned them. Playing in the streets was over.[48]

By this time it didn't really matter since Lapchick was now playing for the Trinity Midgets, a church team organized by a man named Johnny Mears. Joe was 6 feet 3 inches and weighed 140 pounds "and was probably the tallest 'midget' in the world."[47] Lapchick's height determined that he would be a center. He could jump and get the tap or rebound, but his footwork was sadly lacking.

After finishing Public School 20 grade school, Lapchick "went to work for the Ward Leonard Electric Company in Bronxville, New York, making 15 cents an hour for a ten-hour day."[50] At night and on weekends Joe played basketball and at fifteen began to play with the Yonkers Bantams for $5 a game, though players had to pay for their own transportation and meals. He "netted the grand total of $15 the first year and $18 the second year."[51] Joe kept his apprentice machinist job until 1918, when he was making enough money at basketball to go at it full time.

By the age of seventeen, Lapchick had grown to 6 feet 5 inches and was considered exceptionally tall as well as being in greater demand. He had worked out on his own to improve his footwork and could now compete with local players and many top professionals. The Whirlwinds of New York City used him in some games paying him $7 per game. By 1919, he received $10 per game and was known throughout basketball circles in the Northeast while playing for Holyoke of the Western Massachusetts League and Schenectady of the New York State League.

In the 1920-21 season, Lapchick established himself as a top center competing for no fewer than four teams: Holyoke, Schenectady, Mt. Vernon of the Interborough League, and the independent New York Wanderers. The 1921-22 *Reach Guide* pictured Lapchick (identified as Joe Topchick of Yonkers) in a collective photo of "Fifteen Centerman (sic) of the Metropolitan District Present and Future Stars." The only precise record of Lapchick's "work" in that year was the eleven games he played for Holyoke, he scored 68 points for a 6.2 average, which was in the top fifteen in the league. With teams bidding more for good players, Lapchick at times received as much as $75 per game. As he played team offers against one another, he was able to increase that to $100 a game. Lapchick was becoming affluent and, in his own words, "A big shot."

I bought a car and would park right in front of any hall in which we played, throw my bag up in the air, and escort the kid who caught it into the hall for free.[52]

In 1921-22 Lapchick was with the Brooklyn Visitation of the Metropolitan Basketball League, with Schenectady and Troy of the New York State League, and with the Armory Big Five team of Mt. Vernon, New York. In the first half of the New York State League season, Lapchick played in twenty-five of the twenty-six games and he scored 96 points with 80 points coming on free throws. Lapchick's height allowed him to consistently get the center tap, but once the game began, he was fouled rather than allowed to shoot an unmolested basket. His eighty free throws made were third in the league, though he was not even in the top twenty-five in overall scoring.

Schenectady was 19-7, the best record in the league, ". . . but financial trouble caused the destruction and ejection of the team from the league."[53] In the second half, Lapchick played for Troy and performed in seven of their ten games, scoring 23 points.

With the Visitation squad, Lapchick played in ten of twenty games, scoring 32 points. Late in the season (on March 24), Lapchick joined the Armory Big Five team and played in the final three games, all victories, and scored 16 points.

Lapchick at twenty-two was an established star and in the 1922-23 season he solidified that status. Playing again with the Visitation, Troy, and Armory Big Five teams, he increased his scoring and his great tapping. Rebounds were not recorded so one can only speculate how an agile, 6-foot 5-inch player did against players almost all shorter than he. The Visitation had eight wins against six losses in the first half with Lapchick scoring 42 points in nine contests. The original Celtics began that season in the Metropolitan League, where they compiled a record of 13 wins without a loss before leaving the league to make more money elsewhere. Many of the individual Celtics had faced Lapchick in games around the region, but this was probably the first time they had opposed Lapchick as a team and they liked what they saw. By the next year, Lapchick would be the new Celtic center.

In the second half of the Metropolitan season, Lapchick played in twenty-four of the twenty-seven Visitation contests and scored 135 points, third on the team. The leading Visitation scorer was a stocky young player signed at mid-season who scored 178 points in just 26 games, one of only two players in the league to average double figures in scoring. (Benny Borgemann led the league in scoring.) This was the first time Davey Banks and Joe Lapchick had played together. Four years later they would be reunited on the Celtics and help them to consecutive American Basketball League Championships.

Lapchick and Troy were 10 and 9 in the first half of the New York State League Season in 1922-23. Joe had 43 points in seventeen games. He had almost as many (42) in the seven games he played second half but Troy won only three of twelve games.

Nevertheless, Lapchick's individual performances made him highly sought after and the Celtics needed a new center. Horse Haggerty had slowed considerably and his scoring had diminished to almost nothing; he could not jump as well as he had in previous years. Thus, the Furey brothers went after Lapchick and Lapchick was thrilled to be sought by the Celtics and soon signed a contract with them. Lapchick recalled:

In 1923, all my dreams and hopes reached a grand climax. I was asked to sign up with the Celtics. My heart was jumping so hard I could scarcely sign the contract. Now I was really on cloud "9."[54]

Despite Lapchick's excitement and his basketball skills, his first games with the Celtics were very frustrating to him and, most likely, to his teammates. Lapchick, like most players, had learned to play basketball as an individual game. If one outscored one's defender then it was a good game. Winning was an extra bonus, but there wasn't great concern for that among the players since they played on so many different teams in a week. They wanted to win, but a sense of real "teamness" didn't exist because of player and team transience. In 1921, for example, when the Scranton Miners won the Pennsylvania State League title, their lineup during the championship series included Holman, who had played no regular season games for Scranton, and Meehan, who was playing in his fifth, after being added to the roster in March.

The Celtics, however, were different. Team was everything because it led to winning and the Celtics hated to lose. Thus, team and winning became synonymous to Celtic basketball. It took a while for Lapchick to learn this and a longer time to comfortably practice it. It was a difficult transition for Lapchick despite his five years of experience as a professional. Again he recalled:

I was only a beginner in the type of game the Celtics played. I was frustrated because of my ineptness, and the resulting anger which shot through me every time I made a mistake was no help. I had been bred to the theory of individualism, whereas the Celtics were devoted to a team effort.[55]

On defense, Lapchick had to learn to play a switching man-to-man, something no other team did at that time. The Celtics guarded the nearest man, regardless of whose personal opponent he was. When Lapchick had trouble one day, Johnny Whitty, the manager and occasional player took him aside and summed up the Celtics' play. "It isn't how many goals you get or how often you get the tap. . . . It's how you are without the ball that determines how good a basketball player you are."[56]

5

THE 1920-21 SEASON—
NEW SUCCESSES, NEW PROBLEMS

The 1920-21 season was one of the most active in professional basketball. The post-war economic boom fueled both an increase in leisure time and a psychological mode of carefree confidence. Those feelings carried over into the operation of northeastern basketball leagues. The Eastern League had six stable franchises located in and around Philadelphia: Reading, Trenton, Camdem, Germantown, Coatesville, and Philadelphia. The Pennsylvania State League had five teams with four around Wilkes-Barre: Scranton, Pittston, Nanticoke, and Wilkes-Barre and one in New Jersey–Paterson (later Plymouth, Pennsylvania). The New York State League fielded eight teams around the Albany area: Gloversville, Pittsfield (Massachusetts), Schenectady, Utica, Mohawk, Cohoes, Amsterdam, and Albany. The Interstate League had teams around Hartford: Holyoke (Massachusetts), Easthampton, Thompsonville (Bigelow-Hartford), Westfield, Springfield, and Worcester.[1]

The increasingly interconnected railroad system allowed players to move from game to game and league to league. Some of the leagues were partners in agreements about what nights were "theirs," thereby allowing players to play on more than one team and limiting their salary leveraging of one team against another in a different league. The only foe was fatigue, but that seemed to be evenly spread throughout the leagues.

The New York State League was still playing its games without backboards in 1920-21, the last professional league to do so. Scoring averages and totals for that league should be viewed with this fact in mind.

The Pennsylvania State League ended in 1920-21. In both of its last two seasons, Beckman was recognized as "the Babe Ruth of the game"[2] as he led the league in scoring. In 1919-20 he had 346 points in thirty-eight games, an average of just over nine per game. He also led Nanticoke to victory over Scranton in the playoff series, three games to one. In that series, Beckman and Dehnert performed as Nanticoke teammates

The Celtics in 1920.

and were matched against Holman and Reich of the Miners. All four games were refereed by Herman Baetzel, long time and well-respected Eastern League referee. Apparently the best referees "league-hopped" as much as the players.

The next year Beckman set "a new mark in basketball"[3] by tallying 361 points in forty games, but failed to get Nanticoke back in the playoffs. That year Beckman also played for Trenton of the Eastern League after beginning the year with Philadelphia. The other Celtics in the Eastern League were Reich and Haggerty on the Reading Bears; Dehnert, who played briefly for Philadelphia; and Leonard, who played for Coatesville and Holman. Leonard was not yet a Celtic, but played for Germantown where he led the league in scoring with 285 points in thirty-four games and was second in assists with 48.[4] Eastern League teams regularly met the Celtics throughout the 1920-21 season, though somehow players who competed for both squads never seemed to be compromised. Camden was the most popular opponent because of its closer proximity, its position as the most powerful team in the Eastern League, and because it drew large crowds.

The Eastern League season opened in early November with Reading starting off well (five straight wins) behind Reich and Haggerty, but Camden and Trenton were also establishing themselves as powers in the league. Camden routed Philadelphia 51-21 and Newark 34-22 on consecutive November nights. Newark faltered early and rumors of its exit from the Eastern League appeared in the November 20 *Philadelphia Inquirer.*[5] S. O. Grauley, as both league vice president and *Inquirer* pro-basketball reporter, was able to consistently provide an "insider's" view that no other newspapers could match.

Professional Basketball Leagues, 1920-21

<u>Eastern League</u>
Camden Skeeters
Germantown Germs (or G's)
Trenton Bengals
Reading Bears
Philadelphia Phillies
Coatesville
Newark (five games and dropped out)

<u>New York State League</u>
Albany Senators
Schenectady
Cohoes
Gloversville
Mohawk
Utica
Pittsfield
Amsterdam
Glens Falls

<u>Pennsylvania State League</u>
Scranton Miners
Nanticoke Nans
Pittston
Wilkes-Barre Barons
Paterson (NJ/)/Plymouth

<u>Interstate League</u>
Holyoke (MA)
Easthampton (MA)
Thompsonville (Bigelow-Hartford)
Westfield (MA)
Springfield
Worcester

Two days after the first rumor appeared, Grauley noted that both Coatesville and Atlantic City were interested in acquiring the Newark franchise (later awarded to Coatesville). In this article, he took the occasion to question the entire financial structure of the league. Grauley's observations and suggestions certainly have a ring of truth to them when laid upon the context of professional sports in the 1990s. The issue of weak franchises plagues professional sports agreements today much as it did the Eastern League in 1920 and continued to do so leading to the league's demise two years later. Grauley observed that "the absolute unbusinesslike method in which the league exists makes anyone familiar with professional sports wonder how the league exists." Each home team gets all the receipts. It would save the league to install, Grauley felt, a percentage system.[6]

As the Eastern League wrestled with these financial problems, the Celtics enjoyed financial success playing all comers each Sunday at their home court, the Central Opera House at 67th and 3rd Avenue in Manhattan. On November 23, they defeated the Philadelphia "All-Stars" with players from the Philadelphia franchises of the Eastern League. The score was 43 to 31 with Whitty and Beckman leading with 12 and 11 points respectively. Trippe had eight, Reich six, Barry four, and Smolick two.

During the next week Germantown and Holman were frequent topics of *Inquirer* discussion. Camden's loss to Germantown on the

23rd, 26-25, was attributed to Holman outplaying and being faster than the swift and talented Jim "Soup" Campbell. Campbell, it was noted, was "extremely fast, but opposed to Holman, the Camden forward met a tartar last night."[7] Holman's eleven points led all scorers.

Two nights later, Germantown lost to Coatesville in its opening game, 26-11, as Holman "failed to appear." He was most likely in either Westfield, Massachusetts, playing in the Interstate League or New York, coaching CCNY or playing for the Whirlwinds.[8] Despite his absence, Holman was recognized for his greatness as a player with his "only weakness (being) a tendency to play the game himself at times." The next night, Holman had 16 points and set a new assist record with six to lead Germantown to an easy victory over Philadelphia. Holman's six baskets also tied the high for the year set by both Campbell and Tom Barlow of Trenton.[9]

Reading, led by Reich and Haggerty, continued its hot play defeating the Camden Skeeters at the Camden Armory, 23-14 before 5,000 fans. Later that week, Reading defeated Coatesville with Reich scoring 12 points and picking up four assists.[10] When Trenton upended the Bears on December 10, the Potters took over first place in a game where Reich had 6 points. That same night Coatesville defeated Germantown, 19-17, with Holman scoring 14 of the 17 points.[11] Germantown lost again the next night with Holman absent because he was coaching CCNY.[12] The next Saturday Reading easily defeated Germantown, with Holman absent, after defeating them four days earlier with Holman.

By mid-December Trenton, Camden, and Reading led the Eastern League but the Celtics had laid "claim to the championship of the country. They have beaten several Eastern and Pennsylvania State teams. It's doubtful, however, if the Celtics would fare so well if they played some of their games away from their own wooden way."[13] The night before, the Celtics had defeated the Fisk Red Tops, the Industrial Champions of America by a score of 43-27 as Beckman had 12 and Barry 10 before several thousand at the 71st Regimental Armory.[14]

Beckman joined the Philadelphia lineup on December 29, scoring 9 points in a 20-17 upset of Camden. Beckman reappeared in the Eastern League briefly for Philadelphia and then the second half of the season played for Trenton. The first half race, however, remained tight and Grauley highlighted this action in his column on January 3 where he also decried the chasing of dollars by players, thereby weakening all leagues. Soup Campbell, Grauley noted, was playing in three league teams: Camden, Nanticoke in the Pennsylvania State, and Westfield in the Interstate. The Eastern league rule stated that a player could not play in another league if his Eastern team was playing, but Holman missed Saturday nights for coaching and Beckman missed regularly. Grauley noted this rule would be strictly enforced in the second half by President Scheffer.[15]

The Pennsylvania State League was facing the same problems and a revised league rule put the five clubs on notice that they must put a lineup of "State League caliber"[16] on the floor or risk fines as high as $150.[17] The estimate was that 80 percent of the men playing in the Eastern League were also regulars on Pennsylvania State League clubs.

Apparently, the Eastern League was another paper tiger. Just a week later Grauley noted that "Beckman probably plays more basketball and makes more money than any two-cage game stars in the business . . ." Beckman was noticeably weary at times. The *Wilkes-Barre Record* noted that:

Johnny Beckman seemed a trifle worn in Tuesday night's man-killing contest and his flashes came at longer intervals than usual. When he flashed his 100 percent, energy also seemed lacking.[18]

Just five days before, Beckman and his Celtics had played Babe Ruth's All Stars in New York where Ruth was awful. Then Beckman returned to the Philadelphia lineup and with twelve points, led his team to victory over Trenton 29-21. This threw the first half race into a season ending tie with both Reading and Trenton finishing at 15-5 after Reading defeated Germantown 39-16. Holman, however, was absent, coaching in New York.

The Eastern League's first half title would be decided by where the two teams finished the second half. If one finished first in the second half then that team would be the overall winner. If neither did, the one who finished higher would play the second half winner for the championship. Neither club was happy with this decision. Grauley presented the Eastern League point of view:

Both clubs were anxious to stage the big fuss in Camden, which would have meant a big house and a neat sum for each club. The league, however, forced the clubs to decide to tie in the second half, eliminating the idea of commercializing the sport and putting it in a better light before the public.[19]

This is a telling comment on pro basketball and its image at the time. College sports, specifically basketball, were seen as pure, without undue influence, particularly of gamblers. Conventional wisdom was that professional sports were often closely allied with gamblers and the status of the 1919 Black Sox scandal, which was not in an open court setting until 1921, was certainly very important to the feeling Grauley expressed. In professional basketball, including the Eastern League, the public in days gone by saw playoffs and ties as "fixed affairs," notes Grauley, and he felt the league was correct in being overly cautious in this instance. Bole and Lawrence totally missed this aspect of the league decision, instead attributing the plan of William Scheffer, league president, whom they mistakenly refer to as "The Commissioner" to his eccentricities, calling his proposal "convoluted."[20]

The league also adopted a new rule seeking to address at least obliquely, the plethora of players participating in more than one league at a time. President Scheffer had thought the issue had been settled before the 1920 season began when presidents of the New York State, Pennsylvania State, Interstate, and Eastern leagues met in New York City in an effort "to restrict players to one league, forbid exhibition games with independent teams in the territory of teams in the four leagues, and set up a round robin 'world series' among the league champions." The Interstate League backed out and the National Commission never became effective.[21]

Thus, the new rule allowed an Eastern League club to grant one regular player a "leave of absence" for a game; but, if two or more failed to appear, the club would lose one player for the rest of the season. Though the clubs couldn't control the so-called wandering wonders, they hoped this rule would bring the practice under control and not risk further erosion of fan support.[22]

The second half of the Eastern League season began with Ernie Reich not playing for Reading and announcing his intended retirement. He had secured a position with a tire company in New York, a position that would keep him on the road. He might still have been able to play Sundays for the Celtics, but that was not mentioned.[23] Even with Reich in the lineup, Germantown might have won, having strengthened their lineup considerably with the additions of Elmer Ripley from the Pennsylvania State League, Frank Bruggy, "Stretch" Meehan, and George Glasco. Teamed with Nat Holman, this was a formidable five indeed.[24]

On the same evening that Reich did not play for Reading, Beckman *did* play for Philadelphia scoring only three points in a 26-20 loss to Camden. This would be Beckman's final appearance for the Phillies as both he and Dehnert were suspended by the club for "wanting to play too many other games on certain nights."[25] Of course, were they *not* suspended, the new league rule might have resulted in one or both of them being suspended by the league for the remainder of the season. Thus, the Philadelphia club took the initiative, thereby giving themselves some opportunity to renegotiate with either player if either party should so desire.

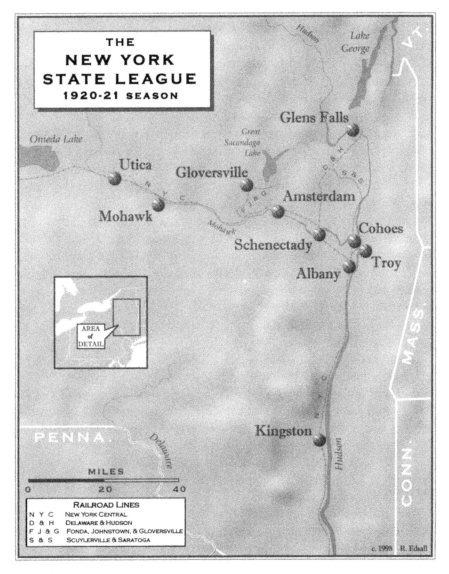

THE
NEW YORK
STATE LEAGUE
1920-21 SEASON

Glens Falls

Onieda Lake

Great Sacandaga Lake

Utica

Gloversville

Amsterdam

Mohawk

Cohoes

Schenectady

Albany

Troy

AREA of DETAIL

PENNA.

Kingston

MILES

0   20   40

RAILROAD LINES
N Y C	NEW YORK CENTRAL
D & H	DELAWARE & HUDSON
F J & G	FONDA, JOHNSTOWN, & GLOVERSVILLE
S & S	SCUYLERVILLE & SARATOGA

c. 1998   R. Edsall

Regarding Dehnert and Beckman, the *Wilkes-Barre Record* noted the tough defense that Dehnert played on Beckman in a State League game. It was impressive since the two were noted as close friends who "play as teammates several nights in the week."[26]

Both Camden and Germantown came out of the second half starting gate quickly while Trenton and Reading, the first half champions, stumbled along at a .500 clip. Philadelphia and Coatesville continued to hold up the rest of the league. Without Beckman and Dehnert, Philadelphia was significantly weakened and similarly so was Reading without Reich.

Beckman and Dehnert were playing regularly in the Pennsylvania State League as were Haggerty and Holman. Beckman, Dehnert, and Reich were also teaming with Barry, Smolick, and Trippe on Sundays in New York for the Celtics. The Celtic fame was growing and some (probably S. O. Grauley) were either skeptical or sought to undermine the Celtic's claims in order to uphold the prestige of the leagues. "The Celtics of New York are making claims to all basketball titles of the county, but they are not overly anxious to stage a series with any of the Eastern League clubs, West Chester, or Parkesburg to decide the much mooted question of supremacy."[27] The Parkesburg Club was a continual "sore spot" with the Eastern League and their teams were forbidden to play Parkesburg, though there were ways around the ban. Parkesburg would end the 1920-21 season, 36-0 playing most of their games in Parkesburg, Pennsylvania, a town about five miles west of Coatesville. The Celtics' Sunday contests, often doubleheaders against two different teams, "had led to the revival of basketball in New York City."[28] In addition, the big crowds and large payoffs had led to all manner of "all star" teams being formed to play the Celtics. On January 23, Babe Ruth and his squad lost to the Celtics, a game in which "Ruth's efforts were laughable and he was hooted off the wooden way."[29]

Players were still playing in multiple leagues and often missing games. On January 29, the Phillies played without one starter because he had played a game in Massachusetts the night before and wired that he had missed his train connections.[30] Reading occasionally had Haggerty missing and, more often Reich, (no longer retired, apparently). President Brislin of the Pennsylvania State League suspended Holman in late January for playing in the New York State League with whom the Pennsylvania State League had a working agreement, i.e., not to use players on the rosters of teams in the other's league.[31]

The *Record* detailed that Holman had appeared with Pittsfield and noted that he had not yet appeared in a game for Scranton, even though he had been on their roster list for several weeks. The suspension was probably to be for a week or more. Two weeks later in an unexplained note, Pittston removed Holman's name from its roster. Somehow his name returned to *Scranton's* roster in March.[32] The working agreement referred to earlier was continually being ignored as the players bargained and dickered regularly to sell their talents to the highest bidder on any one night. Grauley continued to view this habit with disgust noting that an offer of $50 a game was now viewed with scorn by players, many of whom now played in three different leagues.[33]

February saw Holman continue to star, when he showed up. On February 1, he had 16 points and three assists in a 44-18 victory over

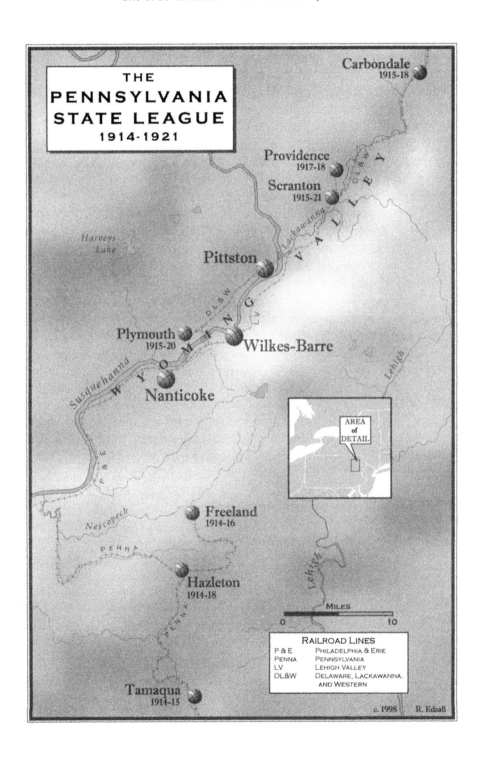

THE
**PENNSYLVANIA
STATE LEAGUE**
1914-1921

Carbondale
1915-18

Providence
1917-18

Scranton
1915-21

*Harveys
Lake*

Pittston

Susquehanna

Plymouth
1915-20

Wilkes-Barre

Nanticoke

AREA
of
DETAIL

Nescopeck

Freeland
1914-16

PENNA

Hazleton
1914-18

MILES
0   10

RAILROAD LINES
P & E   PHILADELPHIA & ERIE
PENNA   PENNSYLVANIA
LV   LEHIGH VALLEY
DL&W   DELAWARE, LACKAWANNA,
         AND WESTERN

Tamaqua
1914-15

c. 1998   R. Edsall

Coatesville.[34] But on February 5, he missed the contest with Reading because of his coaching at CCNY. It was a good game to miss since the "contest became so rough towards the finish that time out was called three times on account of players being knocked out."[35] Four days later the two teams met again and Holman scored eight in the 25-15 Germantown victory. Reich, who had missed the earlier game because of a leg injury, played in the second contest. However, his bad leg limited him to 3 points. Haggerty, who was known for his lack of scoring, was notably horrendous in this game as he "took at least a dozen long chances that never hit the rim."[36] Even in an era where 30 percent was a good field goal figure this performance stands out.

A few days later Beckman, under suspension by Philadelphia, was traded to Trenton for Tommy Dunleavy. Trenton had apparently made a good offer to Beckman that would ensure his playing for the Bengals (at least for a while). In addition, the trade of Dunleavy solved another problem—how to get Tom Barlow back into the Trenton lineup.

Barlow, a future Hall of Fame guard, had a rough year. In November he had swung at referee Herman Baetzel[37] and had been suspended for a month. Upon his return "he injured his arm, probably by cutting it on the cage wire. Subsequently, blood poisoning set in, placing him on the inactive list once more."[38] Dunleavy replaced Barlow in the lineup during the first half as the Bengals tied Reading for the first half title. When Barlow returned, Trenton coach Al Cooper was reluctant to change the lineup despite Trenton's slow, second half start.

Barlow did a slow burn then demanded to be traded or sold, which did not occur. He intimated that he would play in the New York State League and be an "outlaw." Barlow was back in the lineup on February 5 after two games in which neither he nor Dunleavy appeared.[39] This makes Bole and Lawrence's dramatization of Barlow's absence from the lineup less credible (i.e., that Dunleavy's play was keeping Barlow out). Dunleavy came off the bench at the end of the February fifth contest.[40]

Though the trade was seen as helping both teams, Grauley felt that it would help Philadelphia more since "Tommy is bound to be in more games than Johnny," considering his "demanding" schedule. In his first game for Trenton, Beckman outscored and outplayed Holman 14 to 8 in a 24-19 Bengal Victory.[41] The next night against Reading, Beckman "failed to put in an appearance."[42]

The next day Holman was dropped by Pittston of the State League, but he continued to lead the Eastern League in scoring. Germantown no longer had Frank Bruggy, who had quit the team and the league. Still, Germantown continued to win and on February 17, they were in first place, ahead of Camden, Reading, and Trenton.

On Saturday night, February 19, Beckman scored 10 to lead Trenton over Philadelphia 36 to 34 in two overtimes. Dunleavy had 13 for Philadelphia, but of greater interest was the fact that the crowd rode the referee "Midge" Ferguson so unmercifully that at game's end he quit the league.[43]

That same evening Camden defeated Reading 45-28. Each team cleared its bench playing all seven players, but Jim "Soup" Campbell was not one of them. Camden suspended Campbell for playing with the Pennsylvania State League All Stars against Parkesburg that same evening in Parkesburg. The Camden victory moved them into a tie with Germantown at 9 and 3 with Trenton third at 6 and 5.[44]

Despite Grauley's fears of league failures because of money shortfall, there were also rumors of more basketball leagues forming, one of which would be national in scope. In addition, the Eastern League, a six-team league since 1916 except for a brief period in 1916-17, was now thinking of going to eight teams. Clearly this was a reactive response to the fear of encroachment on its territory.[45]

As the year progressed, Germantown and Camden continued to win and Holman continued to lead the league in scoring. After the loss to Trenton, a game in which Beckman outscored Holman 14 to 8, Holman won the next battle ten days later in Germantown leading his team with 12 points in a 33 to 25 victory. Beckman failed to score from the field and finished with five free throws.

A turning point of the season and in professional basketball at the time occurred on February 25 in Trenton. In that game, a 32 to 20 Camden Skeeter victory, neither Beckman nor Grimstead appeared for the game. Under the new regulation, speculation focused on what action President Scheffer would take since he had attended the contest. However, he "refused to state what action he would take, until the facts were in."[46] The Trenton players, possibly encouraged by one of their co-owners, Joe Manze, took preemptive action two days later by announcing they would collectively walk off the floor if Beckman and Grimstead were not allowed to play on Wednesday, March 2, in Camden. Neither player could claim illness or family difficulties since both had played on the 25th in Pennsylvania State League games—Beckman for Nanticoke and Grimstead for Scranton and each had scored six points. Grauley noted that the Pennsylvania State League fines and suspends players while the Eastern League had been allowing players to "escape with a slap on the wrist and told to be good boys."[47] This appeared to be a showdown for power among owners and players. The league race, which now had Camden a game ahead of Germantown, was vying for coverage with this larger power struggle.

On the night of March 2, President Scheffer ordered Trenton to suspend Beckman or Grimstead for the remainder of the season. Trenton co-owner Manze would not yield just before game time. After five minutes, the game was forfeited when Trenton would not remove Grimstead. The 4,000 fans in Camden had their admission refunded (probably 25 or 30 cents apiece) and a league meeting was scheduled for Friday in Philadelphia, according to an *Inquirer* account. Not only was the game forfeited, but so was the Eastern League franchise since league rules stated that a game forfeited would result in forfeiture of the franchise.[48]

This situation also affected the first-half league race. With Trenton out of the league, Reading was the first half champion and would meet the second-half champion for the league title, or so it would seem. Rather than meeting on Friday, the league owners and administrators met Thursday and declared the Manze-Walters ownership of the Trenton franchise null and void. The league then allowed for the open franchise to be bid upon and former co-owner Walters and Jesse Handler, a former Trenton owner, both bid on it. The league powers said they could be approved as co-owners if they would reimburse Camden for its lost admissions. This was agreed upon. Trenton was fined $1,000 and paid that sum which was then granted back to Trenton to reimburse the Camden franchise. Manze, "who was the instigator in informing the players not to play the game against Camden, was banned indefinitely from the league as an owner or any connection with the league whatsoever."[49] The forfeit against Camden would stand and the game against Reading scheduled for that evening was rescheduled for a later date. Grimstead was suspended for the remainder of the season.

As an aside, Manze was not finished as an owner in Trenton quite yet. He contacted the Pennsylvania State League about purchasing a franchise in that league for a team to be placed in Trenton, and on March 6 it was announced that a Pennsylvania State League franchise had, indeed, been awarded to Manze and Trenton. This new team was scheduled to play four games in the league during the remainder of the year. Manze forfeited the rights to Grimstead and Bernie Dunn but succeeded in persuading Teddy Kearns of Trenton's Eastern League franchise to jump to his team. Manze's action widened the breach between the leagues and, following his franchise acquisition, attempts were made with both Allentown and Reading representatives for Pennsylvania State League Franchises.[50] These never came to fruition and the league itself expired after the 1920-21 season concluded.

Nevertheless, President Scheffer of the Eastern League responded to Manze's action by declaring that "Any player, under contract with an

Eastern League team, who played with or against a Pennsylvania State League club, would be barred from playing in the Eastern League."[51]

Also in March, Grauley speculated upon the champions of the Eastern League and the New York State League meeting at the conclusion of their respective league championships. Grauley claimed that "Interest has never higher in basketball than it is this season" and if the New York-Eastern League games materialized, it would be the first such series since Reading and Troy had met in 1913.[52]

Grauley went on in this column to present the Eastern League view of the embarrassing, recent brouhaha. He extolled Scheffer's actions, noting that it showed the Eastern League would not be easily intimidated and that owners would now understand "That rules are rules and must be lived up to."[53]

After the fiasco one might think that Beckman would be a regular "attendee" at subsequent Trenton contests. Instead, Beckman was through with Trenton, failing to appear for their remaining six games including the play-off game with Reading for the first-half title on March 23.[54] Ten days earlier, Reading tried to postpone its game with Trenton and the Bears contended they could not get all of their players to the game. Obviously, the problem of players playing in multiple leagues or teams had not been solved. Scheffer held fast and in a meeting the issue was settled swiftly. Also, it was intimated that the deposit be raised from $200 to $1,000 per franchise for the next year and that a rule would be passed the next year to keep players within the Eastern League and not on outside teams.[55]

The Reading–Trenton game saw Trenton winning 23 to 15 in a contest that featured "fisticuffs, rough play, and intense excitement."[56] The roughness carried into Trenton's next contest with Germantown where Trenton's Brennan "actually held Frankle so that half the time he was unable to move."[57] Despite that handicap, the Germs won handily, 32 to 12 in a contest where Holman had ten points (eight of eight free throws) and Germantown scored 20 of their 32 points on charity tosses. Germantown now led the Skeeters of Camden by defeating Camden 38 to 15 on March 18.

The previous night, Manze's Pennsylvania State League Trenton team had defeated Wilkes-Barre, 33 to 20, a game in which Barney Sedran had six, Marty Friedman five, and Teddy Kearns six for Manze's squad. It is curious that Bole and Lawrence refer to this team as a "rag tag team made up of border-line professional basketballers and a few Trenton City League players."[58] Though past their prime, Friedman and Sedran, one a future Hall of Famer and the other a strong candidate, were hardly borderline.

In other games, Manze was allowed to use players on other Pennsylvania State League rosters and the contests did not count in the league standings, since the purpose of the games was to establish Manze's team in Trenton. In the March 12 game, for example, both Newman and Dunn of Wilkes-Barre played for Trenton in their 30 to 25 defeat of Pittston.[59]

Nanticoke and Scranton were tied at the end of the second half and a best two-of-three playoff was proposed. Instead, the league shifted to a one-game playoff to be held on March 19 at Town Hall in Scranton at 9:00 p.m. A crowd of 2,500 fans waited patiently for the arrival of two Nanticoke players, Horse Haggerty and Soup Campbell, so the Nans could take the floor. Haggerty arrived at 10:40 after hurrying from New York where he had received word of the game via telegram. Attempts to locate Campbell were unsuccessful.

The Scranton owner, R. A. Ammerman, gave the Nans his okay to use any State League players in attendance, which included Chris Leonard and Merle Harris of Pittston and Joe Berger of Plymouth. According to the *Wilkes-Barre Record,* Beckman opposed this and the Nans refused to play without Campbell, opting instead for a postponement. Ammerman refused saying that this was unfair to the fans. "Scranton had its best team on the floor including Meehan, Holman, Harvey, Ripley, Dehnert, Reynics, and Grimstead."[60] Scranton, thus, refused to reschedule the game and the next day President Brislin of the Pennsylvania State League awarded the pennant to Scranton by forfeit.[61]

Scranton, thus, "earned" the right to meet Pittston, the first-half winner, in the State League playoffs. Holman (referred to as Ned Holman of New England) would be playing his first game with the Miners; he would offset, somewhat, the loss of Frank Bruggy, who had left for baseball spring training with the Phillies.[62]

The Eastern League finals opened March 24 in Germantown where the Germs won 30 to 14. Holman's "brilliant playing" was extolled as the "highest heights of basketball" as he scored sixteen points including six of seven free throws. Reich had four for Reading and Haggerty didn't score.[63]

The second contest in Reading was closer but the result was the same as Holman scored eleven to lead Germantown to a 30 to 25 victory. The roughness of these games was again apparent as Holman was momentarily knocked out in a collision with Haggerty in the second half but resumed playing. Reich was a no show for this decisive contest.[64]

In Grauley's column the next day, he again revived the possibility of playing the New York State League Champion, Albany, as long as "George Smith does not play" since he is not a member of Albany and would only be added for the series.[65] Grauley also saw the two-game sweep proof that pro basketball was not fixed in order to play a third game and increase revenues. He might have been comparing his league with the Pennsylvania State League, where a tie for the first-half league title was decided by a best-of-three games playoff between Pittston and Wilkes-Barre. Pittston won the first game 28 to 26 on January 25, then there was a nine-day hiatus until the two teams played on February 4 when Pittston again won, 26 to 23. In those games, Chris Leonard of the Celtics had a prominent role in the Pittston victories, scoring five and seven points respectively.[66]

With the conclusion of the Eastern League season, players' attention could be focused on other teams upon which they played, both independents and league teams. Pittston, with Leonard, was set to play Scranton in the Pennsylvania State League championship. Scranton added Holman and Stretch Meehan in March and teamed with Grimstead and Dehnert of the Celtics, and Ripley who joined the Celts in 1923 for a short stint. Holman, Ripley, and Meehan were the heart of the Germantown team that had just won the Eastern League championship. Or had they?

The Germantown players had agreed to play a series against Manze's Pennsylvania State League Trenton squad in Trenton in early April following the State League playoffs. This prospect caused Trenton's co-owner, Jesse Hendler, to protest to Eastern League President Scheffer. Scheffer warned Germantown that their Eastern League franchise would be forfeited were this series to come about.[67]

The Germantown players were eager to keep playing and make more money. Their position was that the league had no jurisdiction over them after the season was completed. On April 1st, the Germantown squad (minus Holman, Meehan, and Ripley, who were all playing in the Scranton-Pittston series) played in Media (Pennsylvania), a suburb of Philadelphia, edging the Media squad 30 to 26 with Glasco and Hough scoring fourteen and eight points, respectively. Two brothers named Miller filled in for Holman and Meehan.[68]

Now the prospect of the Trenton series was more appealing with each team to get 40 percent of the proceeds and the winning team to get the other 20 percent. With Trenton's large armory, the minimum gate for each team looked to be about $7,000 with another $3,500 possible for the winning team.

Meanwhile the Celtics took to the road with the Eastern League season over and the Pennsylvania State League playoffs beginning. On March 28, they played the New England A - S team before 1,200 fans at Mechanics Hall in Boston. Beckman led with 11 points, Grimstead had 10, Reich 2, Dehnert 4, and Trippe 2 in a 27 to 25 victory.[69]

In the State League Playoffs, Scranton, a team playing together for the first time, defeated Pittston in two straight games. In game one, the Germantown veterans—Meehan, Ripley, and Holman—"gave an exhibition of passing such as had never been seen in this city."[70] Dehnert was ill and unable to play, but in the second game he replaced Grimstead and led the Miner turnaround. According to the *Wilkes-Barre Record,* Dehnert had a half dozen boils on several parts of his body and was not feeling well. It was noted that, "Grimstead was not afflicted with boils but his play indicated that he was the 'weak sister' and his removal made a wonderful difference in the team's play."[71] Holman, Meehan, and Ripley now had two championships for the season.

On the day of the Germantown-Media game, President Scheffer issued an ultimatum. He notified each of the Germantown players— Hough, Frankle, Glasco, Lansing, Meehan, Ripley, Holman, and Powers, and the owner, E. M. Bowers—that they would be liable for fines up to $500 for playing a game in a city where an Eastern League club was located. The players' contention that the league had no jurisdiction after the season had ended was, according to the *Inquirer* (i.e., S. O. Grauley), true only in cities without an Eastern League franchise.[72]

The Germantown players defied Scheffer's threat and played Trenton's State League Club on April 1, losing 26 to 16 or 26 to 23[73] in what was to be the first of a three-game series. Trenton's squad had Barney Sedran, Doc Newman of Parkesburg, Marty Friedman, Bernie Dunn, all top players. For unspecified reasons, games two and three were not played, probably because of a disagreement over money.

The night of the game, the Eastern League owners met at the Hotel Windsor in Philadelphia. Because of the Germantown team's defiance of the playing ban, the league took an unexpected and unprecedented step —it disbanded! Rather than censure Germantown, the clubs simply voted to disband with no 1920-21 championship awarded. They divided $627.43 among the six clubs ($104.58 each) and it was said that they would probably reorganize with a change of name and circuit.[74]

A week later, April 7, 1921, the new Eastern League was formed with Harrisburg being admitted in place of Germantown. The New Eastern League of Professional Basketball also announced that the league would probably go to eight teams since there were four applications for franchises. One of the new rules announced was that "No player would be allowed to play in any other league." Scheffer, Grauley, and William E. Brandt, Eastern League officers, were elected officers of the New Eastern League.

So the upshot of all this was that again the league squared off in a power struggle with a franchise and its players. The players, knowing

THE CRACK NEW YORK
WHIRLWINDS

Organized during the middle of the season
by "Tex" Rickard, to play at Madison Square
Garden, N.Y.City, this club later moved to the
huge 22nd Regiment Armory in the same city
where they won every game played. Made up
of members of the best league teams in the
East, this club immediately became rivals to the
Original Celtics. Just before the season closed
a series of games were arranged between
these two teams, which resulted in each club
winning one game, and owing to the warm
weather a third game could not be staged.
These two games played, drew the greatest
gathering of basket ball fans ever assembled
under one roof anywhere in the world.

Standing—SEDRAN—KENNEDY—RICONDA—HOLMAN
Sitting—FRIEDMAN—LEONARD

The New York City Whirlwinds, 1921.

that the league needed them more than they needed the league, defied
the league with the acquiescence of the owners. The league, seeing that
its threats had been viewed as hollow, disbanded and reformed with Germantown out of the league.[75] The players were apparently not punished
since the New Eastern League allowed them back the next year playing
for various franchises (Hough, Ripley, and Glasco for Coatesville; Frankle for Harrisburg; Meehan for Trenton; and Holman with the Celtics,
who entered the league in December 1921). Germantown was listed as
1920-21 league champion in later league records, despite the earlier
announcement.

The players assumed they could continue to sell their services to the
highest bidders, but at the end of the 1920-21 season, both the Pennsylvania State and Interstate Leagues went out of business. They were
likely driven out by Jim Furey's signing of his Celtics to exclusive contracts for 1921-22, and by a concomitant rise in player salaries to persuade them to sign such exclusive contractual agreements.

The optimism of earlier months, when various new leagues were
formed, was swiftly sobered. The Eastern League ultimately took in two
more franchises after the Pennsylvania State League folded—Wilkes-Barre and Scranton. For Nanticoke, Plymouth, and Pittston, 1921
marked the end of big league basketball status.

Even with their sudden ejection Germantown continued playing,
defeating West Chester 20 to 15 in what the *Inquirer* felt was the final
cage contest of the season. Unlike the Media game, all the Germantown
regulars were there and played, led by Holman's eleven points.[76]

Though Germantown's season had concluded, Holman's had not, nor had those of his Germantown teammates, Meehan and Ripley, or his future Celtic teammate, Dehnert who, along with Harvey, constituted the Scranton Miners Squad. As champions of the Pennsylvania State League, they were to meet Albany who had won both halves of the New York State League season[77] in a series for the world's professional basketball championship.

There were rule differences to be decided. Because the New York State League still had open baskets with no backboards, and because in that league only two men could "dig" in for a loose ball, those rules would prevail in Albany. In Scranton, there would be backboards and three players could go for a loose ball.[78] Before 3,000 fans in Albany's Armory, Albany defeated Scranton 29 to 25. The Albany team was composed of players familiar to the Miners; Sedran, Friedman, and Riconda, all of later SPHA fame, and the former two of Trenton's recent Pennsylvania State League team were the top three players.[79]

Two nights later in Scranton before more than 3,000 fans, the Miners evened the series at one game apiece. Balanced scoring (each player scored between 4 and 8 points) and defense (only one Senator player had more than 2 points—Friedman with 5) were the key to the Scranton win.[80]

The next night, back in Albany before another 3,000 fans, the Senators triumphed 36 to 19. Sedran, the diminutive future hall of famer, had 19 points to match the Miner total. Albany hit 18 or 26 free throws in the victory.

In between these games, it seemed that Holman had been dashing to New York City to play in a three game series for the Whirlwinds against the Celtics. The *Reach Guide* had the games on Sunday, April 10, and Wednesday, April 13, 1921, but both were wrong.[81] On April 10, Holman was in Albany and Sunday was April 9. Assuming that game one was on April 9 and game two on either Tuesday April 11, or Friday April 14, Holman's week looked as follows:

April 7	Germantown at West Chester
April 9	Whirlwinds in New York vs. Celtics
April 10	Scranton Miners at Albany
April 11 or April 14	Whirlwinds in New York vs. Celtics
April 12	Miners in Scranton vs. Albany
April 13	Miners at Albany

It now appears that Holman, Friedman, Sedran, Leonard, and Riconda did not go to New York until after the April 13 game in Albany.

Rather than April 10 and April 13 as the *Reach Guide* stated, and which has been the basis for statements by Peterson as well as Bole and Lawrence, the first Celtic–Whirlwind game was played on Saturday night, April 16, before 10,000 fans. This date (with a different score 40 to 29) resolves the mystery of how players on Scranton and Albany could have been in Albany and New York at the *same time*.[82]

The two games that pitted the New York Whirlwinds against the Celtics led to the completion of the team that would dominate professional basketball for the remainder of the decade. The Celtics players Pete Barry, Oscar (Swede) Grimstead, Ernie Reich, Dutch Dehnert, Johnny Beckman, and Mike Smolick, were an outstanding team as were the Whirlwinds, Tex Rickard's recent foray into the pro game. The squad included Barney Sedran, Marty Friedman, Nat Holman, Chris Leonard, Ray Kennedy, and Harry Riconda, four of whom played for Albany. Holman would play against them three times and with them twice in the two series.

The Scranton–Albany series did not resume until April 26, following a number of postponements. Undoubtedly the Celtic–Whirlwind games interceded and, possibly, previously scheduled Celtic games did also. The *Wilkes-Barre Record* alerted fans that "tickets purchased for postponed games (would) be honored" at the April 26 meeting in Scranton.[83] In that game, the Miners routed the Senators 36 to 15 before 1,000 fans. For the Miners, Grimstead appeared for the absent Holman and Ed Wachter, an old time New York League player, took the place of the absent Riconda. Former Pennsylvania State League and current Eastern League referee, Herman Baetzel, called the game and the next night's contest at the Scranton Armory. The Miners again prevailed 29 to 19[84] and announced themselves World Champions. Though that might be disputed, Holman, Ripley, and Meehan certainly were champions having played on the Eastern League winners and the Pennsylvania State League champions, the latter having also defeated the New York State League victors.

Thus, one of the most tumultuous years in professional basketball ended. Before the next season began, two leagues would fold, one would expand, a new league (the Metropolitan Association League from New York City) would begin and the Celtics would emerge with the addition of Leonard, Holman, and Horse Haggerty as the undisputed leader of professional basketball. The introduction of exclusive, contractual agreements and concomitant higher salaries by James Furey, owner of the Celtics, would later force the Eastern League into salary escalation that ultimately claimed that league as a victim.

The balance of power in the owner/league player dichotomy clearly lay with the players. As long as there were competing leagues and a reliable rail system, players could negotiate for their best deal on a weekly or daily basis. By the end of the decade, that balance would shift decidedly driving professional basketball into the regionalization and low pay where it would remain until after World War II.

6

EASTERN LEAGUE ROMANCE—
THE FIRST GREAT CELTICS SQUAD
1921-22

As the 1921-22 season opened, the Celtics were the highest paid, best organized, and finest team in the world. With the collapse of two leagues and a reluctance on the part of the Eastern League teams to schedule play against the Celtics, it became obvious to the Fureys that the Celtics needed to get into the Eastern League. The league, composed of teams in Trenton, Camden, Scranton, Wilkes-Barre, Reading, Coatesville (a Philadelphia suburb), Philadelphia and Harrisburg, was not looking to expand. It was trying to keep its franchises solvent. After twenty games (most during the first half) the Philadelphia franchise withdrew from the league because of financial exigencies. On November 14, the Harrisburg Club sold its Eastern franchise to New York's[1] Charles Brickley, owner of the Whirlwinds, who used some of those players and some from Harrisburg to form the New York Giants. The change in franchise had no effect on the team and they continued to lose money and games. One month later, on December 15, 1921, the Furey brothers purchased the franchise from Brickley.[2]

The Celtic entry into the Eastern League was a negotiated settlement. First, the Celtics would be permitted to use a net at Madison Square Garden if a cage was not available. (That turned out to be the case and many league members complained long and loud about it.) The Celtics also were to play all their home games at the Garden and "regardless of scheduling problems, be played on Sundays only," a condition that later was to cause considerable contention in the administration of the Eastern League.[3] Third, the Celts would be allowed to choose whom they would play at home to finish out the first half of the Eastern League schedule.

On their part, the Celtics agreed to play with baskets that extended 12 inches rather than 6 inches from the backboard. The *Inquirer* noted that the Celtic players were barred for failure to report to their league clubs (all had formerly played in the Eastern League, while on other teams before the initiation of Furey's exclusive contracts). This was seen as a matter that would be resolved at a league meeting on December 18 in Philadelphia.[4]

The Celtics debuted in Trenton and lost 21 to 18 in a contest called "The greatest game of the present season" amidst "the roughest kind of playing." The Bengals' managers waived on the Celtic players "with the exception of (Pete) Barry who did not play, though Haggerty and Holman, who belong to Reading, and Leonard, on Coatesville ineligible list, did."[5] Of the 18 Celtic points, Beckman had 10 and Leonard 6.

The five-hour league meeting on the 18th brought quite a list of maneuvering in order to keep the Celtic team intact. The Celtic owners —the Furey brothers, Bart Meaney and James Whitty—agreed to pay $1,300 for Brickley's franchise, then proceeded to trade Sedran, Friedman, Riconda, Lawrence, and Schmeelk from the Giant's roster. Coatesville got Riconda for Leonard. Lawrence went to Wilkes-Barre for Malone, who was then sent along with Haggerty to Reading. Reading, in turn, traded Holman and Reich to the Celtics. The Celtics sent Sedran, Schmeelk, Friedman, and $400 to Scranton for Dehnert and Beckman. Friedman was then released to Philadelphia. The Celtics also agreed to give Barry to the New York State League.[6]

Later in the week the "new" Celtics took the floor in Camden where they absorbed a 21 to 14 defeat. The Celtics had many shots but could not hit, scoring only one basket in each half while "Soup" Campbell, Camden's star player, had three and "ran away from Holman, a fast man on the floor." One bright spot for the Celtics was the return of "Horse" Haggerty, whom Reading had sold back to the Celtics rather than pay his high salary.

Things seemed to be promising for the Celtics despite the losses. Unfortunately, the Eastern League was not doing as well. Both Scranton and Philadelphia canceled games, then dropped out of the league, citing low crowds and an uncertain schedule. Rumors had been circulated which had Scranton moving to Nanticoke (Pennsylvania)[7] as well as Brooklyn, Paterson (New Jersey), and Atlantic City.[8] But ultimately, costs drove the Miners out of the league totally. William Scheffer, the president of the Eastern League and the editor of the *Reach Basketball Guide,* described Scranton's demise thusly,

something went wrong in Scranton and the crowds refused to turn out in large numbers. Then, every now and then, games were postponed thus upsetting the schedule. Then the home dates were continually changed so finally the home fans did not know when the next game was going to be played even if they did want to witness it.[9]

The Celtic starting five in about 1921.

Philadelphia's precarious financial position was discussed right up to the start of the second half, though the assumption was that the franchise would continue. Then on January 16, at the outset of the second half of the season, the Philadelphia franchise left the league.[10] Philadelphia's departure was viewed in retrospect, by Scheffer, as noted:

Philadelphia was another club that was badly abused and dropped out after being a member of the league since its organization. A good personality does not make a successful manager and that was the problem with Philadelphia. Then its schedule was badly mixed up and the fans did not know when they would play.[11]

After Scranton and Philadelphia folded, their players were bid on by other teams but the six remaining clubs were being very wary about offering too much money. In articles on January 16 and 18, S. O. Grauley noted that team expenses had doubled in one year and attendance had not risen. The problem, as he saw it, was that the owners signed players on contracts for too much money. Now they needed to ask the players to take salary cuts to save the league. (This, of course, sounds very much like major league baseball in the 1990s.) Grauley went on to discuss the loss of the Philadelphia franchise, claiming that "several clubs in . . . this city could have probably secured the franchise and made a success of it, but the staggering [sic] high salaries paid to the stars evidently frightened them off."[12] Grauley's comments were not just those of an Eastern League beat reporter for the *Philadelphia Inquirer* since he also served as the vice-president of the Eastern League.

Amidst all this structural chaos, the Celtics began the second half of the season with a string of victories. They were not, however, without controversy since the first half of the season had ended most peculiarly. On January 1, Trenton met the Celtics in Madison Square Garden before 8,000 fans, but four Trenton starters—Barlow, Tome, Kearns, and Dunn —were not present. Precisely why is not clear. It may have been a question of money, which was often the case. Bole and Lawrence claimed it was because the players were not consulted on the change of schedule for the games against the new entrant in the league, the Celtics. However, President Scheffer promptly suspended the four for thirty days. The game went on, but because of various snafus, it was played with 6- inch, not 12-inch baskets as the Celtics had agreed to, and a tight net, rather than a cage, was used. The score was 42 to 17, Celtics.[13]

The next night the Celtics beat Reading 28 to 21 while Trenton, with its suspended players playing, was defeating Coatesville.[14] Three days later, on January 5 at a league meeting of owners, it was determined that the president couldn't suspend players—only the team owner could. Thus the league lifted the suspensions and fined the Trenton mangement $100 for not putting their full team on the floor against the Celtics. So as not to appear totally toothless, the league clubs also agreed that next time they would be "hard with a club which is caught practicing any similar stunt of which Trenton was found guilty."[15]

Also at that meeting, the Scranton players were given another week to "look around" for a new home (Carbondale, Pennsylvania, was a site mentioned for the first time), though this search came to naught. In addition, the league provided another concession to its newest member, the Celtics. It was decided that Eastern League players could play in exhibitions against the Celtics, but no more than two players from any one club could play in a game and the team could not use the Eastern League club name.

With these issues settled, speculation centered on whether Trenton, Camden, or New York would take the second-half crown. The Celtics started off fast carrying over from their two victories that ended the first half of the season. The Celtics easily won at Coatesville 32 to 19,[16] then beat them in New York six days later, 40 to 17. After being out of the lineup for more than a week, Johnny Beckman returned. There had been rumors of a trade, but Celtic management announced that all differences (probably money) had been "amicably adjusted" and he would be with the team the rest of the season.[17]

On the 22nd of January, the Celtics went to 3 to 0 with a 38 to 18 win over the Barons of Wilkes-Barre. The essence of Celtic play was captured in one sentence of the *Inquirer*'s account of the contest. "The polished teamwork of the Celtics was again in evidence and repeatedly a basket resulted from snappy passing down the entire length of the court."[18] Chris Leonard had 13 points, Beckman and Reich both had 8, and Holman had 4, plus 5 assists.

The Celtics won on January 30, then a week later swept Reading and Trenton in a day-night doubleheader at Madison Square Garden by scores of 32 to 27 and 23 to 15, respectively. Attendance at the day game was not mentioned, but 6,000 fans attended the Trenton game, one in which "close covering prevented much passing" and where "all (Celtic) shots, but for one last by Reich, were made from beyond the foul mark and side of the court."[19] Referee Baetzel was fingered in the eye[20] and Maury Tome fell over the loose net. It was becoming obvious the Celtics were not going to bring a cage to Madison Square Garden. The use of the loose net was decried as the ball frequently went out of bounds because the net was not fastened to the floor.

Beckman was high against Trenton with 11 points, which included 9 of 13 free-throw shots. The two wins kept the Celtics undefeated for the second half with six wins, even though "Horse" Haggerty did not play in either of the two games at the Garden (for no stated reason).

Finally, on February 10, the Celtics lost in Trenton 17 to 16 in a hotly contested battle. Bole and Lawrence quoted the *Trenton Times* account of the game: "Right from the start it was a contest of strength with all ten players clinging to each other like porous plaster."[21] Stretch Meehan was the offensive leader for Trenton with 6 points while Holman had 9 of the 16 Celtic points. Both teams hit five baskets, but in a rare turn of events, the Celtics lost the game at the line, hitting only six of eighteen free throws to Trenton's seven of fourteen.

The Celts were off from Eastern League play for five days, but two days before their game in Camden, the *Inquirer* ran a story hyping the importance of the game to the Camden franchise. The Celts and the Skeeters were favorably compared in their team play except that the Celts:

take more long and risky flings at the basket . . . They have team play and they also have several long-distance shooting stars who enjoy hearing the swish of the ball through the cord as much as a ball player likes to hear the old twang of the bat as it crashed into the "apple."[22]

Heading into the game, Camden and New York were tied with records of 7 to 1 and Trenton was at 8 to 2 only percentage points behind. The game reflected those close standings as the Celtics edged Camden in overtime, 22 to 21. Again, the Celts were "out freethrown" going 10 for 29 to Camden's 15 for 25, but 6 baskets to the Skeeters' 3 brought the victory. Beckman led with 12 points including 6 for 14 from the line.

Grauley was clearly caught up by the ferocity of the contest.

It was a fierce fight every minute with an extra period tossed in for good measure and then the Manhattan birds won by this squeek—22 to 21.

Every seat had been sold in advance and, despite the inclement night, standing room was at a premium long before the opening whistle shrieked with the biggest crowd ever known at a South Jersey game.[24]

The following Sunday, February 19, the Celtics played another day-night doubleheader in Madison Square Garden, winning twice. Coatesville was the afternoon victim 33 to 31 as Beckman scored 10 and Holman 12. In the evening, before 8,000 fans, the Celtics defeated Camden once again, this time by a score of 25 to 23. Reich did not play due to pneumonia and was "confined to his home."[25]

Ernie Reich about 1920. Within two years he was dead.

The next night the Celtics were upset in Coatesville 23 to 20 before 800 fans, a large crowd for the small Coatesville gym. Johnny Beckman scored all of the field goals (four) that the Celts garnered and finished with 12 points of the 20. Elmer Ripley, who would later have two brief tours with the Celtics, "played rings around Holman." Ten of 24 free-throw shooting to the Coats' 13 to 26 was the difference in the contest.[26] The next night the Celtics were in Atlantic City in a non-league contest against the Atlantic City Knights of Columbus on the Steeple-chase Pier. Holman was absent for no stated reason, as was Ernie Reich, who was still out with pneumonia. Before the largest crowd in Atlantic

City that year, the Celtics edged the Caseys 23 to 20 with Beckman's nine tops for the Shamrock Squad.[27]

Three days later, on February 24, the low point of the season occurred when captain Ernie Reich succumbed to pneumonia and died at his Bailey Avenue home in the Bronx at 3:30 in the afternoon. Reich had been "delirious for hours and kept calling to his teammates to 'pass the ball.'" The *Philadelphia Inquirer*[28] reviewed his career which began in New York City with St. Gabriel's, the National Middleweight Basketball Champions in 1905, when Reich was just thirteen. Two of his teammates on that squad were Chris Leonard and Johnny Beckman, also his Celtic teammates, and they were certainly deeply affected by his sudden loss.

The *New York Times,* which avoided all mention of professional basketball at that time, carried Reich's death notice on February 25 and his funeral service on the next day, but, neither mentioned Reich's career or the Celtics.[29] By contrast, the 1922-23 *Reach Guide* had a full-page article on Reich's death as well as discussion of his loss in the introductory section of the guide.[30] His career was presented in some detail from the St. Gabriel Saints (1905-10) to White Plains of the Hudson River League (1920-12) to the great Sheepshead Bay Five (1912-13), the Jersey City Club of the Interestate League (1913-14) and Norwalk of the Connecticut League (1914-15). In 1915, he ended his minor league career and joined DeNeri of the Eastern League, where he played until the war intervened. In 1918, he was with Reading and in 1919 he was captain of the Scranton team, which the *Reach Guide* incorrectly called the Eastern League champions. (They were the Pennsylvania State League regular season champions.) In that year, Reich had a 6.5 point per-game average while also playing for Reading and scoring nearly 7 points per game.[31] His Miners lost to Beckman's Nanticoke Squad in the post season series, three games to one. In 1920, Reich played with Stamford, Connecticut, and Reading (where he scored 154 points and led his team to the Eastern League finals where they lost to Holman's Germantown squad). Reich joined the Celtics in 1920 and was with them as captain until his death.

Ernie was not a player that showed like Beckman or Holman, but when it came to the fine points of the game and using his head, Ernie had all the "Beckmans" and "Holmans" beat to a frazzle. Reich was a gentleman on the floor and everywhere else, and the game's loss of Reich will be hard to fill.[32]

Reich's funeral was on the 26th, a Sunday, and it was a day that the Celtics were scheduled to play another day-night doubleheader in Madison Square Garden. The funeral was at 4:30 in the afternoon, so it was possible that some of Reich's teammates could have taken the Broadway subway to 231st Street and attended, but before game one against Reading, a tribute to Reich was offered at courtside. According to the *Inquirer* account, this tribute sobered play and had a "saddening effect on the players. After the tribute, 'Nearer My God to Thee' was played while players in the cage stood with bowed heads." Despite not having "the same snap to the ball in passes," the Celtics triumphed, 36 to 29 with Beckman leading with twelve and three assists. Holman had eight and two assists, Dehnert nine, and Barry, now the starter for Reich, had six.

The key game, of course, was the nightcap where the Celtics topped Trenton, 25 to 18. This time Holman led with eleven and Beckman followed with six as the Celts hit 15 of 24 free throws. "The team play of the home boys was in evidence at all stages of the game, and this prevailed against the burlier work of their opponents form the Jersey Capital."[33]

With the victory, the Celtics extended their lead over Trenton to a full game with the Camden Skeeters two games behind. The standings, as of February 27, were:

New York	12	3
Trenton	10	3
Camden	8	3
Wilkes-Barre	3	8
Coatesville	3	11
Reading	2	10

A week later, S. O. Grauley discussed the closeness of the race, which now was a virtual deadlock, as the Celts had not played a league game since the 27th while Trenton had gone 2-0 and Camden 3-0. Since Trenton had won the first half, they were assured of a playoff berth, but the Celtics and Skeeters were still battling for the other slot. Grauley noted that the playoff series should be three games, not five, or it might "look like promoters were making the playoff a money affair."[34] Since Grauley was league vice president, it seemed certain that the playoff would indeed be three games.

The Celtics returned to action on March 10 winning in Trenton 22 to 16. "Beckman and Holman were the whole show for the Celtics" with Johnny getting 7 and Nat 5. The Celtics had only four baskets but their 14 of 28 from the line was the difference.[35] Interestingly, Bole and Lawrence have both the wrong score and the wrong location for this game, calling it 25-16, placing it at the Garden and affixing blame for the loss upon the site![36]

Then on Sunday, the twelfth, the Celts solidified their position with another doubleheader victory in New York. The first game was a breeze over the Barons of Wilkes-Barre 46 to 31. "Even 'Hoss' Haggerty got into the limelight with 3 field goals which added to his large total of 2 for the second half season." Beside Haggerty's six, Holman had 15 with 3 assists and Barry 12 with 4 assists. The Celts had 12 assists for the game and 14 of 20 free throws to coast to victory.

In the evening contest, the Celtics and Skeeters hooked up in what the *Inquirer* reporter called "the greatest game ever played here." Before 6,000 fans, the Celtics triumphed 28 to 25 in double overtime. With 30 seconds left in the first overtime, a double foul was called on Holman and Dolin of Camden with first Dolin, then Holman making their free throw, knotting the score at 25. Johnny Beckman, referred to as "shifty and eagle eyed," was called the hero. He had 16 points plus he hit a long shot in the second overtime following Holman's free throw to assure victory. Holman had no baskets but made eight of ten free throws, so the two of them had 24 of the 28 points. Leonard replaced Barry in the lineup for the evening game.[37]

The Celtics' hold on first place was shaken three nights later in Camden when the Skeeters embarrassed the Shamrocks 26 to 12. New York delayed until 9:30 p.m. because Haggerty hadn't arrived (he also played on the Visitation Squad in the Metropoliatan League and Troy of the New York State League, not having signed an exclusive contract with the Celtics) probably because of a missed or delayed train. Finally they started without him, and by the time he arrived the game was already out of reach. "A Camden crowd of 2,500 roared its approval as its heroes shut the Celtics out without a field goal for the entire first half."[38] The second half made no difference as "the New Yorkers had the ball so little that Camden made them look bad all through the game."[39] Three Celtics scored—Beckman (5), Dehnert (4), and Holman (3).

The last weekend of the season saw the Celtics with a 15-4 record, Camden with 14-5 and Trenton 15-4. The Celtics were to play the Reading Bears in Reading while Trenton and Camden squared off in Camden. Camden won 31 to 26 to tie Trenton, but the Celtics defeated Reading to eliminate Camden and set up the playoff series with Trenton, the first-half winner.[40] The dates, however, weren't set until March 27 in a meeting in Philadelphia. Even though Trenton was thought to be the stronger team, the fact that the Celts took three of four from them gave one pause. The loss of Reich was seen by Grauley as a key. "New York has not fully recovered from the death of Ernie Reich and the team has been playing entirely too many games for the players to be fit and able to stand such a playoff series."[41]

The Potters, however, were also a man short since Teddy Kearns was not in attendance, having left for Portsmouth, Virginia, where he played minor league baseball. Dehnert was reported to have had the flu, so the March 31 matchup was deemed a tossup.[42]

The opener of the best-of-three game playoff series was on March 31 at the Trenton Arena. The Celtics arrived in Trenton after spending the night on a train from Holyoke, Massachusetts, "where they licked the Interstate League team of that place on Thursday (the 30th)."[43] Despite that, the Celtics came out strong "dominating action all the way. At no time were they in danger of losing this basketball game."[44] The Celtics superior ball handling was enhanced by the absence of Kearns, "Trenton's clever ball handler, passer, and playmaker."[45] The Celtics controlled the ball deliberately. "When they did not get a good chance to pass, they made good use of the floor and kept shooting the ball among themselves in the backfield."[46] Indeed, they "followed the leather like a money lender follows his victim."

Dehnert did not play and in his place was Pete Barry (referred to as Tom in the *Inquirer* article), who played "with such skill and ability that he virtually was the man who upset the entire workings of the Trenton defense."[47] Barry made 6 points to support Beckman and Holman who had 7 each in the 24-20 Celtic victory. Once the Celtics had the 15 to 11 halftime lead, they "played safe to the end . . . time and again two and sometimes three Celtics were under their own basket flinging the oval across to prevent a dash for the basket."[48] The Celtics kept sending cutters who were then tackled by Trenton sending the Celts to the line twenty-eight times. This was the aim of the Celtics who converted forteen times to Trenton's twelve (of twenty-six).

The only disappointment was the size of the crowd. There were many empty seats and Grauley speculated that the thirty-cent increase in ticket prices might have precipitated the drop in attendance.

Two days later, in an unexpected reversal, Trenton defeated New York at the 71st Regiment Armory, 22 to 17. "The victory was due primarily to the heady work of 'Stretch' Meehan who upset the New Yorker's play by batting the ball back to the Trenton guards in the final period in such a manner that New York was unable to get their hands on the ball."[49] Barry led the scoring with 8 points and Holman had 6, all free thrown in seven tries. The rest of the Celts shot three of fifteen from the line to total nine of twenty-two compared to Trenton's twelve of nineteen. Beckman had one basket, but assisted on all three of Barry's baskets.

The third game of the series was played at a neutral site, Camden, on April 5. The Celtics, behind Beckman's 14 points, won the Eastern

League Championship 27 to 22. Despite only connecting on one field goal to the Celtic's five, the Potters hung in until the end because of their 20 of 29 free throw shooting. The Celtics were 17-31. The *Inquirer* reported 4,000 fans turned out while the *Reach Guide* claimed 5,000. Another discrepancy saw Holman and Dehnert credited with 8 and 2, respectively, in the *Inquirer* while the *Reach Guide* had Holman with 7 and Dehnert with 3.[50] Whatever the proper scoring, the Celts outplayed them "totally" in the second half.

During the sensational burst of speed, Johnny Beckman, the Babe Ruth of basketball, and Nat Holman, another wooden floor brilliant, played basketball which startled and also wrought havoc with Trenton's defense.[51]

Both the *Inquirer* and the *Reach Guide* lauded one particular play that put the Celtics ahead 20 to 19. Beckman cut to the basket and received a high pass from Holman, which he rose high to receive. With Barlow, the Trenton defender at his heels, "Beckman caught the ball with both hands and twisted his body in the air and tossed the ball through the net with both hands."[52]

The game was the 133rd of the year for the Celtics, of which more than 90 percent were victories, according to the *Inquirer*. The Celtic victory in the final was based on defense, holding Trenton without a field goal for the last 38 minutes of the game.[53] For the year, the Celtics had the best defense in the Eastern League allowing 426 points in the 20 games of the second-half for an average of 21.3 points allowed per game. They scored 535 for a 26.75 average and a league best 5.4 differential.

Thus, the Eastern League season ended with the cocky, arrogant newcomers to the league turning back all comers to triumph. The controversies over the lack of a real cage in the Garden, the favoritism in scheduling, and the higher Celtic salaries were all subsumed in the battles on the court where the Celtics won. The final playoff series was refereed by Herman Baetzel, acknowledged as the finest referee of the era and the *Reach Guide* noted that he "did fine work in all the games."[54] Beckman led in scoring with 23 followed by Holman and Trenton's Meehan with 20.

The 1922-23 Eastern League Season

The Celtic victory and the relative stability of the second half of the 1921-22 season seemed to auger well for the Eastern League's 1922-23 prospects. Six teams were again in the fold, but not the same six as the year before. Wilkes-Barre, unable to win and unable to draw fans, withdrew from the league. Their entire roster, however, became the roster of the Atlantic City Sandpipers—a solid, veteran team, but one that "would not win the championship."[55]

The other new entry was Jasper from South Philadelphia which replaced the Celtics, who felt more money was to be made as a "barnstorming" team than one committed to a rigid league schedule.[56]

Early in the season, 'Horse' Haggerty, who had returned to the Reading Bears, requested and received his unconditional release. He wanted to be committed to playing only for the Celtics, which would be more difficult with their longer and farther trips. The Bears signed Garry Schmeelk, but Reading still had no real center to take Haggerty's place.[57]

A week later Atlantic City's franchise, owned by Tom Hughes, requested league approval to change their night for home games from Tuesdays to Thursdays. The next day it was announced that the Celtics would be replacing the existing Atlantic City roster. The Celtics needed better competition and were guaranteed $900 per week. The league needed the drawing power of the Celtics.[58]

There was criticism, once again, as there had been the year before concerning concessions made to the Celtics. Grauley presented both sides in his article noting that it seemed a good financial move, but some, like the Reading Bears, saw it as bad business to allow them to enter the league again. It was also feared that the Celts could "miss a game or two for a better pay day in New York City or New England. If so, the league should blacklist these fellows forever."[59] Since the Eastern League played only two nights a week, four nights would be left for the Celtics to play exhibitions so the likelihood of early withdrawal was lessened.

The Celtics entered the league with a 2 and 6 win/loss record while Camden led with a 7-1, followed closely by Trenton's 6-2 record.

After the announcement, the manager of Atlantic City, Tom Hughes, sent the contracts for Dehnert, Haggerty, Holman, Barry, Beckman, and Leonard to the league office for approval. Reading put in claims on both Haggerty and Holman, but the *Inquirer* story easily dismissed these since Haggerty had been given his release and Holman had never appeared in a Reading uniform.[61] The League office agreed, which is no surprise since Grauley, the *Inquirer* reporter, was the Eastern League vice president. Thus, the opportunity was there to informally disseminate league views through unsigned and signed columns on the Eastern League.

The Celtic's first game, as returned members of the Eastern League, was against the league leading Camden Skeeters at the Steel Pier in Atlantic City. Before a "capacity crowd," Beckman made six of the eleven Celtic field goals and five of nine free throws to account for 17 of the Celtics' points in a 35 to 22 romp. Holman had nine with five of seven free throws. The Celtics hit 13 of 25 to Camden's 10 of 22. The Celts also had seven assists to Camden's one. In the second half, Jimmy "Soup" Campbell hit two goals from behind mid court.[62] Taking, let alone making, such shots in a modern basketball game is unheard of.

A few nights later Coatesville played what was expected to be its last game at home. The Coats played the Celts, taking them into overtime before losing to Atlantic City 31 to 26. The *Inquirer* noted that former Germantown teammates George Glasco and Nat Holman guarded each other and Glasco got the better of Holman, eleven points to nine. Coatesville also had Elmer Ripley, who joined the Celts for the 1925-26 season, and Lew Sugarman, who became one of the top American Basketball League referees in the 1925 to 1930 life of that league. Coatesville had a "small crowd" (their gym had less than 1,500 capacity so the crowd had to have been less than 100) to watch Beckman and Holman combine for five of the seven baskets. Beckman hit seven of fifteen free throws as the Celts went to the line 33 times and hit seventeen. Coatesville was fourteen of 25.[63]

The next night in Trenton, the Tigers came back from a half-time deficit to defeat the Celtics 29 to 23. It dropped the Celts to a 4-7 record while Trenton tied Camden for first at 8-2. The loss was the last the Celts would suffer in the Eastern League play.

Two nights later, the Celts rolled over Reading in Atlantic City, 49 to 25. Beckman had nine field goals, three of five free throws and 21 points. The *Inquirer* described the attendance as a "monster crowd."[64]

The Celtics were off from Eastern League play for a week during which time they undoubtedly played exhibitions in the Northeast. They returned to league play December 14 in Philadelphia, defeating the Jaspers 30 to 26 in overtime. Beckman had 15 points, but the *Inquirer* was more impressed with one shot of Holman's who "made one of his sensational one hand overhead tosses"—the only goal he scored against the shorter (5 feet 4 inches) and lighter (118 pounds) Barney Sedran, a future Hall of Famer. After the Celtics took the lead in overtime, they "gave a great exhibition of back floor passing after they scored their two field goals."[65] It should be remembered that there was neither a ten-second rule nor a back-court restriction in place then.

The next night back in Atlantic City, the Celtics romped over Coatesville 33 to 21. Directly after that game, it was announced that Thomas Hughes had sold the Atlantic City franchise to Marvin Riley of Trenton.[66] This fact was misrepresented by at least one account of the Eastern League. Bole and Lawrence noted that the Celtics' re-entry into the Eastern League was related to Riley's dissatisfaction with his team's record in November. They also noted: "more important he was not at all pleased with the dwindling crowds and falling gate receipts. Mr. Riley was convinced that it was time for a change." Bole and Lawrence go on to note that, "Marvin Riley's glittering pot of gold was the lure that brought them (the Celtics) back into the fold."[67] This whole description is not only overdramatized speculation; it is absolutely incorrect. Riley came into the Eastern League only in mid-December, although his involvement with professional basketball dated back to the 1890s when he had been a well-respected, professional basketball referee.[68] Riley's entry seemed to have been part of a league plan to save the league from itself. The owners had vastly exceeded their means in paying exorbitant salaries to the players and now this state of affairs was "playing havoc with the clubs' financial conditions."[69] Grauley, the reporter and league official, noted that many players were getting $60 per game and a few were getting more than that. Thus, he noted, an owner had to have a $1,000 house each night to turn a profit. He faulted the owner, not the players, for this predicament. It was the players that would have to give something back or the league's continued existence would be jeopardized.

Riley was to help this "belt tightening" by cutting his team's large payroll—then others would do the same. Thus, no matter how well the Celtics might draw at home or on the road, it was not enough for the league or some of its teams to survive. It was a foregone conclusion that Riley would cut the Sandpiper payroll. Again, Bole and Lawrence dramatize a meeting wherein Riley issued an ultimatum to Jim Furey that "if the Celtics wish to represent Atlantic City, it will be for $400/week and not for $900 weekly as under the old contract."[70] The numbers are correct but there is no indication that such a face-to-face meeting even took place.

After an announcement that the Celts–Jaspers game for December 22 was postponed because of the Celts taking a Western trip, a second annoucement the next day noted that the Celtics were through in Atlantic City and the Eastern League.[71] The latter *Inquirer* article laid out the Riley (and league) plan, i.e., Riley would offer the Furey brothers $400/week which they would refuse and he would then get a new club. Riley was quoted as saying that "The Celts have no Atlantic City pride, all they worry about is the money." That appeared to be the case except there was something they did have—"Celtic" pride and a burning desire to win. Riley was clearly correct that they had no Atlantic City pride, but there is no indication that Trentonian Riley had any either.

The Celtics were caught in a squeeze—the players got $600 per week, which they divided among themselves, and the Furey brothers got $300/week. The Celts could make as much or more in their barnstorming, but the Eastern League seemed like a steady, competitive supplement. As predicted, the Celts replied in December that they wouldn't take the cuts and they were fired. Replacement players would now perform for the Sandpipers.

The Eastern League fans refused to cooperate with the charade and stayed away in droves. In search of league parity, some Eastern League owners supported redistributing some Camden and Trenton players among the weaker teams. The Camden and Trenton owners refused. With no solution, Reading and Atlantic City both pulled out of the league early in January. The remaining teams—Camden, Trenton, Coatesville, and the Jasper club of Philadelphia—tried to continue with four teams. But "On January 19, 1923, the Eastern League quietly expired,"[72] after nearly thirteen seasons of play.[73]

And the Celtics? They went off crisscrossing the country. On a tour that began January 1st, they traveled through three states and 114 cities.

At the end of the season, the Celts made a significant change, cutting George "Horse" Haggerty and signing Joe Lapchick, who had played for a variety of professional leagues and teams since 1918. A younger, more agile and offensive-minded center, Lapchick would make the Celts even stronger and allow them to continue to dominate professional basketball for the next five years.

7

BARNSTORMING

The barnstorming tour that the Celtics had undertaken in 1923 had brought in large amounts of money, sometimes as high as $5,000 for a single appearance. Of the major professional leagues, only the Metropolitan League had survived to play in 1923-24, and the Celtics had already gone that route. Thus, they became full time wanderers bringing the professional game all over the East and the Midwest.

The composition of the 1923-24 squad was the same as the previous two years except for Lapchick's substitution for Haggerty. Lapchick learned quickly and the Celtics proceeded to win another sixty-nine of seventy games from October to December of 1923. Following that record which was largely compiled in the New York City region, the Original Celtics took to the road beginning January 1st. Their travels took them "through New York State, through New England, across the Alleghenies, out to Milwaukee, back through Fort Wayne, Cleveland, Detroit, Toledo, Warren, Ohio; Keyser, West Virginia; Washington, D.C.; Richmond, Virginia; up to Pennsylvania to Pittsburgh, Oil City, Erie, Reading, and Butler, stopping off to play return games in Rochester, Buffalo, Kingston, Catskill and Mt. Vernon, where a previous defeat was wiped out."[1]

At Pittsburgh in February, the Celts met the Leondi club that had been acclaimed basketball's "Negro champions of the world." Led by "Pappy" Ricks' 18 points, and managed by Cumberland Posey (who also scored 2 points in the contest), Leondi lost a tight game to the Celtics at Pittsburgh's Labor Temple by a 42-39 margin. Also in February the Celtics, before 2,000 fans, defeated the Washington Palace team owned by George Marshall, 45 to 28 in a contest that the *Washington Post* called, ". . . virtually a Celtic exhibition." The story noted that "(T)he bullet like passing, the cleverness in team play, the individual brilliancy of the Celtics was marvelous" and claimed further that Holman "ranks with the greatest on the court."

In March, the Celtics returned to Pittsburgh and swamped the Coffey Club 50 to 30 before more than 2,500 fans. The *Pittsburgh Post* raved, "Passing with such speed as to even leave the referee in arrears and tossing the basketball around as if it were a mere baseball, the

Celtics showed a lot of new tricks." The story went on to note that the Celtics could have scored many more points "had they not halted their attack in the final period to give a display of passing that is seldom witnessed on a basketball court."

The Celtics traveled over 150,000 miles, playing in nineteen states and eighty different cities. The tour was a financial success for the Fureys and local promoters, and provided the first indication that professional basketball could have more than a regional appeal. The Celtics played the best teams available as well as some "lesser lights." Of the seventy-one games played, the Celtics lost only four. They swept all three games against the Cleveland Rosenblums anchored by 6-foot 7-inch Stretch Meehan and supported by Marty Friedman, Honey Russell, and Ray Kennedy. The Celtics took five games from the Rochester Centrals, called "one of the four best teams in the county."[2] Against the Brooklyn Visitation, champions of the Metropolitan League, the Celtics won two of three and defeated Kingston in their only contest. The Visitation Squad included Joe Brennan, Red Conaty, Swede Grimstead, Bob Griebe, and Davey Banks.

Many of the best professional players competed in the Metropolitan League and the Celtics handled the best teams of that league as easily as any on their schedule. One loss was to the Ft. Wayne Knights of Columbus team led by Horse Haggerty, Barney Sedran, Elmer Ripley, and a great young shooter named Homer Stonebreaker. The Celtics still won two of the three games played. The only squad of note the Celtics failed to engage was the SPHAs of the South Philadelphia Hebrew Association, who competed in the Philadelphia league, winning the second half after adding Davey Banks and Doc Newman to their squad.

The play of the Celtics was, as usual, totally team oriented on both offense and defense. Despite their scoring capabilities, the Celtics failed to run up the score on weaker opponents, theorizing that "there is no benefit in unnecessarily humiliating a team. When they had a safe lead they usually gave an exhibition of passing and dribbling that opened the eyes of the beholders and made up for all their laxness in endeavoring to pile up the baskets . . ."[3] Only once did the Celtics score 50 points. Rosenwald noted that Beckman, Holman, and Lapchick were the offensive leaders while Dehnert and Leonard "were a stone wall" on defense. Burke, off the bench, was called "one of the best shots in basketball today" while Pete Barry was referred to as 'the miracle man of basketball,' due to his being injected into a tight game late in the play and immediately scoring."

The 1923-24 Original Celtic squad was acknowledged by the professional basketball media as World Champions of professional basketball, and 1924-25 promised to be a repeat of that performance with the entire team back the next year. The Celtics had shown that eastern style basketball would draw crowds in the midwest as well as the northeast. By spreading this basketball "gospel," the Original Celtics probably "did more to advance basketball than any other individual or aggregation. Wherever they have gone basketball has taken on a new lease on life."[4]

The 1924-25 version of the Celtics carried an extra burden with them since "no matter where the New Yorkers played and regardless of the record of the opposing quintet, every game was announced as being for the world's championship." Of the 100 games listed in the 1925-26 *Reach Guide,* the Celtics were victorious in all but six of the contests. The years of playing together paid off and college or high school teams often attended games to learn how the game should be played. "Once more the system of play as used by the Original Celtics of New York City proved itself the best in the country. Despite being battered on their cuts through the middle the Celtics inevitably profited from the excessive fouling by making their free throws with deadly precision."[5]

In mid-season, Burke left the team due to business reasons and was replaced by Elmer Ripley. Ripley was older and not as deadly a shot, but his experience allowed him to blend in easily with the Celtic passing game. Ripley, like Holman, had already begun a college coaching career, at Wagner College and later at Georgetown, Yale, Columbia, Notre Dame, John Carroll, and the U.S. Military Academy for a total record of 298 wins and 228 losses. His fifteen years of playing professional basketball combined with his college coaching career led to Ripley's election to the Naismith Memorial Basketball Hall of Fame in 1972 as a contributor to basketball. The addition of Ripley made little difference as neither he nor Burke could dislodge Beckman, Holman, Lapchick, Dehnert, nor Leonard from the starting five, nor Barry from his sixthman slot. For the season, the Celtics lost to Paterson, but defeated them five times; they lost to the Rochester Centrals but defeated *them* four times; and they lost to Ft. Wayne but defeated them twice. Other losses were to Kingston, who the Celtics beat five times, Pottsville, and Long Island with whom the Celtics split two games, respectively.

The Metropolitan League Champions were again the Brooklyn Visitation whom the Celtics defeated easily in two games at the end of the year. For the first time on record, the Celtics played the New York Renaissance, the "colored champions of basketball" who played the same style of ball as the Celts. In two contests, the Celts won by 8 and 11 points. In reporting on the 11-point loss at the Renaissance Casino in March of 1925, the *Chicago Defender,* probably the best and most well-known of the national Negro newspapers, observed that the "crack white team is too fast." The article went on to summarize the Celtic greatness and pattern of play.

The Celtics seemed to have held most of their tricks for the second half, and when they began to display them, the interest in the game waned, as the fans saw how easily their favorites were being taken in hand. Teamwork was the watchword of this "wonder team" and no particular individual could be named as outplaying his mates.

The *Reach Guide* included six Celtic box scores including two of the losses, since "few of the readers of the Guide have ever seen the Celtics defeated."[6] As many as 10,000 attended individual Celtic games and record crowds were often the rule in many cities where the Celtics had never ventured before.

Again the Celtics did not play the SPHAs, the Philadelphia League champions, nor any of the teams in that circuit. At the end of the year, the Philadelphia league died and a new Eastern League was planned for 1925-26. This was all incidental to the fact that, once again, the Celtics reigned as World's Champions and the Fureys paid them handsomely to wear the Celtic Shamrock.

New Leagues, New Directions

In 1925, three leagues were to begin play and this would impact greatly on the Celtics. The Metropolitan League was to field seven teams from around the New York City region. The Celtics and Jim Furey seemed to have a good working relationship with John J. O'Brien, Metropolitan League president, and the league owners. The Celtics played nearly all the Metro teams to the mutual, financial satisfaction of all concerned. "The Eastern League made an attempt to come back around Philadelphia . . . , but did not meet with the success the promoters anticipated"[7] and the league folded by January, though the best team, the SPHAs left the league and continued as an independent.

In addition to these leagues a new national league, the American Basketball League, began operations in the East and Midwest. Though a nation-wide basketball league had been talked about for years, the failures of various professional leagues in the early 1920s made potential investors/owners wary. Then, the Celtics toured the East and upper Midwest for two years drawing record crowds. The success of the Celtics was the impetus needed to make the league owners begin their league in 1925-26.

Many of the new ABL owners were also involved in professional football or professional baseball such as George Preston Marshall of

Washington, George Halas of Chicago, and Joseph Carr of Columbus, Ohio, who would serve as league president-secretary. Ten teams were located in Boston, Brooklyn, Rochester, Washington, Buffalo, Cleveland, Ft. Wayne, Detroit, Chicago, and East Liverpool, Ohio.

Early in the season the Celts defeated Washington, Brooklyn, and Rochester, later losing a game to the latter squad. With ABL teams playing 36 games in their league and two other leagues playing in the Northeast, the Fureys looked south for a new place to bring Celtic basketball.

The 1925-26 Celtics were a different club. In the middle of the 1925 season, Benny Borgemann, the Paterson Legionnaire star who had led the Metropolitan League in scoring, was signed by Jim Furey. Borgemann had earlier refused offers from Kingston, Ft. Wayne, and Cleveland, all of which were deemed very flattering. Furey obviously offered Borgemann a very high salary and, possibly, a signing bonus.

This meant that the Celtics would have two "scoring machines" in Beckman and Borgemann to go along with Holman, Dehnert, Lapchick, Leonard, and Barry. It also meant that Furey was paying even more in guaranteed contracts and it was likely this contract that pushed his financial resources beyond their limits. Within a year, a $100,000 shortage was reported in the cashier's books of the Arnold Constable Corporation and in October of 1926, Jim Furey pleaded guilty to one of the six indictments of theft brought against him. But all this did not emerge until after the 1925-26 season, one that was filled with success and disappointment.

Borgemann's signing was confirmed at the end of the 1924-25 season, one in which his performance was again outstanding. His signing was not to lead to his first Celtic appearance, however. In late 1922 Borgemann had appeared in the Celtic lineup in a game at Madison Square Garden against the Eastern League Philadelphia Jaspers. This occurred as the Celtics were leaving the league while playing as the Atlantic City Sandpipers. The Celtics with Borgemann and Beckman getting 18 and 14 points respectively, won by a 44 to 33 score.[8] It was this type of forward scoring power which was anticipated for 1925-26.

Unfortunately, Joe Lapchick was in and out of the lineup during the season with illness and a knee injury. In his place, the Celtics had Shang Chadwick, an adequate fill in, but neither the scorer nor the tapper that Lapchick was. Chadwick, however, was an excellent free throw shooter.

The Southern Celtic tour had some excellent games and crowds, but for Miami, "the real estate crowd put binders on their pocketbooks, and the total gate of the three games hardly sufficed to pay the railroad fares."[9] Of the 102 total games played by the Celtics they won 90 and lost 12. On tour in the South, they were 8-1. Following the Southern trip, the Celtics toured the northeast once again.

The Celtics, for the first time, dropped a series, losing two of three to the SPHAs, led by the scoring of Davey Banks. In the Celtic victory, Lapchick made his only appearance of the three contests and scored five points. This was in January of 1926 and the contest was hailed as the first Celtic visit to Philadelphia "after an absence of three years." Fittingly, "The largest crowd that has witnessed a game in this city in this season crowded the hall" at Broad and Bainbridge Streets.

The Celts beat the Paterson Legionnaires in four of five games, defeated both the Visitation team and Rochester two of two, and split six games with the Renaissance, "who have developed into one of the swiftest aggregations in the east."[10] In March of 1926, the Celtics returned to Pittsburgh where they defeated the Morry Club, 27 to 24, after being down the entire game but rallied to outscore the home squad 11 to 2 at the end of the game to win. They also won at McKeesport by 17 and defeated the Lafayette Club at Dusquene's gym, 47 to 40.

As mentioned earlier, the shortage of $100,000 in the cashier's books at Arnold Constable Corporation was announced in April of 1926. By June, the total had increased to $187,000 and Jim Furey was indicted for theft. Furey was head cashier with control of twenty-two ledgers at the company where he had worked for twenty years since he was eleven years old. It was claimed that he lived with a sister in Brooklyn and had done so since his mother died when Jim was a young boy.

In October, the dollar figure was $190,000 missing over the past six months. Furey now was listed as living on the West side at 112th Street and facing six counts of theft. He pleaded guilty in an apparent plea bargain to one count of theft. He was sentenced to three years in Sing Sing prison. His ownership of the Celtics was not mentioned in any of the newspaper accounts.

With Furey's incarceration just before the opening of the basketball season, the Celtics' management became unhinged. The Celtics then became a kind of cooperative enterprise. One of the only personnel moves they made was to sign Davey Banks, the 5-foot, 5-inch deadeye shooter from Brooklyn who had starred for the Visitations and the SPHAs the prior three years. Banks had tormented the Celtics with his great shooting and the Celtics were eager to add him to their roster. He had also agreed to play with the SPHAs, but when they entered the ABL as the Philadelphia Warrior franchise, he chose to not play with them.

Davey Banks

Banks was born in 1901 in New York City on the lower east side where his father, Samuel, was a pretzel baker. This was the reason for one of Banks' nicknames, "Pretzel." He played around the city for various teams as a teen until beginning his professional career with the Armory Big Five of Mount Vernon New York in 1920 when he was nineteen. He also played for the Jersey Separates in Brooklyn. With the formation of the Metropolitan League in 1922, Banks became an immediate "impact" player. Joining the Brooklyn Visitations for the second half of the 1922-23 season, Banks finished fifth in points scored for the season's second half, but his points per game (11.1) were second only to Benny Borgeman's average of 12.1.

Banks was a forward and, though only 5 feet 6 inches or 5 feet 5 inches, his speed and phenomenal shooting made him a dangerous man to defend almost anywhere on the court. Harry Litwack called Banks "a very outstanding shooter" and "very speedy"; Litwack saw Banks play for the SPHAs team.[11] He weighed about 155 pounds and may have appeared to be a bit chubby—thus another nickname, "Fatty." But the most common nickname for Banks was "Flash" because of his speed on the court.

In 1923, Banks began playing for the great SPHA team with "Doc" Newman, "Chicky" Passon, "Red" Klotz, and Eddie Gottlieb, who later became their manager. With the collapse of the Eastern League, the Philadelphia League managed to attract many of the former Eastern League stars like "Soup" Campbell, "Stretch" Meehan, Tom Dunleavy, Bernie Dunn, and Tom Barlow. Banks played only the last forteen games of forty-one but scored 133 points, nearly 10 points per game—the highest league average. In the play-off for the full season's championship, which the SPHA won two games to none, he had 18 points, second to Newman's 19. In the Metropolitan League, Banks finished third in scoring with 278 points in thirty-three games (8.4 points per game) while playing for the Brooklyn Visitations.

The next season (1924-25), Banks finished second in Philadelphia League scoring with 291 points in thirty-two games (9.1 per game), and sixth in Metropolitan League scoring with 290 points in thirty-five games (8.0 per game). But in the opening game of the Philadelphia League playoffs, Banks suffered a broken arm as a result of a fall.[12]

The SPHAs began 1925-26 in the reorganized Eastern League as the Philadelphia League expired. They were tempted to join the Metropolitan League, but "local pride made Passon stick it out to help keep the Philadelphia League afloat."[13] The new Eastern League died before the beginning of 1926, and the SPHAs finished the year playing independently—often against Metropolitan or American League teams. Tom Barlow and Stretch Meehan were added after the Eastern League collapsed, making the SPHAs even more formidable.

At the end of the season, the SPHAs played the Celtics in a three-game series. "Flash" Banks tossed in a two-pointer with the stop watch showing 15 seconds from the finish as the SPHAs won 26 to 25."[14] In the deciding contest, which the SPHAs won by 36 to 27, Banks was again the star as time after time he "would race down the floor through the Celtics' famous defense to receive a pass from Meehan for a goal."[15]

Banks also continued his play with Brooklyn of the Metropolitan League. In 24 contests, Banks scored a total of 188 points (7.8 per game)—good enough for ninth in the League in the first half and third in the second half.

After seeing Banks in the Metropolitan League and as an opponent on the SPHAs, Jim Furey signed him to play for the Celtics in 1926-27. He became the fastest member of the team though he was "no bigger than an average eighth-grader; he made any player who opposed him look like a beginner."[16] Banks and center, Joe Lapchick, the two "extremes" in Celtic height, were sometimes referred to as the "Mutt and Jeff" of professional basketball.

The Celtics barnstormed again in the 1930s but the club and the times had changed. Before that, however, they returned to league play from 1926-28.

8

THE ORIGINAL CELTICS
AND THE 1926-27 AMERICAN BASKETBALL LEAGUE

In the Fall of 1925, the announcement was made of a new league, "almost nation-wide in scope," according to its president, Joeseph F. Carr. The American Basketball League would debut in November with ten clubs, drawn from what was claimed to be a large number of applicants. The teams to be represented were from the following cities— Boston, Brooklyn, Rochester, Washington, Buffalo, Cleveland, Ft. Wayne, Detroit, Chicago, and East Liverpool (Ohio). Before the season even opened, the East Liverpool team withdrew leaving a nine-team circuit to begin play.

The model for the league's operation was based upon that of professional football and major league baseball. This was not surprising since Joe Carr was also the president of the fledgling National Football League, which had begun in 1920 as the American Professional Football Association (APFA). Originally a league based in Ohio, Illinois, Indiana, Michigan, and upstate New York, the NFL had extended itself to include larger East coast cities like New York and Pittsburgh by 1925. The league had originally been a loose association of teams who scheduled their own games with league and non-league opponents; but under Carr, the league drafted a league constitution and by-laws, freely borrowing from major league baseball. Carr was a minor league baseball executive, a Columbus sportswriter, and had been manager of the Columbus Panhandles professional football team before becoming APFA and NFL president. He was able to attract some of his football acquaintances to the new professional basketball venture.

By 1925, the league had acheived stability and recognition and the railroads had allowed the teams easy access to the other cities in the NFL. This was a selling point for the new ABL's possible success. Of course, NFL teams usually played only once a week so travel schedules were less hectic, but the new ABL was to have a full 36-game schedule (which actually became 30 games when the 10th team dropped out).

The ABL included Max Rosenblum, who owned the Cleveland franchise and a department store and sponsored many sports teams in the

Joe Carr, first president of the ABL and president of the NFL, about 1925.

Stationery of the Washington Palace team in the American Basketball League, 1925-27. Shown is George "Horse" Haggerty who was one of the few people able to "palm" the awkward basketball of the time.

region; George Preston Marshall (future NFL Redskins owner), who owned the Washington Palace Laundry and named the team after that establishment; Harry Heilman, the major league baseball star who bankrolled the Brooklyn team; Allie Heerdt, an original Buffalo German basketball star in the early part of the century who coached the Buffalo team; and George Halas, owner and coach of the Chicago Bears. One notable absence was the Original Celtics squad which felt a league too constraining, but a team willing to play the various ABL fives.

It was the Celtics more than any other team who showed that professional basketball could draw big crowds from the East to the Midwest. From the time they left the Eastern League in the winter of 1923, the Celtics had been a road team, playing nearly everywhere in the eastern U.S. against any opponent. In 1923-24, the Celtics played teams from Massachusetts to Chicago and Wisconsin, logging over 150,000 miles. In 1924-25, the Celtics went 67-4 with victories over all the future ABL squads, while playing as far east as Boston and as far west as Chicago, drawing great crowds at almost every game. The ABL figured there was a market for professional basketball and they were going to exploit that. The ABL teams were also happy to play the Celtics in their non-league games during the 1925-26 season. Unfortunately for the ABL, the Celtics defeated the ABL teams consistently. Against Brooklyn they went 3-0; against Rochester they were 3-1; against Boston 1-0; and against Washington 1-0. By the end of the year, Cleveland had won the 1925-26 ABL crown, but the Celtics were still the acknowledged cham-

pion of basketball. By doing that, the Celtics severely damaged the reputation of the ABL as it sought to establish itself as the bastion of the
finest professional basketball teams in the sport.

The Celtics had intended to play in the Metropolitan League but too
few games and too many small venues convinced them to leave the
league almost as soon as the season began. Instead, they played in the
newly formed National Basketball League (NBL), which was really
another version of the Metropolitan League, a regional New York City
league. The Celtics went 14-3 and led the league before dropping out in
November as players jumped from the NBL for better offers with the
year-old American Basketball League. In early December, the Celtics
took over the Brooklyn franchise in the American League and played
under the financial auspices of the Nonpariel Club of Brooklyn, which
they had done in their earlier entrances to the Eastern League in 1921-22
and 1922-23. Johnny Whitty, the old Celtic, was to manage the club.

In 1926, the league offered the Celtics a slot in the league, which
was accepted; but that offer was later rejected just before the opening
game. About that same time Davey Banks, one of the young stars of the
Original Celtics, signed a contract with Philadelphia of the ABL which
would have given them Banks' services had he joined. He decided, however, to stay with the Celtics, who continued to play independently.[1]
There was a new wrinkle added, however, as ABL teams were forbidden
from playing the Celtics, thus shutting out the Celtics from some of their
highest-drawing and highest-grossing contests.

By December, both the Celtics and a number of ABL teams were
hurting financially, most notably Brooklyn, which had gone 0-5. The
owners decided to drop out of the league rather than continue to lose
more games and money. At that point the Celtics were again invited to
join, this time to take over the Brooklyn franchise and schedule. The
Furey brothers, owners of the Celtics since the team had been reconstituted as the Original Celtics following World War I, accepted the offer.
In December 1926, the Celtics became official entrants of the ABL representing Brooklyn.

This was not the Celtics' first foray into a major league after the
season had begun. In 1921-22, the Celtics had taken over the 5-14 New
York franchise of the Eastern League, finishing out the first half with
only two losses. In the second half, the Celtics compiled a 16-4 mark to
win the second-half championship in a three-way struggle with Camden
and Trenton, both of whom finished the half with 15-5 marks.

So the 1926 late entry into the ABL paralleled the events of five
years earlier. Similar, too, was the Celtic lineup. In 1926, Pete Barry,
Johnny Beckman, Nat Holman, and Dutch Dehnert were holdover

The Cleveland Rosenblums of the ABL anchored by center "Stretch" Meehan.

starters from the team of five years before. Davey Banks and Joe Lapchick were the other starters with Chris Leonard, a starter in 1921 and now the first man off the bench. Lapchick had been with Visitation of the Metropolitan Basketball League and he was by far the tallest Celtic at 6 feet, 5 inches. He had joined the Celtics in 1923, so this lineup had been generally intact for three to five years. Few teams had the personnel continuity of the Original Celtics, and it showed in their style of play. Indeed, Gordon MacKay, the ABL beat reporter for the *Philadelphia Inquirer* proffered this view of the team:

The Celtics are by far the best professional combination perhaps that ever played together. Beckman, Holman, Lapchick, Dehnert and the others are high class players, and they have been together so long that the Celtics have welded together the perfect basketball machine.[2]

That machine swung into ABL action on December 6 with a win, and two more followed on the 15th and 16th against Philadelphia, and Detroit before a loss on the 18th in Rochester. The win on the 15th was largely credited to Beckman and Lapchick, the Celtics' "crack jumper who continually got the tap."[3] The Celtics froze the ball, went up 29-20, and won 33-26, led by Lapchick's 14 points and Beckman's 8.

When the Celtics entered the American Basketball League in December 1926, they were the new team "on the block." Yet, almost immediately their contests with the Philadelphia Warriors, also only in their first year of the two-year-old league, became wars with intense heat permeating the games. In the first visit to Philadelphia, the Celtics were greeted by a record 9,000 spectators, the largest crowd to witness a professional basketball game in that city. Gordon McKay, *Philadelphia Inquirer* reporter, praised the Celts as the best professional combination that ever played together. He also noted that "Holman and Beckman . . . were great idols in the old days of the defunct Eastern League." Thus, these two, as well as Dehnert and Leonard, had long basketball histories in Philadelphia.

After attracting 9,000 people on January 4, 1927, to view the Celts in a Warrior victory, they returned on February 22 to play before 6,000 as the Celtics extended their win streak to eight. The Celtics were winning, the Warriors were fading, and frustration was setting in. On March 1, the Celts again defeated the Warriors 39-33 before only 3,000 boisterous fans. This contest was even rougher than usual. Consistent holding, pounding, and aggressive scrambling characterized the contest and set a tone for future games. The final game on March 16 was not much better. The roughness and intensity that characterized professional basketball at the time went up a notch when Brooklyn and Philadelphia met.

In the early part of the 1926-27 season Stretch Meehan, the Warrior center, sustained an injury which kept him out for a time and led to the signing by the Warriors of Al Kellet of Youngstown, Ohio. Kellet was 6 feet 2 (or 3) inches, 200 pounds—a very big, solid performer for that period. Kellet would be the only player on the Warriors without ties to the Philadelphia region, but his size and aggressiveness fit well with Tom Barlow, Meehan, and the other Warriors. Despite the addition of Kellet, the Warriors finished 10-11 in the second half after a 14-7 first half. Regardless, the Celtic-Warrior rivalry was an almost immediate success in the ABL and attracted fans and media coverage.

Celtic-Warrior games had fan intensity stoked by the media. A closer examination indicates how important and obvious that was. The "battle" often had the New York papers not entering into the fray to the extent that the Philadelphia press, notably the *Inquirer,* did. The *Inquirer* reporters had long-standing interest in professional basketball in Philadelphia and that interest often smacked of self-interest, with Stephen Grauley as the best example.

Pro basketball was extremely popular in Philadelphia, but there was still an underlying feeling to some that Philly basketball players couldn't stand up to New York City ballplayers. The game had arisen about the same time in both cities, but most of the top players had New York City roots and Philly was viewed as second best. Beckman, Dehnert, Holman, Lapchick, Borgeman, Ripley, Sedran, Friedman, Reich, and Leonard were all from the New York area and the Philly stars and Philadelphia fans often felt slighted in the greater attention the New York ballplayers received.

There was also the feeling that New York was always taking advantage of Philadelphia in some manner. Gordon McKay, the *Inquirer* reporter, played on this theme in January 1927 when the Celtics entered the ABL with Davey Banks on the Celtic Squad. Banks had played the two years previously with the SPHAs and had signed a Philadelphia-ABL contract but opted to stay with the barnstorming Celtics. When they entered the ABL in December 1926, the Philadelphia team (and the writers) expected Banks to be awarded to them. In articles on January 3rd and January 4th, McKay fomented the anti-Celtic (and New York) feeling by claiming that "Banks is sure to come to Philadelphia" and "Banks is really the property of the Phillies." So even before the Celtics played the Warriors, the Philadelphia fans felt cheated. At the end of the season, McKay couldn't contain the basketball fan he was and wrote admiringly of the Celtics: "Every man is a star in his position. Every man can play any position, and best of all, they have team play, the most essential thing in a basketball game."[4]

Thus, the media of Philadelphia fed the Philadelphia-New York rivalry, one that had existed before basketball. Until 1890, Philadelphia was the second largest city in the United States and through the 1920s it was one of only three cities with a population exceeding one million. Yet, because of its proximity to New York City, Philadelphia had to endure countless jokes and allusions to its supposed status as a less than "major league" city in many ways. The Celtics-Warriors rivalry was a natural extension of this rivalry.

By the end of December the Celtics were 5-2 (5-7 counting the original franchise record), but their style of play was such that even opponents' reporters could admire. Following a 31-29 loss to Philadelphia, the *Inquirer* noted, "The Celtics played remarkable basketball, showing a passing game that was superb. But so closely were they covered that they were outscored in field goals two to one and would have been beaten by a larger score were it not for the uncanny work of Dutch Dehnert at the fifteen-foot line."[5] In fact, the Celtics had only five field goals in the game, but this lack of scoring from the field was not unusual. What was unusual (compared to most teams) was the Celtics' tremendous team consistency at the free-throw line. It seems clear that they often played to be fouled because of their superior free-throw shooting ability. Referring to this quality, specifically for Nat Holman, Hollander noted, "Whenever the Celtics were involved in a tight game, Holman would handle the ball and invariably draw a foul, frequently as a result of imaginary contact that sent Holman careening and drew a sympathetic whistle from the official."[6]

In most of their early season in the 1926-27 games, the Celtics played six players with Banks being the sixth man. Rosters were limited to eight. Rule 20 Section 2 of the official rules stated that a team must play shorthanded or forfeit if four or more players were disqualified.[7]

The first half of the season ended with Brooklyn fourth in the standings with a 13-8 record (but 13-3 since the Celtics had taken over Brooklyn's franchise). The Cleveland Rosenblums, owned by Max Rosenblum, finished in first at 17-4 and they would meet the winner of the second half in the playoffs in April. Second was the Washington Palace team, owned by George Preston Marshall, at 16-5, and third was Philadelphia at 14-7. Deep in last place was the Baltimore Orioles with a 1-20 record.

In early January, the Baltimore franchise had appealed to the Philadelphia team and the league for help. At that point, Philadelphia gave their claim from Banks to Baltimore. Seeking to solve this problem but not wishing to yield Banks, a young player who had starred with the noted SPHAs the previous year, the Celtics instead agreed to sell Beckman to the Orioles as their player coach. Beckman was sold for an undisclosed sum, but it was said to be the largest ever paid for a basketball player. As player coach of the Orioles he would also receive the highest sum ever for a basketball player, according to the *Philadelphia Inquirer* (January 25, 1927: 26). The second half of the season would begin with Banks, the 5-foot, 5-inch sharpshooter, starting in place of Beckman.

In the first week of the second half, the personal foul problem emerged in print. The *Philadelphia Inquirer* stated that good referees were needed as well as equitable treatment. This would mean throwing offending players out of the game, which had never been done in Philadelphia, but occurred when Philadelphia played in Ft. Wayne.[8] A week later Gordon MacKay, the *Inquirer* beat reporter for the ABL, followed this up with a lengthy column that proposed a change in the rules that would make the game more exciting than just a free-throw contest. His proposal was that fouls be shot from the spot committed and the free-throw line eliminated. This was never taken seriously, though it certainly would have changed the complexion of the game.

The Celtics began another win streak in February before amazingly large crowds. A capacity crowd of 10,000 was expected in Cleveland for a hall seating only 7,500, "but the advance sale has warranted installing the utmost possible accommodations." The Celtics played at Cleveland and defeated the first-half champions 24-19 before a crowd of 11,000. Cleveland missed more than two-thirds of their free throws (they made 11 to the Celtics' 14), so again the game was won at the line. The game was so taxing that referee Sugarman, former manager of the Baltimore Club, took time "to recuperate" with eight minutes left to play.[10] On February 16 in the Celtics' 29-28 victory in Ft. Wayne, "the Celts' famous under-the-basket play with Dehnert handling the ball was the big factor in the Easterners' victory. The big guard looped in three baskets from under the net in the last part of the second half to net the victory."[11]

The Celtics' incredible drawing power was also evident during their six game winning streak. Monday they had drawn 11,000 in Cleveland; Tuesday and Wednesday games in Ft. Wayne attracted 7,000; Thursday and Friday in Chicago had 6,000; and Saturday in Rochester there were 3,000 for a total of 27,000 fans. Two nights later (February 22), they were in Philadelphia where they drew 6,000. Previously, the Celtics had drawn 8,000 to the Arena at 45th and Market with another 3,000 denied entry because capacity had been reached. The Celtics continued to win in Philadelphia, 35-22,[12] their eighth straight win. The Celts' 11 of 15 from the line was not much different from Philadelphia's 8 of 12, but the Celtics had twelve baskets to the Warriors' seven. Including exhibition contests, it was the Celtics thirty-fifth straight victory, including one the previous Sunday over the famed New York Renaissance team in New York.

The *Inquirer* account gives some feeling of *how* the Celtics played the game.

The famous Celtic play with Dutch Dehnert doing the pivot work started the Celtics on a scoring rampage with Holman playing the role of scorer. Dave Banks who performed for the SPHAs last season fit nicely and Johnny Beckman was never missed . . . The Celts ran beautiful plays—Dehnert rushed up the floor and with Campbell on his back took a pass and cleverly pivoted the ball to Holman and back to Dehnert and then to Holman on the foul line for a dead shot.[13]

The article also noted Nat Holman's ability to fall on apparent charges and said that "Nat is a great actor in that respect." Not everyone was impressed with Holman's "acting." Early that week, John Dietrich had decried this in commenting on the Celtic-Rosenbloom game.

Holman, in addition to being the world's greatest basketball player, is also the world's greatest foul faker. More than that, he is just about the world's cleverest in getting away with violations of the rules.[14]

The balanced Celtic box score showed:

	Field Goals	Free Throws	Total
Banks	4	2-3	10
Barry	3	2-4	8
Lapchick	1	1-1	3
Holman	3	6-6	12
Dehnert	1	0-1	2
Leonard	0	0-0	0
	12	11-15	35

Later that week, in Cleveland, the Celtics finally lost, 31-23, making them 9-1 midway through the second half. In attendance was Joe Carr, the president of the league who was there to warn the teams about excessive fouling.[15] This was one of those rare off nights that even the great teams have. Playing their ninth game in twelve days, eight of them on the road, the Celts failed to score a field goal until nine minutes remained in the game. (Games were two, twenty-minute halves.) They finished with four, to go with their fifteen free throws.

This game, however, was the last they would lose in the ABL until the last day of the season. Another horrible shooting night occurred in Baltimore when they hit only two baskets, however, this was not enough to deny them victory. The Orioles hit three field goals, but the Celtics again won on free throws 16 to 12 to win 20 to 18. Johnny Beckman did all he could to defeat his former mates with two of the three baskets, six free throws, and ten of the eighteen Oriole points.[16]

The next night Celtic free throws (19 of 22) again were the difference in defeating Philadelphia 39 to 33, which made 15 of 25 from the stripe. The game was very rough as evidenced by this account. "The first half had been slow at times for the players bunched together, there was regular subway-like holding at the rush hour and the scrimmages were not calculated to have helped any sickly individual had he been caught in the press of human bodies."[17] The Celtics' free throws in this type of game caused some writers to question how good the Celtics really were. John Dietrich lamented,

Undoubtedly the Celtics are a better team than Cleveland; better in passing, and maybe better in shooting goals. This latter point is something local fans aren't sure of because the Celtics haven't gone in for it relying on free throw tossing—successfully. In their eight straight victories the Celtics have 68 field goals and 118 free throws.[18]

On March 8, the Celtics were solidly in first, though because of the peculiarities of the schedule they were tied with Washington in losses with only one apiece. The Celts, however, had thirteen victories to only seven for the Palace Quint. Ft. Wayne was 7-5 and Philadelphia 7-7. The next night the Celts again beat the improved Orioles who were 4-7, this time in Brooklyn, 37 to 26. The two teams met again in Baltimore the next night. The result was the same, as the Celts won 28 to 20 before more than 3,000 spectators. Once again free throws were the difference as the visitors canned 16 of 17.

One surprising bump along the Celtics' smooth road to the second half ABL title occurred on March 12. In an exhibition game in Camden, the Celtics were upset by a Camden County League team 31 to 24. Apparently figuring the game would not be difficult, Davey Banks was left in New York and Pete Barry, nursing an injury, was left on the bench. The little-used Chris Leonard and manager John Whittey played instead. Poor shooting from the field and from the line (14 of 23) spelled doom for the New Yorkers. A frustrated Holman resorted to holding and shoving, something "never before seen in this section by the great Nat Holman."[19]

But the Celtics' ABL win streak continued. The next night in Washington, again with Barry on the bench, they defeated the home team 35 to 24. Sixty fouls were called in the game leading to 43 successful free throws, 22 by Washington and 21 by Brooklyn. The Palace team only canned one field goal, however, to the visitors' seven. The two teams met again the next night with the Celts again winning 31-28. Two nights later Barry returned to the lineup to help the Celts edge the Phils in overtime, 45 to 38, as the overwhelming free-throw edge (25 made by the Celts to 14 by the Philadelphia squad) made the difference. The Celtics were now 18-1 and the second place team, Ft. Wayne, was 10-5. With the title clinched, the Celtics eased through their last two games winning in Columbus, Ohio, over the Chicago Bruins and losing in Rochester on March 30. They had a week to rest up for their best-of-five championship series set to begin April 6 in Cleveland.

The Cleveland writers began promoting the series nearly a week before it began, examining the ABL style of play and the teams themselves. Two officials were to be used in the series to try and "do away with most of the roughness that has characterized some of the American League games this year."[20] The hope was that the "fast, dazzling and pleasing sport" would not be marred by "players running roughshod over each other."

The game hype focused on the guarding of Dutch Dehnert who "is built for rough work and he is the man the Celtics use as their

The Public Auditorium in Cleveland, one of the sites of the first and second ABL championships in 1926 and 1927. The building was still standing as of 1998.

'bumper.' " Dietrich went on to comment further on Dehnert's playing technique.[21]

> He has a peculiar crouch which he uses most effectively and once he gets hold of the ball it is all but impossible for a man of ordinary size to guard him. He tucks the ball against his stomach and pivots until he finds a man loose to pass to.

Cleveland had finished the second half below .500 but looked forward to reversing their fortunes against the Celtics, and again claiming the ABL title that Cleveland had won in 1926. However, Cleveland's star, John "Honey" Russell, had been sold at mid-season to Chicago after a dispute with owner Max Rosenblum. Another starter, Vic Hanson, had quit after becoming disillusioned with the rough style of professional ball.[22] The *Inquirer* headline told the story in game one, and it was a familiar one, "Celtics win on foul tossing." Before nearly 10,000 fans, Brooklyn had outscored Cleveland from the field four to three, but the free-throw differential, 21 to 15, was the big difference. As for individual performances, "Lapchick, the Celts' giant center, was the big fly in the ointment, successfully tapping the ball to a fellow player on the tip-off."[23]

The next night in Cleveland the victory was again Brooklyn's, 28-20, with a crowd reduced to less than 7,000, and the teams headed for Brooklyn for what would prove to be the final game on April 9. In the closest game of the series, Brooklyn won 35 to 32 before 2,500 fans to claim the title. Neither the *New York Times* nor the *Cleveland Plain Dealer* covered this contest. In addition to well-played basketball, "the fans got an extra treat when Nat Holman of the Celts and Gil Ely of Cleveland tried out a little fist slinging near the close of the game."[24] Considering Holman had twelve points and he had "basketball's biggest reputation and salary,"[25] it is not surprising that he would be the target. Ely pushed Holman into the crowd and he struck at Ely who "retaliated with a right cross to the head which drew blood from a wound Holman had sustained (in) an accident earlier in the game. Each got a foul and was banished from the game."[26]

On that rugged note, the Celtics wrapped up the ABL Championship and were undoubtedly the finest squad anywhere at that time. "Never had nor would another club dominate the American Basketball League as had the original Celtics in the late winter of 1927."[27]

The 1926-27 ABL season was marked by a number of notable features. The Celtic entry into the league was undoubtedly the most significant. Their style of play was the standard by which others were judged, and they were great innovators. Age more than opponents' skills caught up to the Celtics, who stood head and shoulders above any team from 1921 to 1928. The only team to challenge them was the New York Renaissance, whom the Celtics defeated six times in 1926-27.[28] The success of the Celtics was often frustrating to opponents and led to excessive fouling, something which plagued pro basketball, and the ABL adopted the four foul rule for disqualification in 1927. The problem was not solved, but no longer would nearly unlimited fouling take place.

Despite the Celtic success there was continued optimism among league teams as plans were made for the 1927-28 season. The Celtic victory was not seen as indicative of any long-term trend and at least two teams (Cleveland and Philadelphia) were confident they had strengthened their squads enough to dethrone the Celtics as league champions. The next chapter chronicles that 1927-28 American Basketball League season and the Celtics' continued dominance of professional basketball.

9

CELTICS REPRISE
1927-28

Hoping to ride the crest of sport interest the American people displayed throughout the 1920s, the American Basketball League prepared to open its third season. In 1927, the Celtics returned under new ownership and management. The Furey Brothers, facing financial problems at every turn, allowed Tex Rickard and the new Madison Square Garden to take over the franchise in May of 1927.[1] The Celtics would play home games in both the new garden and their home court of the previous year, Arcadia Hall in Brooklyn.

The league underwent a number of changes in 1927 beginning with the location of franchises. Returnees from 1926-27 were Chicago, Cleveland, Ft. Wayne, Rochester, Washington, Philadelphia, and New York, which shifted from Brooklyn. Gone was Baltimore, which had finished at the bottom of the eight-team league in both halves of the season. Trying once again to make a financial go of it was a Detroit franchise. The previous year Detroit was 0-6. They left the league and these games were then nullified and struck from the standings by ABL president Joe Carr. The Detroit Cardinals started 1927-28 with high hopes and Johnny Beckman, one of the greats of the professional game, on their roster.

There were also structural changes. The league changed from a split season to two divisions, East and West, with the top two teams in each division making the playoffs.

As the season began there were the usual questions of who had strengthened themselves, who might challenge the defending champions, and what effect age might have on various players and teams. In addition, there was still financial uncertainty. Would the league draw better in 1927? Would all eight franchises make it to season's end? Would the excessive rough play which had plagued the pro game continue despite a new "five fouls and out" policy?

The league opened play in late November and the Celtics lost their opener to Philadelphia 54-46 on the Arcadia Hall court in Brooklyn.[2] The next night, November 21, the two teams met once again, this time in

New York at the formal opening of Madison Square Garden. There, before a crowd of more than 5,000 (7,000 according to the *New York Times*), the Celtics won 46 to 44. After leading 10-4, the Celtics extended their lead to 21-16 at the half. The new five foul rule claimed the Phils' Glasco before the end of the half and Lapchick just before the end of the game. Featuring a "dazzling passing attack," the Celtics drew away "as a result of thrilling long shots by Holman and Banks."[3] Five days later, the *New York Times* was still waxing about the Celtics as they prepared to face Washington that evening. "One feature of the contest last Monday that brought delight to the spectators was the clean and fast game played by the local five."[4] The *Philadelphia Inquirer* noted that "Banks, who is the smallest man in the league, was the most elusive player on the floor and always drew a round of applause whenever he scored."[5] Four Celtics—Barry, Banks, Holman and Dehnert—all had four baskets in the win over the Warriors, and the Celtics made 10 of 22 free throws. Banks and Holman had 12 points each though Nat was 4 of 4 from the stripe and Davey Banks only four of nine.

The Celtics returned to league play nearly a week later when they defeated the Washington Palace team in Brooklyn before a capacity crowd by a score of 48 to 36. Leading 27 to 14 at the half the Celtics coasted to victory after a brief Palace rally in the second half. At least two Washington players[6] and Holman all were fouled out of the contest. Lapchick, after fouling out the previous game, came back to score 22 points including 10 from the charity stripe.

The next night the two teams met again in the Garden with the Celtics again triumphing, this time by 48 to 40 before an estimated 4,500 spectators. The *New York Times* piece admired the long periods of passing or tossing by the "Celtic Five," though the article was not bylined and instead was by a local stringer, "special to the *New York Times*." This seems to indicate the lack of respect with which professional basketball was held by certain segments of the press best represented by the *New York Times*. Even for a local contest involving the finest team·in basketball, the *New York Times* was loathe to assign a beat reporter to the game.

In that second Palace contest, the Celtics' balanced scoring was again impressive. Banks led with 15 followed by Pete Barry with 11 and both Lapchick and Dehnert had 10 apiece. At the half the score stood 25 to 23, New York, but the Celtics pulled away at the beginning of the half to lead 41 to 24 before coasting home to the victory.

The next night, the Celtics journeyed to Philadelphia for their third game in three nights and their third meeting of the year with the Philadelphia Warriors. After leading at half-time 22 to 17, the Celtics succumbed to fatigue and fouls, losing on a last second shot 37 to 35 before 4,000 fans at the arena in Philadelphia.

There is some question regarding Joe Lapchick's removal from the game. S. O. Grauley, writing in the *Inquirer* said Lapchick, Holman, and the Phils' Barlow left after fouling out. The *New York Times* article claimed that "Lapchick, the Celtics' centre was put out of the game late in the second half for throwing the ball into a spectator's face. Nat Holman was ruled out a little later for making five personal fouls."[7] Grauley's comment on Holman's removal was "the most ridiculous ruling ever imposed on a professional team."[8] The "five fouls and out" ruling was certainly not pleasing to everyone.

As to determining Lapchick's ejection, either could be true. In the previous contest with the Warriors, he had fouled out early in the second half. In addition, the Celtics-Phils' games had often deteriorated into brawls in the previous year, so it would not be surprising if Lapchick had not been averse to playing roughly from early on. Also in the past year, at least two games in Philadelphia had ended with angry spectators storming the floor. Lapchick may have had enough of the Philadelphia fans and *their* rough play and lashed out at a prior antagonist.[9]

The box scores were inconclusive. They did not include number of fouls or notation as to who fouled out. The *Philadelphia Inquirer* box *did* include free throw shots, a rarity. The Celtics were 13-16, the Warriors five of eight. These numbers lead to some inconsistencies. If Holman had five fouls, that might seem to indicate Lapchick could not have had five. However, since no bonus rule was in effect and free throws were only awarded when shooting, this supposition is only speculative and not conclusive.

Nevertheless, the Celtics were 3-2 as they headed into December, tied for second behind the fast starting Rochester Centrals in the Eastern Division. The Celtics, however, continued to struggle and, on December 4, lost to the Washington Palace team in the capital for the D.C. Quints' first victory of the year in nine tries. It was also the first Washington victory in 14 tries over the Celtics since they had entered the league the year before. Down two at the half, 20 to 18, the Celtics failed to awaken in the second half to lose 36-30. The scoring was evenly distributed between field goals and free throws with ten for each category. Lapchick had eleven to lead the Celtics.[10]

The next night order returned to the universe as the Celtics defeated Washington 30 to 25 before a "capacity crowd," according to the *New York Times*. The Celtics led throughout and coasted to their third win against Washington.[11] The Celtics were now 4-2 but had only played two teams. The Celtics headed West for their first extended road trip. On

December 7, they defeated the Detroit Cardinals 30 to 20 in an embarrassing loss for Detroit. They made no foul shots and at the half were down 20 to 2. The Celtics "cut down their pace in the second half and gave a fine demonstration of passing."[12] They had enough "sitting time" for the starters and Dreyfuss had 6 points, his season high. The box was printed as follows:

	Field Goals	Free Throws	Total
Barry	1	0	2
Banks	4	0	8
Lapchick	1	4	6
Dehnert	0	0	0
Dreyfuss	2	2	6
Holman	3	2	8
Whitty	0	0	0
	11	8	30

The next two nights the Celtics were in Cleveland to face the undefeated Rosenblums. When the Celtics left for Ft. Wayne, the Rosenblums were 8-2 to the Celtics 7-3, the latter second to Rochester's 7-1 in the Eastern Division. The first game, played before 7,500, saw the Celtics take an early lead and they then passed the ball in the middle of the court the rest of the game.[13] The stringer for the *Philadelphia Inquirer* was less charitable.

Completely outclassed, the Cleveland team which prior to tonight had won eight consecutive victories looked foolish on the same court with the New Yorkers.

The Celtics played for free shots and the Clevelanders obliged by fouling every time one of the New Yorkers came anyway near the hoop.[14]

In Ft. Wayne the Celtics slipped briefly, losing the opener at South Side gymnasium 28 to 22, but coming back the next night behind Holman's ten markers to defeat the Hoosiers, 33 to 25.[15] The Celtics caught the train to Chicago where the next night they toppled the Bruins 25 to 16 before 5,000 at the Broadway Armory. Then the story was repeated the next night, again before 5,000.[16] With these victories, the Celtics moved into first place in their division. The December seventeenth standings were as follows:

Eastern Division			Western Division		
New York	10	4	Cleveland	10	2
Rochester	9	3	Ft. Wayne	6	5
Philadelphia	9	5	Chicago	2	10
Washington	2	10	Detroit	1	10

The road trip was over and the Celtics went 6-2. They defeated Cleveland twice and re-established themselves as the best team in the league and in basketball. They would open a home stand December 19 in Arcadia Hall in Brooklyn against the Chicago Bruins.

Before crowds of 2,000, the Celtics defeated the Bruins twice in two nights with scores of 25 to 19 and 32 to 24. The first game was played before a capacity crowd while the second was played in Madison Square Garden with a much larger capacity. This was the Celtics' first appearance there in three weeks. The *New York Times* noted the splendid guarding of Holman and Dehnert and the great passing attacks by both teams, which led to long periods of no scoring. The foul problems earlier in the season seemed to have been somewhat abated or, possibly, the referees were beginning to loosen up a bit. For whatever reason, fewer fouls were called and in the Garden game only six free throws were shot, three by each team with each squad making two.[17]

Four nights later the Celtics continued the home stand playing the Rosenblums in Brooklyn. In a game not as close as the final score indicated, the Celtics, once again, won 33 to 27 after leading 20 to 10 at the half. With the victory, the Celtics had the best record in the league for the first time all season. The *Philadelphia Inquirer* noted both the excellent defense of the Celtics ("Pete Barry and Nat Holman kept mainstays Carl Husta and Vic Hanson in check") and the Celtics' all-around play ("Passing the leather with a speed that dazzled the visitors the Shamrocks were never in danger and rolled up a large lead in each period . . . scor(ing) almost at will").[18]

After two days off for Christmas, which the Celtics got to spend at home and the Rosenblums, most likely, on the road in New York, the teams met once again, this time at Madison Square Garden. The result was the same, a Celtic victory, this time by a 33-29 score but the game showed little of the "spirit of the season." The Celts led 20 to 9 at the half.

In the final period Pete Barry started the scoring with a neat basket from the side of the court, Hickey pushed Barry and the pair went to blows, being separated only by the referee. After the fight both teams quieted down.[19]

The close of the calendar year saw the Celtics atop the league and Cleveland, victimized four straight times by the Celtics, still in first in the Western division. The standings were:

East		
New York Celtics	14	4
Rochester Centrals	11	5
Philadelphia Warriors	10	6
Washington Palace	6	13

West		
Cleveland Rosenblums	13	6
Ft. Wayne Hoosiers	8	7
Detroit Cardinals	3	11
Chicago Bruins	3	16

On New Year's Day the homestand and the winning continued for the Celtics.[20] The next day the league was shaken by internal changes. Following an afternoon and evening doubleheader in which the Detroit Cardinals had swept the Warriors, the owners of the Cardinal franchise, also owners of the Red Wing Hockey Club, quit the league because of lack of fan support. According to the *Cleveland Plain Dealer,* "the fans stayed away in droves and seldom more than a corporal's guard looked in on any of the contests."[21] The article went on to predict the death knell for basketball in this city (Detroit) for the foreseeable future, because of franchise failures in two consecutive years. All players were released and free to sign with other clubs.

Amidst this upheaval, the Celtics' win against Rochester for their ninth-straight win went somewhat unnoticed. Lapchick did not appear in the win and the *New York Times* article also failed to mention any explanation for Lapchick's absence. He did play the next day in an exhibition in Hoboken where the Celtics lost 23 to 19 to the St. Joseph's Club of Hoboken before a capacity crowd of 800.[22]

The next day the upheaval continued. The Washington Palace team was shifting to Brooklyn but George Preston Marshall, the owner, still owned the team. The move was attributed to a lack of attendance in Washington. The new home of the team would be Prospect Hall while the Celtics would play at two home sites in New York City, one in Brooklyn and one in Manhattan.[23] Brooklyn debuted as the Brooklyn visitation in Prospect Hall on January 9. Detroit's place in the standings was frozen at 5 to 13, last in the West (unlike the previous year when their games were expunged from the league's records after the franchise folded).

Despite the exhibition loss, games where the Celtics did not always push themselves to the limit, the Celts were in the midst of a hot streak, which was a time when each player seemed to anticipate the actions of the others. Throughout January they rolled on. They defeated Ft. Wayne on January 8th and 9th, for wins ten and eleven in the streak. Rather than attract fans, the evening seemed to disinterest New York basketball mavens. In their last game of the home stand only 2,500 attended at the Garden.[24]

The opposite effect occurred on the road. Either because they hoped to see the Celtics lose or because they wanted to see the best basketball team going, "5,800 fans, the largest number to witness a professional game in Chicago, crowded into the northside peacetime base of the 202d Coast Artillery" also known as the Broadway Armory. Clearly, the *Philadelphia Inquirer* stringer was impressed by the game and the basketball atmosphere. Led by Banks' 12 points, the Celtics won 26 to 18.[25] The next night before 5,000 more fans, the Celtics won 29 to 25 behind Barry's 10 and Holman's 9.[26]

Returning to Brooklyn, the Celtics extended their win streak to fifteen with victories over Philadelphia and Brooklyn. In the latter contest, the Celtics led 19-0 before coasting to a 47 to 24 victory. The *Philadelphia Inquirer* noted that in the Warrior game, it was "simply a case of a good team, getting beaten by a better one." Leading 22 to 9 at the half the Celtics again eased to victory.[27]

The American Basketball League standings as of January 17 indicated that the Celtics were in top form once again and the Eastern Division race was essentially over. Second place was very much a contest between Philadelphia and Rochester. In the west, Detroit's defection and Chicago's ineptitude seemed to assure Cleveland and Ft. Wayne of the two playoff berths.

Eastern Division			Western Division		
New York	22	4	Cleveland	16	11
Philadelphia	15	22	Ft. Wayne	11	15
Rochester	15	22	Detroit	5	13
Brooklyn	10	16	Chicago	7	20

January 19th saw the streak end in Philadelphia in a game at Philadelphia's Arena at 4th and Market, where admission was $.75 for general admission and $1.10 for reserved seats. This was at a time when the average laborer made about $.70/hr. in wages according to Bureau of Labor Statistics Bulletins.[28] Before 6,500 fans the Warriors triumphed 28-18. The game was extensively described by *Inquirer* beat reporter

Stan Baumgartner but the *New York Times* gave the usual two paragraphs and a box score.[29]

According to Baumgartner, with the score 22 to 16 with Warriors ahead deep in the second half, a Phillies' basket was scored out of a "mass of mingled humanity" and the Celtics "crumbled."

This was the signal for the New Yorkers' demonstrations. They harangued each other and then growled at the officials, dropping their arms at their sides, as if to say; well boys, we're done for the evening.

Twice the ball was tossed up and not a Celtic moved to rush in for the tip off. The Phillies threw two passes and scored unmolested baskets twice.

The 6,500 fans then raised the Arena roof with their hoots and hisses at the quitting tactics of Holman and the other four Shamrocks. New York called time out and were more spirited upon their return but they were licked for the evening and they knew it.[30]

Clearly, the Celtics were upset by the loss and severance of their winning streak, but seeds of this defeat may have been sown three nights before in Madison Square Garden when Philadelphia had been humiliated by the Celtics 47 to 24. In that game the *New York Times* noted:

The locals so far outplayed their rivals that twice during the game the Philadelphia players looked on, helpless, as Holman, Lapchick, and Banks shared honors in building up sustained scoring streaks of more than 15 points. . . . Holman's floor game, until he was ordered out for being unruly, was superb, and most of the Celtic scoring rallies were the result of his clever passing.[31]

Now the Phillies, who had battled (literally) with the Celtics earlier in the season, had gotten a measure of revenge. But it was tainted, somewhat, by the deplorable floor conditions.

As early as the first half a dampness similar to dew had gathered on the concrete which made the court slipperier than a state highway on a rainy day. The rubber soled shoes of the players held no better than automobile tires. The players skidded about in grotesque fashion, sometimes they were sliding on their hips, other times on their knees, more often on their backs. Such a condition of the playing floor made clever teamwork impossible and fast directed passing at certain positions on the floor was lost, when the men attempted to reach their places.[32]

The Celtics came to Brooklyn for a contest on January 22 against their new neighbors, the Brooklyn Visitations, nee Washington Palace. The name Visitations was a paean to a team in Brooklyn that had played in the Metropolitan League earlier in the 1920s and included a young Joe Lapchick. The Visitation of 1928 were no match for the Celtics and lost to them 41 to 23. Unlike the earlier pattern of "coasting" in the second half, the Celtics extended a nine point half-time lead, 21 to 12, to the final 18 point margin. The stringer for the *Cleveland Plain Dealer* described the Celtics as "playing a clever passing game which kept the ball from their opponents during most of the play . . ."[33] The *Philadelphia Inquirer* claimed a crowd of 4,500 was in attendance, the largest to have ever seen a basketball game in Arcadia Hall, which is curious because earlier season newspaper accounts had referred to 2,500 as a capacity crowd.[34]

Following this game the Celtics were 25-5, the Warriors 17-11 and the Rochester Centrals two games back with a 15-13 record in the race for the last eastern playoff slot. In the west, Cleveland had faded to 16-16 and Ft. Wayne improved to 15-15 to leave them tied for the top.

The Celtic destruction of the Visitation had little carryover the next night in Madison Square Garden where the Brooklyn team edged the Celtics 28-24 before either 6,000 or 8,000 people.[35] Either way, it was the Celtics' first loss in Madison Square Garden and was not decided until two Brooklyn free throws and a basket in the last two minutes broke a 24 to 24 tie. The game ended with both Dehnert and Holman on the sidelines, the former having fouled out and the latter,

banished from the game along with Willie Scrill of the Visitations for fighting. Both had been roughing each other throughout the game, but in the last half they came to blows when Holman ran into Scrill. The Visitation player was declared the winner, knocking Holman on his back with several punches to the head.[36]

The score when the players were tossed was 22 to 18 in favor of the Visitation.

The Rochester Centrals played the January 31st contest in Philadelphia and in an article "hyping" that game, Jules Aronson, manager of the Philadelphia Warriors, provided incentive quotes for the Celtic locker room. Aronson was quoted as saying, "we are going to win the Championship of the American League" and "I know we can beat the Celtics. We are the only club that can take their measure." The reporter was much more temperate in his assessment of the chances of defeating the Celtics.[37] Within a week the Phils would have another chance at the Celtics in Philadelphia.

On February 5, the *Inquirer* provided the ABL Standings list of leading scorers and a preview of the Celtics game in Philadelphia that week. The Celtics led the Warriors by 9 1/2 games with a 27-6 to 19-17 record. Rochester was now 17-16. Benny Borgmann of Ft. Wayne led with 253 points in 32 games but Davey Banks of the Celtics had 251. Two other Celtic players, Holman and Lapchick, were eighth and ninth in league scoring with 220 and 218 respectively, all between seven and eight points per game. As for the upcoming contest, it was noted that this was the teams' first meeting since the Celtics' "white feather"[38] (of surrender).

In Philadelphia the Celtics came out smokin', as they say, racing to a 19-3 half-time lead before 4,000 fans, then holding back a late Warrior rally to win 33 to 20. The *Inquirer* used the occasion to remind Philadelphia fans that Davey Banks, the star of the game, who just two years before had "galloped over the SPHA court in spectacular fashion, was at his best last night." In fact the Celtics, as a team, were at their best providing what the *Inquirer* referred to as "one of the greatest exhibitions of basketball seen at the arena this year." In praising both Banks and Celtics it was noted:

It was Banks who always got the ball from tap-off, it was the same little firebrand who picked the ball off the backboard and it was Banks again that stole the balls from clumsy "cavemen" when attempting to start a passing attack . . . [T]he Celts displayed phenomenal passing and floor work. The accuracy of their bullet-like shots from one another was such that in the opening stanza they had complete control of the ball 17 times out of possible 20.[39]

The Celtics now led the Phillies by 9 1/2 games and Rochester was four games behind Philadelphia when the Celtics resumed play that Saturday in Rochester. As on the previous Saturday game date, Holman was not present; instead he was coaching his CCNY team (who finished the year 11-6) to a narrow victory over Catholic University, 31 to 29.[40] In Rochester, the Celtics defeated the Centrals easily 45 to 36 with the four starters upping their scoring to compensate for Holman's absence.

The next night, back in Brooklyn and joined once again by Holman, the Celtics defeated Cleveland 26 to 22 in a match closely contested throughout.[41] Two nights later the Celtics edged the Warriors in Philadelphia 20 to 18 with Holman scoring ten of those. The half-time score was 15 to 10 Celtics, but the Phillies held New York scoreless for twelve minutes of the second half. Despite scoring fewer field goals (seven to Philadelphia's nine), the Celtics had six (of thirteen) free throws to none (of two shot) for the Warriors to edge out the win.[42]

The Philadelphia Warriors of the ABL in 1927-28, the Celtics' archrivals that year.

The Celtics arrived in Cleveland in late February for two games. In the first, Cleveland led the whole game only to fall behind by one on a long basket by Banks with less than a minute to go. Then, "in a driving and dramatic finish that set 5,000 wild and delirious fans absolutely dizzy with delight,"[43] Dave Kerr made a basket from one-third court with seven seconds left to secure the Cleveland victory. Dietrich of the *Plain Dealer* observed that the Celtics lost because they could not freeze the ball for 45 seconds. The *Plain Dealer* provided more data than usual for the game, offering a more insightful look at shooting accuracy. The Celtics were 8 for 46 from the floor with Banks at 3 of 22 and Holman with 4 of 13. Cleveland was slightly better at 10 of 47. The Celtics hit nine of sixteen free throws.

The next night the Celtic shooting improved to 13 to 36 while the Rosies sunk to 7 of 56 and the Celtics romped 33 to 18. Before a crowd of 7,500, the Celtics led 20 to 3 at the half in a contest that "should have been halted early in the first half."[44]

In a column on the 25th, the *Plain Dealer*'s Sports Editor, Sam Otis, said that the "Celtic's visit proves the pro game is honest" and that the Celtics didn't lose the first game "for the interest of the upcoming Fort Wayne series."[45] Even in 1928, nine years after the infamous scandal in the World Series, there was still great concern and sensitivity about the honesty of professional athletic contests.

From Cleveland, the Celtics headed back to Rochester for a Saturday contest, again without Holman whose CCNY Lavender defeated NYU in their last game of the season, 29 to 26.[46] In Rochester, the Celtics were upset 43 to 41 after leading 19 to 18 at half-time. Leading 41 to 35, the Celtics lost as Topol of the Centrals scored eight points in the last two minutes as he finished with 13 for the game.[47]

February ended with a Celtic victory in Brooklyn over Chicago. March began the same way with victories over Ft. Wayne and Brooklyn, both in Brooklyn. The Celtics' next challenge of note was to meet the Warriors in Philadelphia for the Eastern Division playoffs. The Celtics had finished the season 40-9, the Warriors 30-21, with the Celts taking the season series five games to three. The Phillies had beaten the Celtics in Brooklyn, their first loss on the Arcadia Hall floor and were convinced they could master the Celtics in the playoffs. Originally, the first two games of the best-of-three series had been scheduled for the Arena in Philadelphia, but it was now to be one and one because the Celtics had wanted to bring their own referee, according to Philadelphia Manager, Jules Aronson.[48]

In game one the Celtics turned a 13-13 half-time score into a hard fought 27-21 victory before 5,000 to 7,000 fans, depending on which account was accurate.[49] Controversy began early in the contest, when "the victors threatened to quit, claiming the floor was too slippery but decided to play. The crowd roared its disapproval during the interruption."[50] The *Philadelphia Inquirer* was more pointed in their remarks:

Due to the slippery conditions of the floor, caused by the sweating of the concrete, the battle was not all that a great basketball game should be. At times the men skidded, slipped and slid over the court as if it were hockey night. Early in the game the Shamrocks registered a strong protest because of this, and for a time it looked as if the game would be called on account of "wet grounds," but after rival managers and officials had gone into a huddle play was resumed.[51]

Despite the conditions, the Celtics played excellent basketball working the ball in "by clever teamwork and fast passing." In addition, "the New York defense was so perfect that, but twice in the entire 40 minutes of play did the Aronsonmen have easy tosses for the rim."[52]

The two teams headed for Brooklyn, where the Celtics ended the Warrior season with a 32 to 24 victory. This game, too, was not without controversy, this time because of rough play—rough even by standards that prior Celtic-Warrior games had established. Dehnert pushed the referee to the floor early in the game and was ejected but returned later. At the half referee Lew Sugarman, former Eastern League player, denied

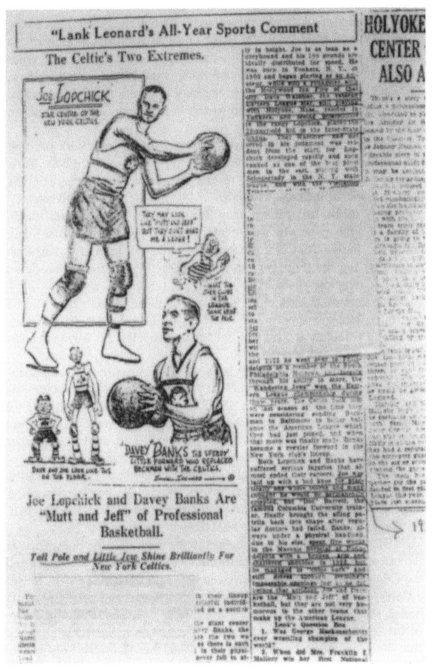

A newspaper depiction of Lapchick and Banks noting them as both the "Mutt and Jeff" of pro basketball and as the "Tall Pole" and the "Little Jew."

ejecting Dehnert and explained that he had warned the big Celtic that he *would* eject him if Dehnert pushed him again. The 3,000 fans in attendance saw this as a lack of courage and hooted at Sugarman mercilessly from then on.[53] Banks was the most physically damaged, receiving a deep gash in his forehead and "the blood spurted out and his face crimsoned." After a doctor had attended to his wound, "the young Hebrew, dizzy but courageous, returned to the battle."[54] Both the Celtics and Ft. Wayne now had a week off until the series opened in Indiana on March 21.

The championship series was a best-of-five games with the first three scheduled for Ft. Wayne and the next two (if need) for New York. Despite their decidedly inferior record, the Hoosiers had gone 16-9 the last six weeks of the season to finish 27-24 atop the Western Division.

Early in the first game Benny Borgman, the leading scorer for Ft. Wayne, left the game with a knee injury and did not return. This severely hampered the Hoosier offense and the Celtics ran up a 19-8 half-time score "leaving the (Fort Wayne) guards fairly bewildered by the Celtic passwork and close shots."[55]

The next night the Celtics broke out to a lead at the half of 15 to 8 but tough Hoosier shooting and defense in the second half (the Celts were held without a second half field goal), propelled Ft. Wayne to a 28-21 triumph before 4,000 fans.[56]

The Celtics did not usually play two bad games in a row, particularly against the same opponent. That pattern continued in game three as the Celtics came back to win 35-18. Interestingly, the *Philadelphia Inquirer* awarded the title to the Celts prematurely with an incorrect headline, apparently thinking it was a best-of-three series. The paper then failed to cover the next, and last, game of the series.[57]

Borgman did not return after leaving in game one and the Celtic victory seemed assured after leaving Ft. Wayne, leading two games to one. Nevertheless, the Hoosiers did not fold. Down 16 to 4 at the half, Ft. Wayne put on a furious rally but fell short and lost 27 to 26.

The Celtics had proven once again that they were the finest team in the league and in the world. Questions about the future of the league and the Celtics had begun, however, even before the playoffs ended. In two articles on the sixteenth of March, as the first round of the playoffs ended, writers in the *Cleveland Plain Dealer* wondered about the future of the league. In his bylined column, sports editor Sam Otis observed that there had been "considerable talk that the American League will break up at the close of the season. That does not seem likely now."[58] John Dietrich, ABL beat writer, also speculated about the future of the league. He noted that meetings about the league would be held during the playoffs. He felt that Philadelphia and Rochester had fared poorly and would not be surprised if they dropped out of the league. He also thought the Chicago franchise, despite losses, would be willing to try again. He concluded that:

Of the present league, at least five clubs—Cleveland, New York, Brooklyn, Ft. Wayne and Chicago—are looked upon as certainties for the 1928-29 campaign. The game hasn't paid, but it is no secret that business conditions this winter have made it bad for all winter sports, fights, hockey and everything included.[59]

Of course one could respond, "If you think 1928 was bad, wait until you see 1929 when things would get even worse." But of course, the Great Depression was hardly anticipated in these future considerations. What *was* considered was the role of the Celtics in the league in 1928-29.

The Celtics had, in two years, completely dominated the American Basketball League, winning over eighty percent of their regular season games and winning league titles under two different playoff formats. The Celtics had great players, with all five starters capable of scoring in double figures on any given night. Team play, however, was their strength and after nearly eight years of playing together they were, by far, the most innovative and cohesive team in basketball.

Unfortunately, the success of the Celtics was one of the reasons for the financial distress of the rest of the league. Fans in the cities flocked to the Celtics games to see their great performances and, just maybe, to see them lose to the hometown favorites. The other games did not draw crowds nearly as well and the league was close to financial disaster. Thus, to achieve greater parity, the original Celtics were broken up by the league. Lapchick, Dehnert, and Barry were signed by Cleveland and led them to another league title in 1928-29. Holman and Banks returned to the league with the New York Hakoahs, an all (or nearly all) Jewish team.

The next year Holman started with New York, then was sold to Syracuse when the New York Club was about to fail. He was later sold to Chicago when Syracuse also quit the league. After that series of experiences, his full-time professional career ended and his coaching career became paramount.

Thus, the Celtic squad ended its dominance much more quickly than it had taken to develop that dominance. The 1927-28 season was truly the last hurrah for this great team. Though efforts were made to reunite them in later years, they never played together on a regular basis ever again. In the next chapter there is an effort made to put the Celtics and their success into some perspective, to examine how good they actually were in the overall success, and in the contributions they made to the playing and conceptualizing of basketball.

10

THE MEASURE OF GREATNESS

I first encountered the Celtics when reading about various aspects of early professional basketball. The more I read and researched, the more acknowledgments I encountered that attested to their greatness such as books, basketball encyclopedias, and other reference works. These acknowledgments conceded the remarkable gifts of the Celtic squad and their obvious superiority to their contemporaries in all aspects of basketball.

What was troubling in all these laudatory expostulations was the utter deficiency of accurate, well-presented information. What was readily available was similar from account to account—the same stories, the same data, the same comments. It was clear that a great deal of intellectual borrowing was prevalent. Less obvious were the sources and accuracy of the data. Separating myth from reality was the initial intent of this work. Who were these guys? How good were they, really? What was the sport of basketball like in the late 1910s and what role did the Celtics have in shaping the game? What reasonable comparisons can be made with other basketball teams of subsequent eras? Were these players and their team truly great?

It is this latter question that bothered me the most. There seemed to be a consensus that the Celtics were one of the greatest basketball squads ever assembled, but some of the questions about their performance were disturbing. Early on, I talked with William Himmelman, a basketball researcher whose company is compiling data on all early professional league games under a contractual agreement for the National Basketball Association. Himmelman was openly skeptical of the performances of the Celtics, or any team not in a league. He saw their records as "padded," filled with "pick up" players almost always consigned to lose to barnstorming professional squads.

The lingering question, then, continued to be "How great were the Celtics?" However, answering the question was dependent upon being able to assess, in some way, the measurement of greatness. It was this chronological conundrum that I will address in this chapter in order to satisfy the reader's (and my own) curiosity as to how good the Celtics really were—as a team and individually.

The Celtics Measured

In the period 1920-28 the Celtics played an average of 100 games per season, at times surpassing 200 contests in a year, and they had a winning percentage of over .900. This record has never been surpassed. A "down" year might have the Celtics with as low a percentage as .833, but years at over .930 offset this anomalous performance.

The Celtics were hardly "one-year wonders." The Furey brothers built their team over an initial three-year period, then made small, necessary adjustments in the subsequent six or seven years, consistently improving areas of the team that were in need of strengthening. This deliberate building process, a function of both Jim Furey's eye for talent and his ability to pay top dollar, brought the best players to the Celtics. It also, however, allowed for the development of a sense of team—a rare commodity in the 1920s. From 1921 when Furey acquired Leonard, Holman and, later Haggerty, the core of the team remained intact. The roster of 1921 was virtually the same in 1922 except for Burke, who was added after Reich's death. Burke was an excellent player in the Metropolitan League but never seemed to excel as a Celtic and hardly replaced Reich in the lineup. In 1923, Lapchick replaced Haggerty on the roster. Haggerty had gotten slower and his shooting, which had never been his forte, was now horrendous and he was clearly on the downside of his career. In 1924, Ripley was added and Burke left in mid-year. Ripley knew the game but was also at the end of a good career when he joined the Celtics, so his addition was certainly intended to be temporary. In 1925, Borgmann replaced Johnny Whitty and, when Lapchick was injured, Shang Chadwick was signed. Borgmann had the talent to continue with the Celtics, but because of his desire to be the star or because he welcomed the stability of a league team (or both), he left after the 1925-26 season and signed on with the Ft. Wayne franchise in Ft. Wayne. In 1926 Banks replaced Borgmann, Lapchick returned, Beckman was traded in mid-season, and Whitty returned from Ft. Wayne as a "player-manager." The 1927 roster was unchanged.

In a period of tremendous team instability, the Celtic personnel changes for nearly a decade can be summarized in one paragraph. No other team of the period could approach the Celtics in steady commitment to a consistent team roster. This stability was one factor in the development of teamness, but it is clear that the selflessness all Celtics players felt was just as vital. Holman was the expert at taking charges, real and imagined; he consistently gave himself up for the team. He also had been the leading scorer in the Eastern League just before joining the Celtics, but he became the second option to Beckman after joining the team. After Lapchick joined the Celtics in 1923, he became the second leading scorer and Holman was often the third option.

Dehnert was viewed by his teammates as the ultimate team player making jarring picks to set up his teammates. Dehnert, too, had been a top scorer, finishing tenth in the Pennsylvania State League in 1919-20 and seventh in 1920-21, but his scoring was also subsumed by team demands. The account of Dehnert playing a game with severe boils indicates his tenacity and self-sacrificing ways.

Though Beckman was the leading Celtic scorer, he was also the heart of the club's drive, particularly after Reich's death and Beckman's appointment as Celtic captain. Reich, another top scorer with other teams, became a passer and top defender with the Celtics.

Chris Leonard and Pete Barry recognized their particular roles early on, despite their earlier successes with other squads. Leonard was versatile enough to play any position and was the equal to anyone at shutting down the opponent's leading scorer. In 1919, he had been referred to in the *Reach Guide* as "the best of the present-day centers," yet he became a backup guard when Lapchick joined the Celtics in 1923. Barry was also relegated to coming off the bench, but he became a 1920s version of "instant offense"—entering a game and quickly scoring.

In terms of scoring and their physical needs, the Celtic players regularly thought of the team first and self second and, as they played, their knowledge for other's moves and respect for their abilities made them an even better team.

One area where the Celtics were unique was in coaching/managerial leadership service, since most professional teams of the time had neither. Furey scheduled games and handled administrative duties. In the late 1920s Johnny Whitty had a quasi-coach role. More normative, however, was the self-coaching the Celts did, which ultimately led to the lengthy coaching careers of Holman and Lapchick and the less celebrated efforts of Dehnert. It seems clear that Beckman and Holman ran the team— Holman through analytical methods and Beckman through emotional demands. In various retrospective accounts, Dehnert, Lapchick, and Barry all point to these two men in their roles as coach/leaders.

The Celtics are credited with the invention or perfection of both offensive and defensive basketball standards. On defense, teams played man to man, but players often slipped free in the scrum-like conditions under the baskets or as the ball was advanced up court. The Celtics were the first to employ, then perfect, a switching man-to-man defense. Being picked off on defense either intentionally or accidentally was no longer an excuse for an offensive player being free to score. Baskets were scored on the team, not the individual. Lapchick described how the "rent a player" philosophy permeated the thinking of most professional players. Since individuals regularly played for the highest bidder, success was measured by outscoring one's man. Wins and losses were almost incidental. The Celtics ended that type of thinking and created the concept of team defense. Talking on defense, unheard of previously (so to speak!), became a part of the Celtic's manner of play and, eventually, that of all good teams.

On offense the Celtics perfected a fluid, open style of play, responding to various defensive situations as one entity rather than five individuals. Back door cuts (though not called that) were a part of that repertoire —one that other teams had great difficulty imitating until years later. Short, crisp passes and sharp cuts characterized Celtic play. As Lapchick noted earlier, the Celtics made the ball "sing" as they whipped it from player to player. And from every newspaper account available it is evident the Celtics were nearly flawless in their ball handling.

Though not the inventors, the Celtics perfected the pivot play. Many media accounts attest to Dehnert's contention on his Hall of Fame nomination that the play, as they ran it, was nearly unstoppable. The three-second violation was created to assist the defense, but the Celtics still ran it perfectly outside the lane. In the last years of the ABL, the league tried to impose a two-second time limit for possession of the ball without dribbling or shooting and this was claimed to be the reason the Cleveland Rosenblum Celtics left the ABL in 1930.

As noted earlier, almost all the Celtic players had been top scorers in various professional leagues. This ability to score served them well when opposing teams would resort to extraordinary measures to stop Beckman or later Banks, from scoring. Though scoring was predominately "forward biased" in the 1920s, the Celtics were unusual in having top-scoring guards (most notably Holman) and, later, a high-scoring center in Lapchick whenever they needed to use them. Thus, despite the lack of a coach, the Celtics were the best coached and most flexible team in basketball.

In examining the record of the Celtics against top competition of the 1920s, the Celtics were consistently victorious. From 1921-22 to 1927-28 the Celtics played in three leagues. In 1921-22 they won the second half of the Eastern League season title and defeated the first-half winner, Trenton, 2-1, in a three-game series. It should be recalled that the Celtics had not entered the league until December. The next season they also entered the Eastern League after the start of the season, but left after winning five of six games. Prior to rejoining the Eastern League, the Celtics had gone undefeated in the Metropolitan League. The Celts left both leagues for the same reason—not enough money.

The Celts did not play in formal league play again until 1926-27, when they joined the short-lived National Basketball League (NBL), which suspended operations and melded with the Metropolitan League. Before leaving the NBL, the Celtics compiled a 14-3 record, best in the league. The Celtics then took over the Brooklyn Franchise in the American Basketball League (ABL) and proceeded to go 13-3 in the first half and 19-2 in the second half to qualify for the league playoffs. There, they defeated the Cleveland Rosenblums three games to none to claim the Championship.

In the next season, the Celtics started in the ABL and ran up a 40-9 record to win the league title by eleven games. In two rounds of playoffs, the Celts defeated Philadelphia two games to none in the first round, and Ft. Wayne three games to one in a five-game series.

Thus, the Celtics won all three league championship series in which they played and had the top record in two other leagues before they dropped out of those leagues. In their barnstorming years the Celtics played all comers, ducking no teams,[1] and until 1925-26 had a winning record against every squad they played. Despite some criticism for "padding" their record, the Celtics played and defeated every quality basketball team in the United States that would play them from 1923-28. This last caveat is necessary because beginning in 1925-26, the American Basketball League pressured its members not to play the Celtics and this was enforced in 1926-27—a major factor in the Celts joining the ABL.

Peer evaluation of the period 1920-40 is nearly unanimous in concluding the Celtics were the greatest team of that era. The rankings of writers then and since are also unanimous in awarding the mantle of greatness to the Celtics. It is clear that the election of the team to the Naismith Memorial Basketball Hall of Fame was instrumental in influencing more modern writers like Hollander, Neft and Cohen, and Padwe to offer such plaudits. The media of the 1920s, however, saw the Celtics play and these writers were singular in their pronouncement that the Celtics were the best team of the 1920s. Writers in Philadelphia, Boston, New York, Chicago, Rochester, and scores of smaller cities in between, wax effusive about the superior quality of the Celtics as a team and individually. The scrapbooks of Nat Holman, Joe Lapchick, George (Horse) Haggerty, Henry (Dutch) Dehnert, and Nat Hickey are replete with clippings that bestow the title of the "greatest" upon the Celtics. Even recognizing the media propensity for hyperbole, no team comes anywhere near the Celtics in laudatory recognition.

Unfortunately, the historical retrospective view of the Celtics is largely empty. People both outside and inside basketball are ignorant of the professional game prior to World War II. As great a team as the Celtics were, even they had been unable to overcome this ignorance. In junior high school I wrote one of my first "research" papers, presumptively entitled "History of Professional Basketball." I, too, dated the game from the NBL-BAA and their merger to create the NBA. The struggle to present the story of professional basketball before 1945 is largely met with indifference. The richness of this aspect of American sport and culture remains largely unmined. This is due largely to a pattern of media indifference from the beginning of professional basketball. The game, nevertheless, was often played before capacity houses and no team was as big a draw as the Original Celtics.

The Celtics were the source of so much that is a standard part of basketball played even today. As the inventors and perfectors of "Eastern style" basketball, they were the model for the great teams from the 1930s to the 1970s. The New York Renaissance team and the Harlem Globetrotters both copied the techniques of the Celts and shaped them in their own way. Even the clowning of the Globetrotters was first perfected by the Celtics. From the 1920s into the 1930s, when a reorganized team toured under the Celtic banner, newspaper accounts chronicle the ability of the Celtics to win *and* entertain. The ball handling of Dehnert and Lapchick, the dribbling of Holman, and the antics of Davey Banks all foreshadow the later behavior of the "Clown Princes of Basketball." It is interesting to note the disdain with which some basketball "purists" view the Globetrotters, often viewing their behavior as indicative of the lack of reverence for the game held by the Trotters. This thin veil of racism is undermined by the realization that a team of white players first marketed their basketball and entertainment skills simultaneously while barnstorming in the mid 1920s.

The tight passing, sharp cutting, and team defense became the hallmark of the Boston Celtics of the late 1950s and 60s, as well as the New York Knickerbockers of the late 1960s and early 70s. The latter, of course, were coached by Red Holzman, a former star of the 1941-43 CCNY squads of Coach Nat Holman.

Another measure of imitation was the hordes of high school teams (players and coaches) that attended Celtic games in the 1920s and 30s. The Celtics were a model for these teams. Today, film and videotape would be acceptable, possibly superior substitutes, but in that era live games were the only alternative and teams flocked to view the "master teachers" at work.

So, How Good Were They, Really?

In the last decade, the comparison of teams across eras has grown more popular in all sports. Computer-generated virtual games have led to the 1927 Yankees facing the 1961 Yankees, the 1967 Cardinals, or the 1954 Indians. The undefeated Dolphins of 1972 have battered the 1966 Green Bay Packers. The success of the Chicago Bulls will lead to challenges against the Celtics of the early 1960s, the Lakers of George Mikan in the 1940s and 50s and the Knicks of Reed, Frazier, Bradley, et al. Plugging the Celtics data into such a program would be a possibility. What might the result be?

There seems to be no question that the Original Celtics would get destroyed by any of the above mentioned teams. Unlike baseball, where the game is largely unchanged and player size is less important, basketball is radically different from the game the Celtics played. The Celtics play emphasized ball control; this would be of little use with a twenty-four second clock. The Celtics hardly left the floor in a game, largely because of the generally rougher play. Celtic shooting was far less accurate with a larger, more irregular ball and the looser foul calls of the era. Until 1926, the Celtics played as often in a cage as in an open gym.

The Celtic players were also shorter, slower, and less accurate shooters than today's professionals. The Celts essentially made up the game as they progressed through their careers; today's professionals have been coached in shooting, team defense, and passing since pre-adolescence. Players begin weight training in high school. Nutritional advances have allowed players to eat smarter, though many do not.

The Celtic players, interviewed in 1960, agreed wholeheartedly with this assessment of their abilities measured against the teams of today. A summary of their comments was made by Hal Lebovitz. These included the following:

- Their team, if they suddenly became young men again, could not compete against the present pro teams under the present rules.
- There are better shooters today and better board men, also much bigger ones, but too few playmakers.
- Big men are now agile. In the old days a big man was an awkward goon.
- It's an entirely different game now.[2]

Individually, most of the Celtics felt they would be able to compete today. Holman noted in 1970 the following:

The game as played today is an entirely different game than the one we played
. . . Individually, the men on the Celtics were outstanding and in my honest
opinion, they could make any club playing the pro circuit today. Bear in mind,
the personnel of the team would have to have the necessary height to take care
of the opposition! The Celtic man would have the speed, shooting ability, passing, shooting, and deceptive ability to go along with any club. True-most of our
shots from the outside were the two-hand shot and would use the one hand
ONLY on the drive to the basket; the boys today with their one-hand shots are
simply fantastic. I wish someone would have stressed the one hand shot when I
was a kid. I have always been reluctant in making comparisons or giving an
opinion as to how the Celtics would go do against other teams.[3]

Thus, as noted earlier, the Celts would have little chance of beating
today's bigger, faster, stronger players using the better equipment of
today. Even giving the virtual Celtics a year to prepare could not significantly alter their size, speed, and techniques that would enable them to
beat the worst team in the NBA, let alone the best ones, unless today's
professionals met the Celtics at *their* game.

Since this kind of fantasy is so outrageous I would propose testing
the Celtics against today's teams with the Celtics' rules and equipment
such as using the "medicine ball" that the Celts played with, playing
with no-shot clock or ten-second line, using a cage, and having a jump
ball after each score. Allowing for the "subtle roughness" that characterized pro ball in the 1920s might make the odds much closer. Even allowing for the dramatic size differential, I would predict some Celtic
victories in our make-believe series. Just as one can't "coach height,"
one can't "teach heart" either. The Celtic pride was founded on teamwork and heart. Holman noted the following:

The Celtics were a great team and I enjoyed playing with a group of men who
have done a great deal for the game. They were overwhelming and overpower-
ing with lots of pride, determination, hustle, and sacrifice. [It] made no difference who got the points and they played as a team all the time, which made
them so dangerous![4]

It is fitting to speculate about Celtic success against teams of other
eras, since the Celtics were initially the standard against which all other
teams were once judged. When the Celtics began, basketball was a wild,
rough house sport where skill, technique, and teamwork were rare commodities. By the time the Original Celtic name disappeared in the early
1940s, those commodities were the coin of the basketball realm. It was
through Celtic play that the game of basketball was created, not trans-

formed, because what was there before the Celts was raw material. So much of Celtic creation is second nature to players and teams today, but it was through the determination and skill of a group of great individuals who hated to lose that the team concept of winning basketball came about.

11

THE ORIGINAL CELTICS AFTER 1928

The end of the 1927-28 American Basketball League season left the Celtics the undisputed champions and the league with declining attendance. It was clear that there would have to be changes in the franchise locations and in the team compositions for the league to succesfully continue in 1928-29. A major problem was the Celtic success and the league members felt it was in their own best interest to break up the Celtic team and redistribute the players among the other franchises. With Jim Furey in jail and the Celtic players more or less running the team themselves, there was not a strong owner advocate to discourage the league's contemplated action. Though Nat Holman disputed this version of the Celtic break-up, all the other players who addressed this topic were in agreement, the dissolution of the Celtics was initiated by the ABL.

The players went their separate ways, but the Celtics' presence was still felt in the make-up of the Cleveland Rosenblums. When the league broke up the Celtics, the plan was to distribute the players to reestablish some parity in the league. Thus, Barry and Dehnert went to Rochester, Lapchick to Cleveland, Beckman to Baltimore, and Holman and Banks to the newly formed New York Hakoahs franchise. Things changed shortly before the season began, however. After trying to make a "go" of playing independently, the Celtics folded, with Lapchick, Barry and Dehnert still carrying the standard. Lapchick finally signed with the Rosenblums two games into the ABL season, but Dehnert and Barry could not come to terms with the Rochester Centrals so they also signed with Cleveland. This made the Rosenblums a bit too dominant. With these Celtics, combined with Carl Husta and Nat Hickey, and fearing another case of fan ennui, "the league forced owner Max Rosenblum to sell Hickey to Chicago in December."[1] The Baltimore franchise folded before the season began and Beckman ended up with Rochester, but later was traded in mid-season to Cleveland. "With ex-Celtics Lapchick, Dehnert, Barry, and Beckman in the lineup with Carl Husta,"[2] the Rosenblums were able to win the first half of the season, finish a game behind Ft. Wayne in the second half, and then sweep the Hoosiers in four straight games to claim the 1928-29 ABL title.

SPORT KINGS GUM

NAT HOLMAN

1933 Gum Card. Gum Cards were part of the "Sport Kings" set which had American athletes drawn from all sports. Of the four basketball players depicted, three were former Celtics (the third was Eddie Burke, a minor Celtic contributor but a well-known New York City professional).

Husta led the Rosenblums in scoring and was second in the league. Beckman, at age 34 or 37, still was a fine shooter and finished second to Husta in total points, but had a slightly better scoring average. Lapchick noted that, "(I)n addition to the league games, we played against independents anywhere and everywhere. All the players were doing well financially (I was earning $1,500 per month) but the league was losing

— No. 3 —

NAT HOLMAN

(BASKETBALL)

Unlike most of our athletic contests, which had their origin with ancient peoples, Basketball is distinctly a modern game. It was originated by a teacher at Springfield College in 1891, and immediately became popular all over the world. Few men have done more to increase the popularity of the game than Nat Holman. Nat was born in New York City in 1896. He played Basketball in school where he became a star. In 1919 Holman was a member of the Germantown Professional team and helped the club to win the Eastern Professional League Championship that year. For the next seven years, he played with the New York Celtics, members of the American Basketball League, helping his team to win the Championship in 1927. He has continued his interest in the game and is the author of "Scientific Basketball", an excellent book on the sport.

This is one of a series of noted athletes and sportsmen. The complete series includes all the leaders in every branch of sport. START YOUR COLLECTION NOW.

SPORT KINGS CHEWING GUM

THE GOUDEY GUM CO.   BOSTON

Made by the originators of

INDIAN and BIG LEAGUE GUM

1933 Gum Card.

money."[3] The Rosenblums won the league title again in 1929-30 but the league folded after the 1930-31 season, due to the Celtic/Rosenblum success and the onset of the Great Depression. Rosenblum had pulled out of the league before it folded because of the league's initiation of a 2.5-second rule for an offensive player's presence in the center lane. According to League president John J. O'Brien, "Mr. Rosenblum felt that we had no right in putting any curb or restrictions on any type of

1933 Gum Card.

play . . . He then withdrew in the middle of the first half of the season
. . . It was primarily an argument—that Mr. Rosenblum felt we were
handicapping the play of the man who actually started the pivot play,
namely Dutch Dehnert."[4]

During these years, Holman and Banks tried leading the New York
Hakoahs, an all Jewish team, to prominence in the ABL. Besides
Holman and Banks, the team consisted of Passon from the Warriors,
Marron of the Visitation and three league rookies—Red Sheer from the
Philadelphia Hebrew Club and Penn; and Shein and Wolfe from CCNY

MAR—No. 3 1934

JOSEPH LOPCHICK

BASKET-BALL

Basket-ball was originated at Springfield College in 1891, and has grown in a sensational manner all over the world. It is one of the most popular of all indoor games. Leagues were soon formed, and later, amateur stars became professional players. One of the greatest of these basket-ball Sport Kings was Joe Lopchick, who played with the Original Celtics, a team organized in 1918, and became the greatest basket-ball squad ever to play the game. Won the Eastern League Championship from Camden, 1921, won thirteen straight games in Metropolitan League, 1921-22, then traveled around the country meeting the best teams available. Joined the American League, 1926-27 season, and took over the Brooklyn franchise which had already had five losses, but went on to win the championship from Cleveland. Won championship, 1927-28, defeating Fort Wayne, 3 out of five games. The next year, to even the league strength, Lopchick went to Cleveland, which team won title for two successive years.

This is one of a series of noted athletes and sportsmen. The complete series includes all the leaders in every branch of sport. START YOUR COLLECTION NOW.

SPORT KINGS CHEWING GUM

THE GOUDEY GUM CO.   BOSTON

Made by the originators of

INDIAN and BIG LEAGUE GUM

Ⓐrⁿↄ △ 140602

1933 Gum Card.

where they had played for Holman. Two other former players for Holman at CCNY, Rube Goldberg and Doc Edelstein, also appeared for the Hakoahs during the year. Despite the presence of Holman and Banks, the Hakoahs came in fifth with an overall 18-25 record. Banks led them in scoring, but his 5.8 points-per-game were decidedly less than his records of the previous two years with the Celtics. At the end of the year, the Hakoahs franchise withdrew from the league and the team disbanded.

Despite playing on different squads the old Celtics still played together at times, both for money and because they enjoyed the pleasure of teamwork established over many years. In April of 1929, after the ABL season had ended, Beckman, Barry, Banks, Lapchick, Dehnert and Holman reunited to play a notable contest against the New York Renaissance team with "Pappy" Ricks, "Bruiser" Saith, "Tarzan" Cooper, "Fat" Jenkins, Hilton Slocum, and Harold Mayers. The contest was held at the 71st Regiment Armory at 34th Street and Park Avenue in Manhattan and was witnessed by 10,000 fans. In what the *Chicago Defender* called "the greatest game ever played in this city,"[5] the Celtics defeated the Rens 38 to 31. It is interesting to note that few "white" newspapers gave the game any significant coverage and that the reporter for the *Defender*, Jack Murray, was a white, former basketball star in New York who had played on the old St. Gabriels team with Beckman, Leonard, and Reich.

In the Rens contest, the Celtics held a 20 to 18 halftime lead but the Rens pulled out to a 28 to 20 lead early in the second half. In the last seven minutes, the Celtics outscored the Rens 18 to 3 for the final 38 to 31 margin. Holman led with 15 while Dehnert had 5 and both Beckman and Lapchick had 5. For the Rens, Jenkins led with 11 and Cooper scored 10. This contest foreshadowed some great Celtic-Rens games in the 1930s as the Rens matured to become the dominant team in basketball, while the Celtics aged and slowed down.

Nat Holman

Holman continued coaching while playing for the Hakoahs and the next year his coaching became more difficult, though still was maintained. Holman played with Jim Furey's attempt at a resurrected Celtic team. "Furey had been paroled from Sing Sing prison after serving three years for embezzlement and he immediately signed Nat Holman, Davey Banks, and Johnny Beckman to play for the new team."[6] As before, Furey ran out of funds as the older, slower Celtics failed to draw a sufficient number of fans to Madison Square Garden or to their other playing site on Long Island. In early December, Furey sold his veterans to other teams and restocked with younger players, but the team folded after playing only two games. The Celtic record of five wins and five losses was stricken from the ABL standings.

Holman ended up with Syracuse, but they, too, ran into financial problems and folded, on January 6, 1930. They left the league after compiling a record of four wins and sixteen losses, which became twenty losses when league president John O'Brien made their last four games of the first half forfeits. The league continued with six teams and Holman moved on to the Chicago Bruins. He finished tenth in the ABL in scoring with a 4.8 points per game average and helped Chicago finish third in the second half of the season. All the disruption had clearly affected Holman, however, and he decided to leave the professional game and concentrate on college coaching and organizational administration.

I reached the point where it was time to quit. I decided I had my camp, which was very successful, as well as the coaching job at CCNY. A new YMHA was opening and Harry Henchel, who was on the board, offered me a job to run the gymnasium as director of health and physical education. I was able to make adjustments in my schedule at CCNY so I could take the YMHA job.[7]

Holman retained his administrative position and ran a popular summer camp (Camp Scatico) in the Catskills for many years; but his greatest fame was based on his highly successful coaching. Holman compiled a record of 422 wins and 188 defeats in his nearly 37 years of coaching.[8] Coaching was much different in the period when Holman was active at CCNY. Teams played about a dozen games in a season and at CCNY his players were restricted to New York City residents.[9] The most well-known and singular events of Holman's coaching career occurred in 1951 when his CCNY squad won both the NIT (a more prestigious 16-team tournament) and the NCAA (an eight-team event) titles within a ten-day period with both finals in Madison Square Garden. Holman recalled,

What a great thrill it was that night, when we left Madison Square Garden, the students and fans were on Seventh Avenue waiting for us. Flags were being waved and the students were singing our alma mater.[10]

Not long afterward, the college basketball scandals of 1951-52 were revealed and CCNY players were implicated. That loss of faith in his players affected Holman for the rest of his life. He felt betrayed and could never reconcile the players' actions toward basketball with his views of right and wrong. He forgave his players for their actions, but he never understood and he never had the same undying trust in his players again.

Mr. Holman was suspended by the New York City Board of Higher Education in 1951 for "conduct unbecoming to a teacher." Contending he had known nothing of his players' deceit, he rejected the option of an early pension and fought for vindication and won. He was re-instated at CCNY two years later, but the school had de-emphasized its basketball program.[11]

Holman retired in 1960, but remained active in basketball. He coached in Israel and became a Goodwill Ambassador for basketball and Israeli sports. Into the 1970s, he retained the position of president on the United States Committee of Sports for Israel and actively engaged in coaching and fundraising. One of his former players, Dr. Irwin Dambrot, the captain of the 1950 team who became a successful dentist recalled Holman's contact with him in retirement.

He kept in touch with us. . . . He would call me and say "How are you doing, Irwin?" I'd say, "I'm doing well" and he'd say, "If you're doing well, send $200 to Sports for Israel. We need the money." He raised millions for Sports for Israel.[12]

Though Holman lived a long life, in his last years he withdrew more and more from almost all contact with sport and society. Many people found it difficult to deal with his critical nature, accurate though he might have been in his comments. His age also was a factor in his withdrawal from public view; all of his old friends and his wife had died and, being childless, he may have felt that he had lived too long. In visits with his nephew and with Sam Goldaper (an old newspaperman and friend) as well as rare contacts with basketball researchers, it was clear that his mind remained sharp, though his interest in modern basketball no longer keen.

Holman died in February 1995, at the age of 98 at the Hebrew Home for the Aged in Riverdale, Bronx. He had been elected to the Naismith Memorial Hall of Fame in 1964 after being nominated by long-time friend, teammate, and rival coach, Joe Lapchick. In an undated letter nominating Holman, Lapchick stated that:

this man was one of the greatest basketball players that ever lived. This man was very fast . . . a great shot and best of all was a great ball handler—one who could really thread a needle from any distance with passes so fast that interceptions were rare.[13]

In a column printed just after Holman's death, Dave Anderson described Holman's conduct during basketball practice. Holman would regularly address a player who had made a mistake by asking a series of questions, getting the player to explain why he did or did not do certain actions.

And if any of the other players were talking while he was speaking, he would stop and stare. "I'm teaching," he would say. "Do you speak when your philosophy professor is teaching?"[14]

"He taught team basketball," said Red Holzman, a former CCNY player for Holman before coaching the Knicks to two NBA Championships in 1970 and 1973. Holman, recalled another former player, could see all ten players at once.

The combination of great player, great coach, great student of the game, and long association with it, led to Holman being known as "Mr. Basketball" for much of his life.

Joe Lapchick

There was a bit of irony in Joe Lapchick nominating Nat Holman for entrance into the Basketball Hall of Fame. Clearly, Lapchick was a most appropriate nominator, since his career had paralleled and intertwined with Holman's from about 1920 until 1960 when Holman retired as coach at C.C.N.Y. The irony, of course, was that Lapchick had joined the Celtics in 1923 when Holman was already a veteran and, along with Beckmann, was one of the acknowledged leaders of the Original Celtics team. But Lapchick had preceded Holman in being elected as an individual to the Hall of Fame, partly because Lapchick was more liked by the sportswriters of New York and nationally. He always had time to talk to them, he played golf with them, and he was a genuinely friendly person.

As mentioned previously, Lapchick went to the Cleveland Rosenblums after the Original Celtics were disbanded in 1928. In December 1930, following the withdrawal of the Rosenblums from the ABL, Lapchick and two of his former Celtics and Rosenblum teammates, Barry and Dehnert, were signed by the Toledo Redman, who had entered the ABL that year. Despite the presence of the old Celtics (including Davey Banks), the Redman failed to either win much or draw many spectators. Age seemed to have caught up with the former Celtics and Lapchick's knees, which had plagued him since he had missed much of the 1925-26 season, again slowed him greatly. The Redman finished the second half of the 1930-31 season with four wins and eleven losses, last in the league.

After the Redman and the American Basketball League went out of business, Lapchick gathered together some of the old Celtics and went back to their roots, that is, barnstorming. Lapchick had remained good friends with his former employers, Max Rosenblum and Irving ("Nig") Rose. Lapchick convinced them to sponsor the Celtics as a traveling team and Lapchick helped Rose put the team together.

Max Rosenblum was the owner of a family credit clothing store in Cleveland and "Nig" Rose was the credit manager of the store from the early 1900s until the 1940s. Rosenblum and Rose had married sisters and both were sports fans. They saw sports as an avenue for promoting advertising for the store, so Rosenblum sponsored teams and activities in the Cleveland area and Rose moved into heading up sales and sports promotion. When the ABL was formed in 1925, Rosenblum became league vice-president and Rose was elected secretary-treasurer.

Whereas the old Celtics traveled first class by train, this new version of the Celtics would have to be a bit more frugal with the Depression affecting the lives of everyone in the United States. As Lapchick recalled

Hickey, Dehnert, Barry, Banks and I formed a road version of the Celtics and barnstormed. We had an old Pierce Arrow that we bought for $125, and we played for $125 per night with an option of 60 percent of the gate. It sounded good, but we traveled light (usually the five of us with another player when we could find one).[15]

Norton Rose, the youngest child of "Nig" Rose, recalled many of the Rosenblum Celtics having dinner at his house (particularly enjoying his mother's beef brisket). He remembers them as a rough, raw-boned group of ethnics. He also noted that his father went on some of the Celtic trips in the early 1930s, usually ones to Indiana or to Chicago. The team traveled in two touring cars (the equivalent of stretch limos today). The team often stayed in so-called tourist homes which seemed to be analogous to today's bed and breakfasts. Despite being a top team, money was always tight in those times so staying in posh hotels was very unusual.[16] This corroborates the view offered by Lapchick in his autobiography even though the second car was not mentioned.

The Rosenblum Celtics combined their great skill with a sense of entertainment, and Lapchick was most popular in that regard. He recalled one account of his play that appeared in the *Knoxville (Tennessee) Journal* in 1933 that illustrated his comedic qualities.

As is always the case, it will undoubtedly be Lapchick who will give the fans the most laughs. He can do more tricks with the basketball than a monkey can with the proverbial peanut. Palming the ball, wrapping his slim arms around it, and the like, is just a part of his repertoire.[17]

During the early 1930s most teams needed to tour incessantly merely to survive; the Celtics often met the best of them. Lapchick grew to appreciate and admire the skills of the New York Renaissance team, an African American squad the Celtics often met in big cities. The Rens were younger and stronger but the Celtics had more experience. Their battles were legendary, but in the 1930s the Rens won more often. Lapchick battled "Wee Wille" Smith, the Rens center who was the same height but outweighed him by more than 30 pounds.

Age, travel, and small crowds all began to wear on Lapchick, the road warrior. In 1931 he married Elizabeth Sarubbi and soon had two children. "In 1936 Lapchick was asked by Father Rebholz, the Athletic Moderator at St. John's University," to be the coach at that institution.[18] He leapt at the chance even though he had never formally coached before; in fact he had never really *been* coached so his eagerness was certainly tempered with anxiety.

I never had the opportunity to come under the influence of a coach, as such. In fact, there were no coaches in professional basketball when I played. You learned basketball from experience.[19]

Despite this handicap, Lapchick was one of the greatest college coaches of his time from 1937 to 1947 and again from 1957 until mandatory retirement in 1965. Lapchick compiled a record of 334-130. His teams won the National Invitational Tournament Championship in 1943, 1944, 1959, and 1965.

In between his St. John's coaching stints, Lapchick was the coach of the New York Knickerbockers of the Basketball Association of America and the National Basketball Association. At the time of his induction into the Basketball Hall of Fame in 1966, he noted that he was the "only pro (NBA) coach to never have (a) losing season, three times to finals. In all playoffs!!"[20] Indeed, Lapchick's Knicks were in the NBA Finals in 1951, 1952, and 1953, but were defeated in all of those playoffs. Nevertheless, Lapchick's professional coaching record of 326-247 over twelve years was outstanding.

Throughout his coaching career Lapchick's health suffered; he slept poorly, had his stomach "tied up in knots," and suffered two heart attacks. At a reunion of the old Celtics in New York in 1960, Lapchick joked of his ailments. Referring to his continued coaching he noted, "I'm still at it, getting ulcers on my ulcers."[21]

After retiring at 65, the mandatory age at St. John's University in 1965, Lapchick was sports coordinator for Kutscher's County Club in Monticello, New York. He also kept his long association as athletic footwear consultant for G. R. Kinney Shoe Company.

In August 1970 Lapchick suffered a heart attack while playing golf at Kutscher's. On August 10, after a brief hospitalization, Joe Lapchick died. Eulogized as a player, coach, friend, and humanitarian, he was buried in his boyhood home of Yonkers. As Claire Bee noted in the introduction to Joe Lapchick's autobiography, "Basketball has been Joe's life and his life has been basketball."[22]

As noted earlier, when the Celtics were broken up, Dutch Dehnert joined with Lapchick, Beckman, Barry, Dave Kerr, Carl Husta, and Rich Deighan on the Cleveland Rosenblums to produce two more ABL championships. And, as also noted, after the league folded in 1931 Dehnert joined with Lapchick, Banks, Barry Hickey and Husta (later adding Herlihy and Paul Birch to replace Barry and Husta) to barnstorm under the Celtic banner into the 1940s. In order to keep the fans coming back, the Celtics extended the "clowning" they had begun in the 1920s to attract fans to a team that almost never lost. One newspaper article noted that the Celtics' "leapfrog play" was their latest with either Davey Banks or Pat Herlihy doing the leaping. Another popular "play" noted was where the Celtics played with four players while one sneaked off to play the piano.[23] It was difficult for the players, financially, at this time. Les Harrison, long-time pro basketball impressario noted, "No one could make a living playing pro basketball in the 1930s. If someone got a coaching offer, they got out of playing."[24]

Dutch Dehnert

In the 1940s, Dehnert coached professional teams in Detroit, Harrisburg, Cleveland, Sheboygan, Chattanooga, and Saratoga Springs, New York as well as a high school team, Bishop Loughlin Memorial in Rockaways, New York, near his home. His Detroit Eagles won the 1941 World Professional Tournament in Chicago Stadium, defeating the Oskosh All-Stars 39 to 37 after upsetting the New York Rens and the Harlem Globetrotters in previous rounds. Dehnert's Sheboygan Redskins won the Western Division of the National Basketball League in 1944-45 and 1945-46, but were defeated by the Ft. Wayne Zollner Pistons both times in the league championship series. The league had only six teams in 1944-45 and eight in 1945-46. In articles about Dehnert's teams, he was often the focus. In a Detroit paper in 1941, the writer recalled that "Dutch Dehnert was a tall, slender blonde kid with big hands and laughing eyes when you first saw him in the long ago" (playing with DeNeri of the old Eastern League).[25] Dehnert recalled those days at times also, remembering himself as a 6-foot, 1-inch, 175 pounder when Johnny Beckmann brought him up to Reading in the Pennsylvania State League when he was 17 or 18.[26] Dehnert's coaching was often praised, despite the performances of his teams. In an article in which the New York Rens were to play Dehnert's Detroit Eagles, the reference was to "Dehnert, one of the smartest of the country's basketball brains at the helm."[27] An article in a Cleveland paper noted that the "Detroit Eagles thrived on

Dehnert's coaching"[28] and another writer referred to Dehnert as "one of the really great cage coaches of the land."[29] Dehnert turned to coaching at the local high school when the Detroit Eagles had to disband in 1943 because of "doubtful transportation facilities because of the war."[30]

This view of Dehnert as coaching genius was in contrast to that held by Hal Lebovitz, who expressed his surprise at Dehnert's lack of basketball knowledge when he talked with and observed Dehnert as coach of the Cleveland Rebels of the BAA in 1946-47.[31] Dehnert had a 17-20 record with Cleveland when he was fired just over halfway through the season. Of course, there is a world of difference between performing a task and explaining it verbally. Trying to get explanations from artists or athletes who do not necessarily excel in written or spoken communication often leaves an interviewer dissatisfied.

In the 1950s and 60s, Dehnert was on the payroll of the Harlem Globetrotters as a part-time coach and scout. However, his "real" job was at the New York Racing Association, where he worked as a mutual clerk at Aqueduct and Belmont before retiring in the late 1960s. Dehnert was an inveterate gambler; he never saved much and never had much after he left basketball. When he worked for Belmont, he often would carry money to the park to place bets for friends. Inevitably he lost it betting on his own picks. His inability to keep money for very long is illustrated by the fact that he never owned a house in his life.[32] Dehnert was nominated for the Hall of Fame a number of times and was voted on in 1966 and 1967 before being elected with 12 of 13 votes in 1968.[33] He died in 1979 at the age of 81. Just before his death, Dehnert received a letter from then NBA Commissioner Larry O'Brien in which he (O'Brien) noted his pleasure at finding how well Dehnert was doing after surgery. O'Brien then went on to extol Dehnert's achievements as a pioneer of professional basketball. He concluded by noting that "All of us concerned with the NBA are aware of your special skill in developing what is so commonplace in our league today—the hook shot."[34] This was a nice effort but a sad result by the commissioner.

Johnny Beckman

Johnny Beckman went into professional coaching while still a player. He had been sold to Baltimore in 1927 to shore up that franchise, but he was their only playing asset and the club folded after that year. Beckman played the next year for Detroit and Chicago before rejoining his former teammates in Cleveland. When the franchise folded and the Celtics returned to barnstorming, Beckman declined the opportunity to tour with the Celtics. Later in the 1930s, he played on a new barnstorming Celtics squad after Lapchick had turned to full time coaching at St.

John's. Beckman finally retired as a player in 1941 when he was in his late 40s.

In 1931, Frank Morgenweck (long-time coach of Kingston in the New York State League, and a Hall of Fame member) placed Beckman on his second team for his all-time squad. Lew Wachter, the Hall of Fame player whose career was also played largely in upstate New York, in 1940 named Beckman to the second squad on his all-time team behind Chris Leonard, Beckman's long-time teammate. Beckman was "a master of the fast break."[35] In 1918, Beckman was "considered the most dangerous shot in the game today and the equal of any the game has produced."[36] Beckman's teammates recognized his greatness. In a letter to the executive secretary of the basketball Hall of Fame, Nat Holman had this to say about Beckman:

He was an aggressive leader, highly respected for his scoring ability and unmatched for his capacity to break away from his closely guarded opponents in his lightning drives for the basket. He was always a threat on the offense because of his outstanding shooting ability from the outside or his drive ins for the basket. Those who played against this great player will vouch for the authenticity of my remarks.

John Beckman was the pro's basketball player. He was one of the greatest and is deserving of our praise and adulation. He was feared by all when he took to the court because of his speed and shooting ability.[37]

Dehnert echoed these sentiments as he described his initial apprehensions regarding the use of the pivot play, "When told . . . that Beckman thought it was a great basketball weapon, Dehnert breathed a sigh of relief and confessed 'We knew that if Beckie liked it we had something, because Johnny was the smartest man who ever played basketball.' "[38] In 1935, Stanley Frank examined competitiveness in athletes in a series of articles carried in the *New York Post*. Frank claimed that the retired Beckman brought to basketball:

the perfect physical equipment: above the waist he was built like a young bull with most of his 155 pounds distributed there. Downstairs, he had the lithe, tapering legs of a sprinter. And somewhere within his five feet, eight inches he had an abnormally aggressive spirit which never communicated to the brain the knowledge of fear.[39]

Following his playing career, Beckman—whose grit, insights, and basketball intelligence were widely known and admired—declined numerous coaching offers. His son Edwin offered an explanation:

Dad had offers to coach at Yale, Harvard, NYU, Columbia and others but was smart enough to realize that his personality was not the kind a good coach wants. His philosophy was a "do it yourself, not tell others" kind and a "must win at all costs attitude" which a pro must have.[40]

This attitude was acknowledged (and feared, to a degree) by Beckman's teammates. He refused to lose and refused to accept excuses for giving less than a total commitment to one's performance. As Joe Lapchick recalled, "The Celtics had no time for alibis, excuses or explanations. The big asset was *guts,* and the only objective was to *win* basketball games."[41]

In 1957, Beckman moved to Miami from New Jersey to be closer to his son Edwin and his family. For a number of years, Johnny Beckman "served as athletic director for the Sunland Training Center, a facility for retarded children."[42] Despite his fears about coaching, Beckman was gentle and patient with the children; he treasured this work.

In 1959, the Original Celtics team (including Beckman) was inducted into the James Naismith Memorial Basketball Hall of Fame and in 1972 Beckman was inducted as a player. At the end of his life, Johnny Beckman was afflicted with Alzheimer's and he died of that disease in 1968.

Davey Banks

The last of the "coaching Celtics" was their last addition, Davey Banks. Banks established himself as one of the major sources of "entertainment" with the barnstorming Celtics in the 1930s. In about 1940 Wirt Gammon, a well-known writer in Chattanooga, anticipated the arrival of the Celtics in that city in his column which stated:

What's Davey Banks going to do tonight? In recent years his appearance in a game here has been the signal for the point making to stop and Banks' fun to begin-the dribble between a foe's legs . . . the hot pass fired at an astonished foe or referee or fan . . . the goal in the opponent's baskets . . . the fifth column, hide-out play, in a lady fan's lap . . . He used to do everything with a ball but eat it; now it looks like he's swallowed one. But don't sell him short.[43]

Obviously, the always chunky Banks had gained weight as he reached his forties, but he was still feared as a shooter. Bill Brunning, a Detroit newspaper writer, referred to him as "their funny little man," and noted that "Banks' clowning might have to be set aside, but keeping that lad quiet is about as easy as making a one dollar fedora hold its shape in a rainstorm."[44]

After touring with the Celtics, Banks turned to coaching Kingston and Troy between 1939-41 and the Chicago Gears between 1946-47. His Gears record was 3-3 in the midst of a three coach season for the Gears, a tumultuous year for them.[45] Banks also coached the Troy Celtics of the American Professional Basketball League in 1946-47 and was active in racing circles. In August of 1952, Banks died suddenly in an auto accident in Troy while returning from a trip to Saratoga Springs race track in New York. Newspaper accounts indicated he was in negotiations with the University of Notre Dame to take their head coaching position for the 1952-53 season. He was buried in Queens, New York. He was just fifty years of age.

Chris Leonard

Like Holman, Chris Leonard was a college graduate, but Leonard was the only Celtic to see active duty during World War I. By 1928 Leonard's career was nearly at an end. When the Celtics were disbanded he left the game and went into business with apparently no regrets or interest in coaching as a profession. Ed Wachter selected Leonard as one of the ten players on Wachter's first team. Despite the publicity garnered by Holman, Lapchick, and Dehnert, Leonard was recognized by his teammates and opponents as a great player—versatile and capable.

Leonard's father had headed a piano moving concern and Leonard was familiar with the transportation industry. In 1933, he began Leonard Delivery and Warehouse Corporation. He also did volunteer coaching as a hobby at nearby Long Island high schools, Great Neck and Manhasset. In May 1957, Leonard, who had never married, died at home on Long Island at the age of sixty-seven. His basketball memorabilia were left, for some reason not even clear to the curators, to the New York City Sports Hall of Fame which, as of 1998, had lost its lease and had their materials in storage while they sought another site.

Pete Barry

John Peter Barry was one of the original Celtics from McCormick's squad of 1915 and he remained a Celtic (except for the war years when the team was disbanded), until 1936 when he retired from basketball. Barry, nearly forty years old was neither interested in, nor apparently asked, to enter coaching. Instead he took a job working in the checking department of the W. R. Grace Shipping Lines and remained there until retiring from that company in 1965. He died three years later on Long Island at the age of sixty-eight.

Except for Lapchick, the Celtic players were all born and raised in New York City—specifically Manhattan—though Banks moved to Brooklyn as a youngster.

All learned basketball on the streets of New York—at outdoor courts, settlement houses, "Y"s, and church gyms. Beckman, Leonard, and Reich were basketball teammates while playing for the St. Gabriels light or middleweight national champions (from as young as fifteen). Most were not college graduates (Leonard and Holman being exceptions) and not attending high school was the norm for this group. Nevertheless, they were not dumb. They taught themselves and others how to master a game only recently invented. They were masterful at devising new plays, techniques, and concepts of basketball that had never been considered—let alone practiced. Playing together night after night they not only perfected their basketball, they also became as close to each other as to their families. In a delirious state on his deathbed in 1922, Ernie Reich kept calling for Beckman and Leonard, teammates since childhood, to pass the ball.[46] For most of these Celtics, their years on the team were not only the highlight of their lives, but the rest of their lives were lived in relative quiet—bordering on obscurity. Haggerty lived and died quietly in Reading. Leonard put his college degree to use in forming his trucking business. Barry worked as a clerk—as did Dehnert after coaching.

Reich and Banks died prematurely, while Beckman played basketball into his forties before retiring. Only Joe Lapchick and Nat Holman had second careers as notable as their playing careers. Only Holman and Lapchick are still widely recognized names in basketball history—largely because of their coaching.

Yet these players maintained contact through notes, cards, and occasional visits. They remained in the New York City metropolitan region and were able to get together at times, though there is no record of all of them ever getting together in one place ever again after the 1930s. However, Holman, Lapchick, Barry, Dehnert, and Beckman were together in Springfield, Massachusetts, for the induction of the original Celtics team into the Naismith Memorial Basketball Hall of Fame. One other possible meeting place was the Old Time Pro Basketball Players Association annual meetings. In 1960, most of the old Celtics attended the meeting at White's Restaurant in Manhattan. Barry, Lapchick, and Dehnert were joined at their table by Elmer Ripley, Stretch Meehan, and Joe Dreyfuss (all of whom played briefly for a Celtic team) and Nig Rose, the secretary of the old ABL and general manager of the Rosenblum Celtics. Beckman, retired in Florida, was unable to attend and Holman was ill. However, the Celtics were able to relive some of their adventures, according to the notes taken by Rose and shared with Hal Lebovitz.[47] Those adventures may seem today to be the stuff of legend, but the Celtics were larger than life and remain so today.

APPENDIX I

CELTIC PLAYERS

1919-20 Pete Barry, Johnny Witte, Ernie Riech, Joe Trippe, Eddie White, Mike Smolick

1920-21 Whitty, Barry, Reich, Dehnert, Smolick, Grimstead, Beckman, Trippe

1921-22 Smolick (early part of season), Barry, Reich, Dehnert, Beckman, Haggerty, Leonard, Holman, Witte

1922-23 Barry, Dehnert, Beckman, Haggerty, Leonard, Holman, Burke, Whitte

1923-24 Barry, Dehnert, Beckman, Whitte, Lapchick, Leonard, Holman, Burke

1924-25 Barry, Dehnert, Beckman, Witte, Lapchick, Holman, Leonard, Ripley, Burke (left mid-year)

1925-26 Barry, Dehnert, Beckman, Lapchick, Holman, Leonard, Borgmann, (Shang Chadwick when Lapchick out)

1926-27 Beckman (off in January), Dehnert, Barry, Lapchick, Holman, Leonard, Banks, Whitte

1927-28 Dehnert, Barry, Lapchick, Leonard, Holman, Banks, Dreyfuss, Witte

1928 - The Original Celtics were disbanded

	1912-13	1913-14	1914-15	1915-16	1916-17	1917-18	1918-19	1919-20
Beckman		Metro Big 5, Kingston (NYL), St. Gabriels	Kingston (NYSL), Blue Ribbons (CT State), St. Gabriels, St. Michaels	DeNeri (EL) Paterson (In. L)	Reading (EL), Bridgeport & Denmark (Int), Turners	DeNeri (EL), Nanticoke (PAL), Norwalk (CT), Newark Turners, Blue Ribbons (CT)	Standard Shipyard, Persons Big 5, Troy (NYS), Newark Turners	DeNeri (EL), Nar (PAL), St. James, Triangles, New Y
Leonard		Metro 5 St. Gabriels	Paterson (IL), St. Gabriels, Blue Ribbons (CT)	Paterson (IL)	Hazleton (PAL), Glens Falls, Danbury (IL), Newark (IL)	Jasper (EL), Hazelton (PAL), Norwalk (CT SL)		Pittston (PAL), T (NYL), Utica (N
Holman							Bridgeport (CT), Newark Whirlwinds	Bridgeport (EL), (PA), Germantow Albany (NL)
Reich		Metro 5, Cohoes (NYL), Reading (EL), St. Gabriels	Jersey City, Troy (EL), St. Gabriels	Jersey City (IL), Norwalk, Smith Co., DeNeri (EL)	Jersey City (IL), DeNeri (EL)	Norwalk, Troy, Hoboken, Wright-Martian Aero Co., Ansonia (CT)	Downey Shipyard, Whirlwinds-Newark	Downey Shipyard, Scranton (PAL), (EL), Celtics
Haggerty	Gloversville (NYL) Cohoes (NYL)	Troy (NYL) Reading (EL)	Reading (EL)	Reading (EL)	Reading (EL)	Reading (EL)		Reading (EL), Pit (PAL)
Dehnert						Ansonia (CT), Newark Turners	Downey Shipyard	Nanticoke (PA), Bridgeport (IL), (NYL)
Lapchick								Holyoke (W-MA Schenectady (NY
Barry		Paterson (NYL)	St. Michaels	Celtics	Celtics	Celtics		Celtics, Bridgepo St. Anthony's, Tr (NYL), Van & S (Brooklyn), Broo
Banks								
Grimstead	Oswego Indians	Utica (NYL)	Utica (NYL)	DeNeri (EL)	?	?	?	Gloversville/Troy Pittston (PA), Ce Paterson (IL), Br (IL), Nonpareils
Ripley					Hoboken (IL)	Blue Ribbons (CT)	Standard Shipyard	Scranton (PA), P (IL)
Whitty				Celtics	Celtics	Celtics		Celtics
Smolick						Hoboken Knickerbockers		Celtics, Albany (
Trippe								Celtics, St. Anthe
Borgmann								Paterson (IL)
Burke								St. Stephens

1920 - 21	1921 - 22	1922 - 23	1923 - 24	1924 - 25	1925 - 26	1926 - 27	1927 - 28
& Philadelphia (EL), onville (IL), All-rooklyn), Celtics, ce (PAL), Jordan Big	New York Celtics (EL)	Celtics, (Atlantic City (El, New York (Metro)	Celtics	Celtics	Celtics	Celtics, Baltimore (ABL)	Chicago(ABL), Detroit
lle (EL), Prospect stston (PAL), (IL), Danbury (CT)	New York Celtics (EL)	Celtics, Atlantic City (EL), New York (Metro)	Celtics	Celtics	Celtics	Celtics (ABL)	Celtics (ABL)
own (EL), NY nds, Scranton (PAL), d (IL)	New York Celtics (EL)	Celtics, Atlantic City (EL), New York (Metro)	Celtics	Celtics	Celtics	Celtics (ABL)	Celtics (ABL)
(EL), Celtics, d (CT) (IL)	New York Celtics (EL)						
ce (PAL), Danbury ading (EL)	New York Celtics (EL), Troy (NYL), Visitation (Metro)	Celtics, Atlantic City (EL), New York (Metro)	Paterson (Metro)	St. Henry (Philly)	Brooklyn (ABL)	Washington (ABL)	
phia (EL), Scranton , James, Celtics, onville (IL)	New York Celtics (EL)	Celtics Atlantic City (EL), New York (Metro)	Celtics	Celtics	Celtics	Celtics (ABL)	Celtics (ABL)
rk Wonderers, (IL), Schenectady Mt. Vernon ough)	Visitation (Metro), Troy (NYL), Armory Big 5	Visitation (Metro), Armory Big 5, Troy (NYL)	Celtics	Celtics	Celtics	Celtics (ABL)	Celtics (ABL)
Westfield (IL), St.	New York Celtics (EL), Amsterdam (NYL)	Celtics Atlantic City (EL), New York (Metro)	Celtics	Celtics	Celtics	Celtics (ABL)	Celtics (ABL)
		Visitation (Metro)	Brooklyn (Metro), SPHAS	Brooklyn (Metro), SPHAS	Brooklyn (Metro), SPHAS	Celtics (ABL)	Celtics (ABL
a (PA), Trenton (EL), onville (IL), Celtics	Dodgers (Metro), Camden (EL), Scranton (NYL)	Elizabeth (Metro), Schenectady (NYL)		Shanahen (Philly), Brooklyn (Metro)	Washington (ABL)	Rochester (ABL)	Washington (ABL)
a (PA), Germantown	Dodgers (Metro), Scranton (EL), Coatesville (EL)	Elizabeth (Metro), NYL - Cohoes, Albany	Paterson (Metro)	Celts	Brooklyn (Metro)	Washington (ABL)	Washington (ABL)
	New York Celtics (EL)	Atlantic City (EL), New York (Metro)	Celts	Celts	Fort Wayne (ABL)	Celts	Celts
Whirlwinds rn), Easthampten/ all (IL)	Powers (Metro), Schenectady (NYL), Amsterdam (NYL)	McDowell (Metro), Amsterdam (NYL)					
	Knights (Metro), Cohoes (NYL)	Knights (Metro), Cohoes (NYL)	Greenpoint (Metro)	Paterson (Metro)			
	Kingston (NYL), Powers (Metro)	Paterson (Metro), Kingston (NYL)	Paterson (Metro)	Paterson	Celtics, Paterson (Metro)	Fort Wayne (ABL)	Fort Wayne (ABL)
Barre (PA), Brooklyn	Visitation (Metro)	Visitation (Metro), Schenectady (NYL), Celtics	Celtics		Brooklyn (Metro)		

NOTES

Introduction

1. See J. Durso, *Madison Square Garden,* Simon and Schuster, New York, 1979, for a fuller discussion of Rickard and Madison Square Garden.

2. R. Peterson, *Cages to Jump Shots,* Oxford University Press, New York, 1990.

3. See B. Postal, J. Silver, and R. Silver, *Encyclopedia of Jews in Sports,* New York, Block Publishing Co., 1965, for fuller descriptions for the careers of Friedman and Sedran.

4. See recollections of "Flip" Dowling, a New York State League player starting in about 1917 in R. Peterson, pp. 6-7.

5. National Rules in *Reach Official Basketball Guides* from the period of 1919-22.

6. "N.Y. Whirlwinds Turned Perfect Cage Combination," *Wilkes-Barre Record,* 21 Apr. 1921: 18.

7. *Reach Official Basketball Guide,* A. S. Reach Co., Philadelphia, PA, p. 56.

8. The *Record* said 40-29, the *Reach Guide* 27. Most other accounts, quote the *Reach Guide* so that the score has been seen most often.

Chapter 1

1. G. Perret, *America in the Twenties, a History,* New York, Simon & Schuster, 1982, p. 10.

2. D. Snowman, *America Since 1920,* New York, Harper and Row, 1968.

3. D. Snowman, *America Since 1920,* New York, Harper and Row, 1968, p. 13.

4. D. Snowman, *America Since 1920,* New York, Harper and Row, 1968, p. 21.

5. D. Noverr and L. Ziewacz, *The Games They Played,* Chicago, Nelson Hall, 1983, p. 67.

6. D. Snowman, *America Since 1920,* New York, Harper and Row, 1968, p. 16.

7. D. Snowman, *America Since 1920,* New York, Harper and Row, 1968, p. 23.

8. G. Perret, *America in the Twenties, a History,* New York, Simon & Schuster, 1982, p. 222.

9. F. Allen, *Only Yesterday,* New York, Bantam Books, 1931.

10. P. Carter, *The Twenties in America,* Arlington Heights, IL, Harlan Davidson, Inc., 1968.

11. G. Perret, *America in the Twenties, a History,* New York, Simon & Schuster, 1982, p. 222.

12. D. Noverr and L. Ziewacz, *The Games They Played,* Chicago, Nelson Hall, 1983, p. 68.

13. D. Noverr and L. Ziewacz, *The Games They Played,* Chicago, Nelson Hall, 1983, p. 68-69.

14. B. Rader, *American Sports,* Englewood Cliffs, NJ, Prentice Hall, 3rd, 1996, p. 117.

15. D. Noverr and L. Ziewacz, *The Games They Played,* Chicago, Nelson Hall, 1983, p. 71.

16. G. Rice, "The Golden Panorama," *Sport's Golden Age,* ed. A. Danzig and P. Brandwein, New York, Harper Bros., 1948, p. 1.

17. J. Kiernan, "Foreword," *Sport's Golden Age,* ed. A. Danzig and P. Brandwein, New York, Harper Bros., 1948, p. ix.

18. A. Danzig and P. Brandwein, "Editor's Preface," *Sport's Golden Age,* New York, Harper Bros., 1948, p. ix.

19. R. Harker, "Bourdieu—Education and Reproduction," *An Introduction to the Work of Pierre Bourdieu,* London, MacMillan, 1990, p. 87.

20. P. Bourdieu, "Sport and Social Class," *Social Science Information,* 17.6 (1978): 819-40.

21. P. Bourdieu, "Sport and Social Class," *Social Science Information,* 17.6 (1978): 823.

22. P. Bourdieu, "Sport and Social Class," *Social Science Information,* 17.6 (1978): 828.

23. P. Bourdieu, "Sport and Social Class," *Social Science Information,* 17.6 (1978): 830.

24. P. Bourdieu, "Sport and Social Class," *Social Science Information,* 17.6 (1978): 831.

25. H. Litwack, interview. Cheltenham, PA, July 27, 1995.

26. S. Riess, *City Games, the Evolution of American Urban Society and the Rise of Sports,* Urbana, IL, University of Illinois Press, 1989, p. 185.

27. R. O'Connor, *German Americans,* Boston, Little & Brown, 1968, p. 355.

28. R. O'Connor, *German Americans,* Boston, Little & Brown, 1968, p. 359.

29. R. O'Connor, *German Americans,* Boston, Little & Brown, 1968, p. 395-96.

30. R. O'Connor, *German Americans,* Boston, Little & Brown, 1968, p. 309.

31. L. McCaffrey, *Textures of Irish America,* Syracuse, NY, Syracuse Uni-

versity Press, 1992, p. 27.

32. L. McCaffrey, *Textures of Irish America*, Syracuse, NY, Syracuse University Press, 1992, p. 28.

33. S. Riess, *City Games, the Evolution of American Urban Society and the Rise of Sports*, Urbana, IL, University of Illinois Press, 1989, p. 185.

34. L. McCaffrey, *Textures of Irish America*, Syracuse, NY, Syracuse University Press, 1992, p. 27.

35. B. Silverman, *The Jewish Athletes Hall of Fame*, New York, Shapolsky Publishing Co., 1989, p. 73.

36. P. Levine, *Ellis Island to Ebbets Field*, Chicago, Oxford University Press, 1992, p. 6.

37. G. Gems, *Windy City Wars*, Lanham, MD, Scarecrow Press, 1997, p. 113.

38. I. Rosenwaike, *Population History of New York City*, Syracuse, NY, Syracuse University Press, 1982.

39. P. Levine, *Ellis Island to Ebbets Field*, Chicago, Oxford University Press, 1992, p. 14.

40. B. J. Postal and R. Silver, ed., *Encyclopedia of Jews in Sports*, New York, Bloch Publishing Co., 1965, p. 83, 92.

41. J. Healy, "Nat Holman Player and Coach," copy in Holman file, Naismith Memorial Basketball Hall of Fame, (n.d.). p. 1.

42. P. Levine.

43. H. Litwack interview. Cheltenham, PA, July 27, 1995.

44. T. Vincent, *Mudville's Revenge*, New York, Seaview Books, 1981, p. 248.

45. P. Levine, *Ellis Island to Ebbets Field*, Chicago, Oxford University Press, 1992, p. 38.

46. P. Levine, *Ellis Island to Ebbets Field*, Chicago, Oxford University Press, 1992, p. 72.

47. B. Silverman, *The Jewish Athletes Hall of Fame*, New York, Shapolsky Publishing Co., 1989, p. 73.

48. P. Gallico, *Farewell to Sport*, New York, Alfred A. Knopf, 1938, p. 325.

49. E. Sullivan, "Ed Sullivan's Sport Whirl," *New York World*, Joe Lapchick Scrapbooks, 1926.

50. I. Rosenwaike, *Population History of New York City*, Syracuse, NY, Syracuse University Press, 1972, p. 56.

51. Z. Hollander, *The NBA Official Encyclopedia of Pro Basketball*, New York, 1979, p. 272.

52. H. Bradley, "Dempsey to Open Basketball Duel by Tossing Sphere," Joe Lapchick Scrapbooks, Boston, MA, Richard Lapchick, 1927.

53. "Lank," Leonard, Joe Lapchick, and Davey Banks are "Mutt and Jeff

of Professional Basketball" in Joe Lapchick Scrapbooks, Boston, MA, Richard Lapchick, 1927.

54. *Philadelphia Inquirer,* 15 Mar. 1928: 23.

55. P. Levine, *Ellis Island to Ebbets Field,* Chicago, Oxford University Press, 1992, p. 73.

56. P. Levine, *Ellis Island to Ebbets Field,* Chicago, Oxford University Press, 1992, p. 281-84.

57. T. Vincent, *Mudville's Revenge,* New York, Seaville Books, 1981, p. 247.

58. T. Vincent, *Mudville's Revenge,* New York, Seaville Books, 1981, p. 248.

Chapter 2

1. A. Martin, *Railroads Triumphant,* New York, Oxford University Press, 1992, p. 122.

2. J. F. Stover, *Life and Decline of the American Railroad,* New York, Oxford University Press, 1970, p. 199.

3. J. F. Stover, *Life and Decline of the American Railroad,* New York, Oxford University Press, 1970, p. 199.

4. R. Saylor, *The Railroads of Pennsylvania,* Penn State University, University Park, PA, 1964. J. Weller, *The New Haven Railroad,* Hastings House, New York, 1969.

5. State League Cage Notes, *Wilkes Barre Record,* 3 Feb. 1921: 17.

6. C. Hood, *722 Miles, The Building of the Subways and How They Transformed New York,* Baltimore, Johns Hopkins Press, 1993.

7. J. F. Stover, *Life and Decline of the American Railroad,* New York, Oxford University Press, 1970, p. 199.

8. J. F. Stover, *Life and Decline of the American Railroad,* New York, Oxford University Press, 1970, p. 200.

9. J. F. Stover, *Life and Decline of the American Railroad,* New York, Oxford University Press, 1970, p. 202-03.

10. J. F. Stover, *Life and Decline of the American Railroad,* New York, Oxford University Press, 1970, p. 165.

11. J. F. Stover, *Life and Decline of the American Railroad,* New York, Oxford University Press, 1970, p. 170.

12. "Hoover May Head U.S. Owned Railroads," *Washington Times,* 10 Mar. 1921: 1.

13. J. F. Stover, *Life and Decline of the American Railroad,* New York, Oxford University Press, 1970, p. 179.

14. F. Hubbard, *Encyclopedia of North American Railroading,* New York, McGraw Hill, 1981, p. 93-94.

15. F. Hubbard, *Encyclopedia of North American Railroading,* New York,

McGraw Hill, 1981, p. 252.

16. A. Martin, *Railroads Triumphant,* New York, Oxford University Press, 1992, p. 119.

17. J. Lapchick, *50 Years of Basketball,* Englewood Cliffs, NJ, Prentice-Hall, 1968, p. 11.

18. N. Holman, "Basketball 50 Years Ago," 1971, n.p.

19. "Basketball in Connecticut," *The Reach Official Basketball Guide,* ed. William Sheffer, A. J. Reach Co., Philadelphia, 1918, pp. 55-63.

20. S. O. Grauley, "To Decide Tie in Second Half Race," *Philadelphia Inquirer,* 10 Jan. 1921: 13.

21. J. Lapchick, *50 Years of Basketball,* Englewood Cliffs, NJ, Prentice-Hall, 1968, p. 11.

22. R. W. Peterson, *Cages to Jump Shots,* New York, Oxford University Press, 1990, p. 53-54.

23. R. W. Peterson, *Cages to Jump Shots,* New York, Oxford University Press, 1990, p. 54.

24. J. Lapchick, *50 Years of Basketball,* Englewood Cliffs, NJ, Prentice-Hall, 1968, p. 11.

25. "Controlling Body for 'Pro' Basketball Leagues in East," *Reach Official Basketball Guide,* 1920-21, A. J. Reach Co., Philadelphia, PA, p. 46-47.

26. "Two Teams After Eastern Franchise," *Philadelphia Inquirer,* 22 Nov. 1920: 16.

27. J. Murray, "Professional Review for 1921-22," *Reach Official Basketball Guide,* 1922-23, A. J. Reach Co., Philadelphia, pp. 67-69.

28. S. O. Grauley, "Eastern Basketballers Face Crisis at Meeting to Be Held Here Tomorrow," *Philadelphia Inquirer,* 16 Jan. 1922: 15.

29. "Metropolitan Professional League Season," *Reach Official Basketball Guide 1923-24,* A. J. Reach Co., Philadelphia, 1923, pp. 20-34.

30. R. W. Peterson, *Cages to Jump Shots,* New York, Oxford University Press, 1990, p. 64.

31. F. Basloe, *I Grew Up with Basketball,* New York, Greenberg Publisher, 1952.

32. H. Litwack, interview, Cheltenham, PA, July 27, 1995.

Chapter 3

1. *Official Rules of Basketball,* Philadelphia, A. J. Reach Company, 1922-23, p. 3.

2. S. Povich, telephone interview, July 16, 1997.

3. J. Lapchick, *50 Years of Basketball,* Englewood Cliffs, NJ, Prentice-Hall, 1968, p. 5.

4. W. Scheffer, "Bill Scheffer Says—," *Reach Official Basketball Guide, 1924-25,* Philadelphia, A. J. Reach Company, 1924, p. 7.

192 · *Notes to Chapter 3*

5. J. Lapchick, *50 Years of Basketball,* Englewood Cliffs, NJ, Prentice-Hall, 1968, p. 6.

6. J. Lapchick, *50 Years of Basketball,* Englewood Cliffs, NJ, Prentice-Hall, 1968, p. 7.

7. *Official Basketball Guide for 1922-23,* Philadelphia, A. J. Reach Company, 1922-23, p. 18.

8. W. Scheffer, "Bill Scheffer Says—," *Reach Official Basketball Guide, 1924-25,* Philadelphia, A. J. Reach Company, 1924, p. 211.

9. M. Rosenwald, "New York Celtics," *Reach Official Basketball Guide, 1925-26,* Philadelphia, A. J. Reach Company, 1925, p. 154.

10. R. Curtis, "Ansonia, Connecticut State Champions," *Reach Official Basketball Guide, 1919,* Philadelphia, A. J. Reach Company, 1919, p. 59.

11. R. Curtis, "Ansonia, Connecticut State Champions," *Reach Official Basketball Guide, 1919,* Philadelphia, A. J. Reach Company, 1919, p. 62.

12. J. Murray, "Professional Basketball Review," *Reach Official Basketball Guide,* 1923-24, Philadelphia, A. J. Reach Company, 1923, p. 51.

13. State League "Cage Notes," *Wilkes-Barre Record,* Wilkes-Barre, PA, 29 Jan. 1921: 23.

14. Litwack interview, Cheltenham, PA, July 27, 1995.

15. J. Lapchick, *50 Years of Basketball,* Englewood Cliffs, NJ, Prentice-Hall, 1968, p. 5.

16. J. Lapchick, *50 Years of Basketball,* Englewood Cliffs, NJ, Prentice-Hall, 1968, p. 20.

17. S. Povich, telephone interview, July 16, 1997.

18. Lapchick in Dehnert file, James Naismith Memorial Basketball Hall of Fame.

19. S. Povich, telephone interview, July 16, 1997.

20. B. Reedy, Running Column, *Reading Eagle,* Reading, PA, Jan. 31, 1942. (Haggerty Scrapbook, Naismith Memorial Basketball Hall of Fame, Springfield, MA.)

21. H. Lebovitz, "Teams Better Now, Admit Old Celtics," *Cleveland Plain Dealer,* 1 May 1960: n.p. (Lapchick file, Naismith Memorial Basketball Hall of Fame, Springfield, MA.)

22. J. Lapchick, *50 Years of Basketball,* Englewood Cliffs, NJ, Prentice-Hall, 1968, p. 30.

23. "Phillies Fail to Check Celtics Winning Streak," *Philadelphia Inquirer,* 23 Feb. 1927: 22.

24. "Celtics Vanquish Philadelphia Fire," *New York Times,* 22 Nov. 1927: 34.

25. 1927 Untitled News Clippings, Dec. 8, 1927, Joe Lapchick Scrapbooks, Richard Lapchick.

26. "Cleveland Swamped by Celtic Quintet," *Philadelphia Inquirer,*

24 Dec. 1927: 18.

27. S. O. Grauley, "Celtics Defeat Brooklyn Sons Trouble, 41-23," *Cleveland Plain Dealer,* 23 Jan. 1928: 18.

28. "Warriors Make Great Second Half Rally, but Bow Before Attack of Shamrocks," *Philadelphia Inquirer,* 8 Feb. 1928: 19.

29. "Cleveland Edges Celtics in Final Seconds, 26 to 25," *Cleveland Plain Dealer,* 24 Feb 1928: 18.

30. "Sedran, Barney," *Encyclopedia of Jews in Sports,* Postal, Silver and Silver, Bloch Publishing Co., 1965.

31. R. Peterson, *Cages to Jump Shots,* New York, Oxford University Press, 1990, p. 144.

32. R. Peterson, *Cages to Jump Shots,* New York, Oxford University Press, 1990, p. 145.

33. R. Peterson, *Cages to Jump Shots,* New York, Oxford University Press, 1990, p. 145.

34. J. Lapchick, *50 Years of Basketball,* Englewood Cliffs, NJ, Prentice-Hall, 1968, p. 9.

35. F. J. Basloe, *I Grew Up with Basketball,* New York, Greenberg Publishing, 1952, p. 87.

36. F. J. Basloe, *I Grew Up with Basketball,* New York, Greenberg Publishing, 1952, p. 83.

37. F. J. Basloe, *I Grew Up with Basketball,* New York, Greenberg Publishing, 1952, p. 78.

38. Newspaper clippings and team stationery can all be seen in George Haggerty's Scrapbook, Naismith Memorial Basketball Hall of Fame Archives, Springfield, MA.

39. J. W. Smith, "Haggerty and Original Celtics Picked into Court Hall of Fame," *Reading Eagle,* Reading, PA, 17 Jan. 1960.

40. B. Reedy, *Reading Eagle,* Reading, PA, 31 Jan. 1942 (Haggerty Scrapbook, Naismith Memorial Basketball Hall of Fame, Springfield, MA.)

41. R. Bole, and A. Lawrence, *From Peachbaskets to Slam Dunks,* Canaan, NH, B & L Publishers, 1987, p. 28.

42. R. Bole and A. Lawrence, *From Peachbaskets to Slam Dunks,* Canaan, NH, B & L Publishers, 1987, p. 113.

43. R. Bole and A. Lawrence, *From Peachbaskets to Slam Dunks,* Canaan, NH, B & L Publishers, 1987, p. 30, 53.

44. R. Bole and A. Lawrence, *From Peachbaskets to Slam Dunks,* Canaan, NH, B & L Publishers, 1987, p. 53.

45. J. Lapchick, *50 Years of Basketball,* Englewood Cliffs, NJ, Prentice-Hall, 1968, p. 20.

Chapter 4

1. J. Williams, letter to Edward J. Hickox, Springfield, MA, Celtics file, Naismith Memorial Basketball Hall of Fame, Nov. 4, 1962.

2. G. T. Hepbron, editor, *Spalding Official Basketball Guide for 1912-13,* New York, American Sports Publishing Co., 1912.

3. *Reach Official Basketball Guide, 1919-20,* p. 54.

4. Pete Barry, *New York Times,* 30 Aug. 1968: 33: 2, Obituary.

5. *Reach Official Basketball Guide, 1920-21,* Philadelphia, A. J. Reach Co., 1920, p. 109; R. W. Peterson, *Cages to Jump Shots,* New York, Oxford University Press, 1990, p. 70.

6. *Reach Official Basketball Guide, 1920-21,* Philadelphia, A. J. Reach Co., 1920, p. 109.

7. J. Williams letter to Edward J. Hickox, Springfield, MA, Celtics file, Naismith Memorial Basketball Hall of Fame, Nov. 4, 1962.

8. *Reach Official Basketball Guide, 1920-21,* Philadelphia, A. J. Reach Co., 1920, p. 113-15.

9. Murphy quoted in *Reach Official Basketball Guide, 1920-21,* Philadelphia, A. J. Reach Co., 1920, p. 112.

10. F. Basloe, *I Grew Up with Basketball,* New York, Greenberg Press, 1957, p. 87.

11. R. Curtiss, "Basketball in Connecticut—Ansonia, Conn., State Champion," *The Reach Official Basketball Guide, 1918-19,* ed. W. Scheffer, A. J. Reach Company, Philadelphia, p. 63.

12. "Champion Newark, N.J., Turner Quintet," *The Reach Official Basketball Guide, 1918-19,* ed. W. Scheffer, A. J. Reach Company, Philadelphia, 1918, p. 69.

13. B. Reedy, "Beckman Echoes Opinion of Old Pal That Defense Is Gone in Basketball," *Reading Eagle,* 31 Jan. 1942: 10.

14. H. Dehnert, Hall of Fame nomination in Dehnert file in Naismith Memorial Basketball Hall of Fame archives, 1964.

15. N. Holman, *Winning Basketball,* New York, Charles Scribner's Sons, 1932, p. x.

16. Dehnert, file.

17. N. Isaacs, *All the Moves,* New York, Harper and Row, 1975, 1984, p. 34.

18. Z. Hollander, *The Modern Encyclopedia of Basketball,* Garden City, NY, Dolphin Books, 1979, p. 275.

19. Dehnert file, Naismith Memorial Basketball Hall of Fame, Springfield, MA.

20. "City to Have Court Entry," *Harrisburg Patriot,* 5 Dec. 1942: 17.

21. Dehnert, file.

22. It is not clear which weight the team was. Most of the time there were only two divisions—light and heavyweight. Beckman's Hall of Fame file indicates they were a lightweight squad—contradicting all accounts in the 25 Feb. 1922 *Philadelphia Inquirer* and the *Reach Guides* for 1922-23.

23. Smith.

24. R. Bole and A. Lawrence, *From Peachbaskets to Slam Dunks,* Canaan, NH, B&L Publishers, 1987, p. 148.

25. J. Lapchick, *50 Years of Basketball,* Englewood Cliffs, NJ, Prentice-Hall, 1968, p. 21.

26. M. McDohaghy, "New York State Basketball League," in *Reach Official Basketball Guide 1920-21,* A. J. Reach Company, Philadelphia, 1920, p. 59.

27. The *Encyclopedia of Jews in Sports* lists Oct. 19 as does his biography in the *Biographical Dictionary of American Sport.* Holman's obituary authored by long time acquaintance Sam Goldaper lists Oct. 16 as Holman's birthday, and The Hall of Fame lists Oct. 18.

28. J. Healy, "Nat Holman Player and Coach." Copy in Holman File, Naismith Memorial Basketball Hall of Fame, 1988.

29. B. Postal, J. Silver, R. Silver, ed., *Encyclopedia of Jews in Sports,* New York, Bloch Publishing Co., 1965, p. 87.

30. S. Goldaper, "Nat Holman Is Dead at 98; Led C.C.N.Y. Champions," *New York Times,* 13 Feb. 1995: B7.

31. J. Laney, "Why Jews Excel in Basketball," *New York Evening Graphic Magazine,* 5 Mar. 1927: 1.

32. J. Healy, J., "Nat Holman Player and Coach." Copy in Holman File, Naismith Memorial Basketball Hall of Fame, p. 2.

33. *Reach Official Basketball Guide, 1917-18,* A. J. Reach Company, Philadelphia, 1917, p. 41; J. Healy, "Nat Holman Player and Coach." Copy in Holman File, Naismith Memorial Basketball Hall of Fame, p. 2.

34. Holman quoted in B. Postal, J. Silver, and R. Silver, ed., *Encyclopedia of Jews in Sports,* New York, Bloch Publishing Co., 1965, p. 87.

35. Holman, 1973.

36. Holman, 1973.

37. J. Healy, "Nat Holman Player and Coach." Copy in Holman File, Naismith Memorial Basketball Hall of Fame, p. 5.

38. Holman, 1932.

39. T. Meany, "Basketball," *Sports Golden Age,* ed. A. Danzig and P. Barandwein, New York, Harper Bros., 1948.

40. T. Meany, "Basketball," *Sports Golden Age,* ed. A. Danzig and P. Barandwein, New York, Harper Bros., 1948, p. 271.

41. *Reach Official Basketball Guide, 1920-21,* A. J. Reach Co., Philadelphia, PA, 1920, p. 46-47.

42. T. Meany, "Basketball," *Sports Golden Age,* ed. A. Danzig and P.

Barandwein, New York, Harper Bros., 1948, p. 272.

43. *Reach Official Basketball Guide, 1923-24*, A. J. Reach Co., Philadelphia, 1923, p. 22.

44. *Reach Official Basketball Guide, 1923-24*, A. J. Reach Co., Philadelphia, 1923, p. 50.

45. *Reach Official Basketball Guide, 1923-24*, A. J. Reach Co., Philadelphia, 1923, p. 51.

46. J. W. Smith, "Haggerty and Original Celtics Picked into Court Hall of Fame," *Reading Eagle*, 17 Jan. 1960: 27.

47. J. Lapchick, *50 Years of Basketball*, Englewood Cliffs, NJ, Prentice-Hall, 1968, p. 9.

48. R. Lapchick, *Five Minutes to Midnight*, Lanham, MD, Madison Books, 1991, p. 145.

49. J. Lapchick, *50 Years of Basketball*, Englewood Cliffs, NJ, Prentice-Hall, 1968, p. 9.

50. R. Lapchick, *Five Minutes to Midnight*, Lanham, MD, Madison Books, 1991, p. 146.

51. J. Lapchick, *50 Years of Basketball*, Englewood Cliffs, NJ, Prentice-Hall, 1968, p. 10.

52. J. Lapchick, *50 Years of Basketball*, Englewood Cliffs, NJ, Prentice-Hall, 1968, p. 12.

53. Stolz, 1922, 77.

54. J. Lapchick, *50 Years of Basketball*, Englewood Cliffs, NJ, Prentice-Hall, 1968, p. 12.

55. R. Lapchick, *Five Minutes to Midnight*, Lanham, MD, Madison Books, 1991, p. 151.

56. Z. Hollander, *The Modern Encyclopedia of Basketball*, Garden City, New York, 1979, p. 275.

Chapter 5

1. See Appendix B of Peterson, op. cit., S. O. Grauley, "Two Teams After Eastern Franchises," *Philadelphia Inquirer*, 22 Nov. 1920: 16, and S. O. Grauley, "Camden Must Beat Trenton This Week to Stay in Eastern League Basketball Race," *Philadelphia Inquirer*, 26 Dec. 1920: 16.

2. "Pennsylvania State League," *Reach Official Basketball Guide 1921-22*, A. J. Reach Co., Philadelphia, 1921, p. 20.

3. Ibid.

4. *Reach Official Basketball Guide 1921-22*, A. J. Reach Company, Philadelphia.

5. "Newark Reported Out of Eastern League," *Philadelphia Inquirer*, 20 Nov. 1920: 16.

6. S. O. Grauley, "Two Teams After Eastern Franchise," *Philadelphia*

Inquirer, 22 Nov. 1920:16.

7. "Camden Defeated in Last Minute Play," *Philadelphia Inquirer,* 24 Nov. 1920: 18.

8. S. O. Grauley, "Wilkes-Barre Club Defies Commission," *Philadelphia Inquirer,* 29 Nov. 1920: 17.

9. "Germantown Rolls Up 35-18 Score," *Philadelphia Inquirer,* 1 Dec. 1920: 24.

10. "Camden Fails to Stop Reading Five," *Philadelphia Inquirer,* 2 Dec. 1920: 16.

11. "Trenton Wins and Takes First Place," *Philadelphia Inquirer,* 11 Dec. 1920: 20; "Coatesville Beaten by Reading, 31 to 24," *Philadelphia Inquirer,* 11 Dec. 1920: 17.

12. "Germantown Nosed Out by One Point," *Philadelphia Inquirer,* 12 Dec. 1920: 22.

13. "Local Clubs Will Stick Out Season," *Philadelphia Inquirer,* 20 Dec. 1920: 15.

14. "Fisk Red Tops Lose to Celtic Goal Getters," *Philadelphia Inquirer,* 20 Dec. 1920: 14.

15. S. O. Grauley, "Eastern Title at Stake This Week," *Philadelphia Inquirer,* 3 Jan. 1921: 15.

16. "State League Cage Notes," *Wilkes-Barre Record,* 3 Feb. 1921: 17.

17. "State League President Announces New Schedule," *Wilkes-Barre Record,* 2 Feb. 1921: 18.

18. "State League Cage Notes," *Wilkes-Barre Record,* 3 Feb. 1921: 17.

19. S. O. Grauley, "To Decide Tie in Second Half Race," *Philadelphia Inquirer,* 10 Jan. 1921: 13.

20. R. D. Bole, and A. C. Lawrence, *Peach Baskets to Slam Dunks,* B & L Publishers, Canaan, NH, 1987, pp. 44-45.

21. Peterson, op. cit., 55.

22. S. O. Grauley, "To Decide Tie in Second Half Race."

23. "Reading Loses to Germantown, 23-15," *Philadelphia Inquirer,* 12 Jan. 1921: 16.

24. S. O. Grauley, "Germantown Five Looks Formidable," *Philadelphia Inquirer,* 17 Jan. 1921: 13. Also see Bole and Lawrence, op. cit., p. 45.

25. S. O. Grauley, "Germantown Five Looks Formidable."

26. "Scranton Gains First Place in League," *Wilkes-Barre Record,* 8 Feb. 1921: 18.

27. "Basketball Chatter," *Philadelphia Inquirer,* 24 Jan. 1921: 11.

28. "Will Get $2,000 for 4 Basketball Games," *Philadelphia Inquirer,* 31 Jan. 1921: 13.

29. Ibid.

30. "Germantown Wins from Phils, 25-15," *Philadelphia Inquirer,* 30 Jan.

1921: 21.

31. Ibid.

32. "Bans Scranton Player for Breaking Agreement," *Wilkes-Barre Record*, 25 Jan. 1921: 16; "State League Cage Notes," *Wilkes-Barre Record*, 8 Feb. 1921: 18.

33. "Will Get $2,000 for 4 Basketball Games," *Philadelphia Inquirer*, 31 Jan. 1921: 11.

34. "Germantown Has Easy Time of It," *Philadelphia Inquirer*, 2 Feb. 1921: 16.

35. "Germantown Wins Rough Battle," *Philadelphia Inquirer*, 5 Feb. 1921: 21.

36. "Germantown Wins and Ties Camden," *Philadelphia Inquirer*, 9 Feb. 1921: 14.

37. Baetzel was often praised for his work. In 1917-18 he had been *the* league referee in the Pennsylvania State League according to the *Wilkes-Barre Record* of Feb. 3, 1921 ("State League Cage Notes"), but now was reffing mostly in the Eastern League and exhibition contests. The Pennsylvania State League was reliant upon Ward Brennan of Brooklyn, but used Baetzel and others to cover for Brennan's exhaustion in January. See "State Cage League Notes," *Wilkes-Barre Record*, 29 Jan. 1921: 23.

38. Bole and Lawrence, op. cit., pp. 48-51.

39. Neither played in either the Jan. 26 or Jan. 28 Trenton contests.

40. "Basketball Flashes," *Philadelphia Inquirer*, 14 Feb. 1921: 14.

41. "Trenton Checks Germantown Rush," *Philadelphia Inquirer*, 12 Feb. 1921: 12.

42. "Reading Defeats Trenton, 26-12," *Philadelphia Inquirer*, 13 Feb. 1921: 19.

43. "Phils Lose Close One, Referee Quits," *Philadelphia Inquirer*, 20 Feb. 1921: 21.

44. "Camden Runs Away from Reading 45-28," *Philadelphia Inquirer*, 20 Feb. 1921: 21.

45. "More Basketball Leagues Loom Up," *Philadelphia Inquirer*, 21 Feb. 1921: 11. Two weeks later on March 2, the National Basketball League awarded franchises to Brooklyn, Philadelphia, Boston, and Paterson. The American League was to include Chicago, Cleveland, Cincinatti, Detroit, Akron, Toledo, Louisvill, Buffalo, and Dayton. "National Basketball League Awards Four Franchises," *Philadelphia Inquirer*, 3 Mar. 1921: 14. The leagues never came to be.

46. "Camden Rallies at Finish and Wins," *Philadelphia Inquirer*, 26 Feb. 1921: 16.

47. S. O. Grauley, "Trenton Threatens to Walk Off Floor," *Philadelphia Inquirer*, 28 Feb. 1921: 13.

48. Again Bole and Lawrence's account is in conflict with the *Inquirer*.

The former claim Walters designated Beckman, not Grimstead, for suspension. In addition the *Inquirer* only noted that Trenton was given five minutes to get Grimstead off the floor before forfeiting. Bole and Lawrence included the flourish of a jump ball and an uncontested basket.

49. "Trenton Fined $1,000 and Retains Franchise," *Philadelphia Inquirer*, 4 Mar. 1921: 16. This article appears with no byline nor even a "Special to the *Inquirer*" comment. It was undoubtedly written by Grauley who may have felt uncomfortable putting his name on such "privileged data."

50. "Trenton Admitted to Pennsylvania State League," *Philadelphia Inquirer*, 7 Mar. 1921: 12.

51. Bole and Lawrence, p. 57.

52. S. O. Grauley, "New York and Eastern May Meet," *Philadelphia Inquirer*, 7 Mar. 1921: 13.

53. Ibid.

54. Of course by then Beckman was ineligible.

55. "League Orders Reading to Play Tonight," *Philadelphia Inqirer*, 14 Mar. 1921: 13.

56. "Trenton Wins Rough Game from Reading," *Philadelphia Inquirer*, 15 Mar. 1921: 16.

57. "Germantown Wins Strenuous Game from Reading," *Philadelphia Inquirer*, 16 Mar. 1921: 16.

58. Bole and Lawrence, p. 57.

59. "Trenton Defeats Pittston," *Wilkes-Barre Record*, 12 Mar. 1921: 22.

60. "Nan-Scranton Game Fizzles," *Wilkes-Barre Record*, 23 Mar. 1921: 20.

61. "Forfeits Flag to Scranton," *Wilkes-Barre Record*, 24 Mar. 1921: 20.

62. Ibid. Also "State League Grants Franchise to Trenton," *Wilkes-Barre Record*, 7 Mar. 1921: 17.

63. "Germantown Wins First of Series," *Philadelphia Inquirer*, 25 Mar. 1921: 20. The *Wilkes-Barre Record* said Holman "played an unusually sensational game." "Reading Drops First Game to Germantown," 25 Mar. 1921: 26.

64. "Germantown Wins Basketball Title," *Philadelphia Inquirer*, 27 Mar. 1921: 21.

65. S. O. Grauley, "Germantown May Clash with Albany," *Philadelphia Inquirer*, 28 Mar. 1921: 13. Earlier in the season, Albany had withdrawn from the league, but after discussions ensued, they reconciled and returned to win the championship.

66. "Cage Teams to Play Off Tie," *Wilkes-Barre Record*, 24 Jan. 1921: 20; "Pittston Wins First Contest," *Wilkes-Barre Record*, 26 Jan. 1921: 19; "Pittston Wins Pennant in First Half of Race," *Wilkes-Barre Record*, 5 Feb. 1921: 22.

67. "Germantown to Play Trenton State Team," *Philadelphia Inquirer*, 30 Mar. 1921: 14.

68. "Media Team Makes Germantown Hustle," *Philadelphia Inquirer,* 1 Apr. 1921: 20.

69. "Celtics Stage Late Rally," *Philadelphia Inquirer,* 29 Mar. 1921: 12. The player totals (29) do not reconcile with the 27 point total reported.

70. "Scranton Wins First Battle," *Wilkes-Barre Record,* 30 Mar. 1921: 19.

71. "Scranton Wins 1921 Pennant," *Wilkes-Barre Record,* 1 Apr. 1921: 22.

72. "Germantown Warned," *Philadelphia Inquirer,* 1 Apr. 1921: 20.

73. The headline for the game claimed 26-16, the players' points total 23. "Germantown Loses at Trenton 26 to 16," *Philadelphia Inquirer,* 2 Apr. 1921: 12.

74. "Eastern League Disbands," *Philadelphia Inquirer,* 2 Apr. 1921: 12.

75. "New Eastern League Arises from Ashes," *Philadelphia Inquirer,* 8 Apr. 1921: 16. This entire episode is ignored by both Peterson and Bole and Lawrence.

76. "West Chester Loses Final Cage Contest," *Philadelphia Inquirer,* 8 Apr. 1921: 16.

77. The change of seasons must have caught up *Inquirer* sportswriters who called the contests for the "baseball" championship in their account of the opening game on Apr. 19, 1921; also "Scranton and Albany Fives to Fight for Championship," *Wilkes-Barre Record,* 16 Apr. 1921: 19.

78. "Arrange World Series Games," *Wilkes-Barre Record,* 9 Apr. 1921: 22.

79. "Scranton Beaten in Opening Game," *Philadelphia Inquirer,* 11 Apr. 1921: 12.

80. "Scranton Routs Albany and Evens Up Series," *Philadelphia Inquirer,* 13 Apr. 1921: 14.

81. *Reach Official Basketball Guide,* 1921-22, A. J. Reach Co., Philadelphia, 1922, pp. 56-57.

82. "N.Y. Whirlwind Termed Perfect Cage Combination," *Wilkes-Barre Record,* 21 Apr. 1921: 18. "Whirlwinds Beat the Celtics," *Albany Journal,* 18 Apr. 1921: 10.

83. "Scranton to Play Albany Tonight," *Wilkes-Barre Record,* 26 Apr. 1921: 15.

84. "Scranton Defeats Albany before 1,000 Fans," *Wilkes-Barre Record,* 27 Apr. 1921: 17, and "Scranton Wins Championship," *Wilkes-Barre Record,* 28 Apr. 1921: 18.

Chapter 6

1. Bole and Lawrence claim this as "about mid-November" (*From Peach Baskets to Slam Dunks,* p. 67). The *Philadelphia Inquirer* story of 15 Nov. 1921 15 noted that the Harrisburg cage was shipped to New York to use in the 22nd Regiment Armory.

2. Bole and Lawrence, op. cit., p. 70. Also "Celtics Enter Eastern Basket-

ball League by Purchasing New York Franchise," *Philadelphia Inquirer,* 16 Dec. 1921: 19.

3. Bole and Lawrence, op. cit., p. 70.

4. "Celtics Enter Eastern Basketball League by Purchasing New York Franchise," *Philadelphia Inquirer,* 16 Dec. 1921: 19.

5. "Celtics Unable to Stop Trenton's Rush," *Philadelphia Inquirer,* 17 Dec. 1921: 14.

6. S. O. Grauley, "Celtics Get Eastern League Franchise and Many Players are Shifted in New Deal," *Philadelphia Inquirer,* 19 Dec. 1921: 15. In this story, Witte's name is misspelled as Whittey and Pete Barry is called Tom—these mistakes were common in newspapers of the time.

7. *Philadelphia Inquirer,* 28 Dec. 1921: 12.

8. *Philadelphia Inquirer,* 9 Jan. 1922: 14.

9. W. J. Scheffer, "Introductory" in *Reach Official Basketball Guide, 1922-23,* Philadelphia, A. J. Reach Co., 1922, p. 5.

10. S. O. Grauley, "Eastern Basketballers Face Crisis at Meeting to be Held Here Tomorrow," *Philadelphia Inquirer,* 16 Jan. 1922: 15.

11. W. J. Scheffer, "Introductory in *Reach Official Basketball Guide, 1922-23,* A. J. Reach Company, Philadelphia, 1922, p. 6.

12. S. O. Grauley, "Eastern League to Play with Six Clubs," *Philadelphia Inquirer,* 18 Jan. 1922: 16. Also see Grauley's Jan. 16, 1922, article cited earlier as well as Scheffer's "Introductory" in the 1922-23 *Reach Guide,* also cited earlier and chapter 4 of Bole and Lawrence's *From Peachbaskets to Slamdunks.*

13. "Trenton Regulars, Eastern Leaders, Suspended Because of Refusal to Play Celtics," *Philadelphia Inquirer,* 2 Jan. 1922: 9.

14. "Celtics Win from Reading 28 to 21" and "Trenton Beats Coats with Suspended Players," *Philadelphia Inquirer,* 3 Jan. 1922: 17.

15. S. O. Grauley, "Reinstate Potters; Owner Pays Fine," *Philadelphia Inquirer,* 6 Jan. 1922: 16.

16. "With Brown Out, Coats Were Easy," *Philadelphia Inquirer,* 10 Jan. 1922: 14.

17. "Celtics Keep Slate All Clean Defeating Coats," *Philadelphia Inquirer,* 16 Jan. 1922: 14.

18. "Celtics Run Away from Wilkes-Barre," *Philadelphia Inquirer,* 23 Jan. 1922: 13.

19. "Celtics Tame Bears; Then Trim Potters," *Philadelphia Inquirer,* 6 Feb. 1922: 14.

20. For their $20 per game, referees were frequently abused, physically injured by players and, occasionally, threatened with their lives.

21. Bole and Lawrence, op. cit., p. 87.

22. "Camden's Future at Stake This Week," *Philadelphia Inquirer,* 13 Feb. 1922: 13.

23. S. O. Grauley, "Celtics Trim Camden in Extra Period and Take Eastern Lead," *Philadelphia Inquirer,* 16 Feb. 1922: 14.

24. Ibid.

25. "Celtics Win Twice, Camden One Victim," *Philadelphia Inquirer,* 20 Feb. 1922: 12.

26. "Coatesville Downs Celtics," *Philadelphia Inquirer,* 21 Feb. 1922: 14.

27. "New York Celtics Nose Out Atlantic City Caseys," *Philadelphia Inquirer,* 22 Feb. 1922: 15.

28. "Ernie Reich, Celtics Basketball Star, Is Dead," *Philadelphia Inquirer,* 25 Feb. 192: 13.

29. Died—Reich, Ernest B. *New York Times,* 25 Feb. 1922: 13. Death notice—Reich, Ernest B. *New York Times,* 26 Feb. 1922: 26.

30. "The Death of Ernie Reich," *Reach Official Basketball Guide, 1922-23,* A. J. Reach Company, Philadelphia, 1922, pp. 18-19. William J. Scheffer, "Introductory," *Reach Official Basketball Guide, 1922-23,* A. J. Reach Co., Philadephia, pp. 5-7.

31. See *Reach Official Basketball Guide*(s) for leagues' data on Reich each year.

32. Scheffer, "Introductory."

33. "Celts Trim Potters, Take Eastern Lead," *Philadelphia Inquirer,* 27 Feb. 1922: 14.

34. S. O. Grauley, "Camden Half Game Behind Leaders," *Philadelphia Inquirer,* 6 Mar. 1922: 13.

35. "Celtics Take Lead Beating Trenton, 22-16," *Philadelphia Inquirer,* 11 Mar. 1922: 13.

36. Bole and Lawrence, *From Peachbaskets to Slamdunks,* p. 88.

37. "Camden Beaten in 50-Minute Game," *Philadelphia Inquirer,* 13 Mar. 1922: 13.

38. Bole and Lawrence, p. 88.

39. "Skeeters Are Too Fast for Celtics Winning by 26 to 12," *Philadelphia Inquirer,* 16 Mar. 1922: 16.

40. "Camden Rallies and Beats Out Trenton," *Philadelphia Inquirer,* 23 Mar. 1922: 16.

41. S. O. Grauley, "Arrange Dates for Playoff Tonight," *Philadelphia Inquirer,* 27 Mar. 1922: 13.

42. S. O. Grauley, "Potters and Celts in Post Cage Frays," *Philadelphia Inquirer,* 31 Mar. 1922: 19.

43. S. O. Grauley, "Celtics Take First Game from Potters," *Philadelphia Inquirer,* 1 Apr. 1922: 14.

44. Bole and Lawrence, p. 95.

45. Ibid., p. 95.

46. S. O. Grauley, "Celtics Take First Game from Potters," *Philadelphia*

Inquirer, 1 Apr. 1922: 14.

47. Ibid.

48. Ibid.

49. "Eastern League Playoff Series," *Reach Official Basketball Guide 1922-23,* A. J. Reach Company, Philadelphia, 1923, p. 17.

50. "Celtics Grab Final Fray and Cage Title," *Philadelphia Inquirer,* 6 Apr. 1922: 19, and "Eastern League Playoff Series" in *Reach Official Basketball Guide, 1922-23,* p. 9.

51. "Celtics Grab Final Fray and Cage Title."

52. "Eastern League Season, 1921-22," *Reach Official Basketball Guide, 1922-23,* p. 9.

53. Bole and Lawrence, p. 100.

54. *Reach Official Basketball Guide 1922-23,* p. 18.

55. Bole and Lawrence, p. 106.

56. "Haggerty Quits Bears, Schmelk Is Signed," *Philadelphia Inquirer,* 17 Nov. 1922: 23.

57. Ibid.

58. "Camden's Speed Too Much for Resorters," *Philadelphia Inquirer,* 23 Nov. 1922: 18. S. O. Grauley, "Celtics at Shore Will Add Punch to Eastern Cage Race," *Philadelphia Inquirer,* 27 Nov. 1922: 19.

59. Grauley, Ibid.

60. Bole and Lawrence incorrectly claim it was 2 and 4 on pages 111 and 112.

61. "Celtics Stars Sign with Shore Five," *Philadelphia Inquirer,* 29 Nov. 1922: 22.

62. "Atlantic City Stops Camden Five's Rush," *Philadelphia Inquirer,* 2 Dec. 1922: 23.

63. "Coates' Swan Song Becomes a Dirge," *Philadelphia Inquirer,* 5 Dec. 1922: 19.

64. "Tigers Rally, Beat Atlantics and Tie Camden for Lead," *Philadelphia Inquirer,* 6 Dec. 1922: 23.

65. "Atlantic Basketeers Defeat Jasper Five in Extra Period Fray," *Philadelphia Inquirer,* 15 Dec. 1922: 22.

66. "Atlantics Run Away from Coatesville," *Philadelphia Inquirer,* 16 Dec. 1922: 21.

67. Bole and Lawrence, p. 119.

68. S. O. Grauley, "Eastern Cage Fives Must Cut Expenses," *Philadelphia Inquirer,* 18 Dec. 1922: 19.

69. Grauley, Ibid.

70. Bole and Lawrence, p. 121.

71. "Celtics—Jaspers Game Postponed," *Philadelphia Inquirer,* 19 Dec. 1922: 19. "Jaspers Bar Three; Celtics Done at Shore," *Philadelphia Inquirer,*

20 Dec. 1922: 22.

72. Bole and Lawrence, p. 132.

73. The first game was held Nov. 20, 1909, in Reading where Reading defeated the Sixth Regiment Team of Philadelphia, 21-20.

Chapter 7

1. M. Rosenwald, "Original Celtics of New York," *Reach Official Basketball Guide, 1924-25,* A. J. Reach Co., Philadelphia, 1924, p. 167.

2. *Reach Official Basketball Guide, 1924-25,* A. J. Reach Co., Philadelphia, 1924, p. 216.

3. M. Rosenwald, "Original Celtics of New York," *Reach Official Basketball Guide, 1924-25,* A. J. Reach Co., Philadelphia, 1924, p. 168.

4. M. Rosenwald, "Original Celtics," *Reach Official Basketball Guide, 1924-25,* A. J. Reach Co., Philadelphia, 1924, p. 167.

5. M. Rosenwald, "New York Celtics," *The Reach Official Basketball Guide, 1925-26,* A. J. Reach Co., Philadelphia, 1925, p. 151.

6. M. Rosenwald, "New York Celtics," *The Reach Official Basketball Guide, 1925-26,* A. J. Reach Co., Philadelphia, 1925, p. 153.

7. Wm. J. Scheffer, "Review of Basketball in Philadelphia," *Reach Official Basketball Guide, 1926-27,* A. J. Reach Co., Philadelphia, 1926, p. 223.

8. Benny Borgemann file, Naismith Memorial Basketball Hall of Fame.

9. M. Rosenwald, "Original Celtics," *The Reach Official Basketball Guide, 1926-27,* A. J. Reach Co., Philadelphia, 1926, p. 213.

10. M. Rosenwald, "Original Celtics," *The Reach Official Basketball Guide, 1926-27,* A. J. Reach Co., Philadelphia, 1926, p. 215.

11. H. Litwack interview, Cheltenham, PA, July 27, 1995.

12. A. Radel, "South Philadelphia Hebrew Association," *Reach Official Basketball Guide, 1925-26,* A. J. Reach Co., Philadelphia, 1925, p. 191.

13. A. Radel, "South Philadelphia Hebrew Association," *Reach Official Basketball Guide, 1925-26,* A. J. Reach Co., Philadelphia, 1925, p. 193.

14. A. Radel, 1926, p. 221.

15. A. Radel, 1926, p. 221.

16. Lapchick, p. 21.

Chapter 8

1. G. MacKay, "Expect Record Crowd When Celtics and Quakers Clash Tonight at Arena," *Philadelphia Inquirer,* 4 Jan. 1927: 19.

2. G. MacKay, "Expect Record Crowd When Celtics and Quakers Clash Tonight at Arena," *Philadelphia Inquirer,* 4 Jan. 1927: 19.

3. G. MacKay, "Phils Fail to Stop Celtics and Lose Their Sixth American Court League Tilt," *Philadelphia Inquirer,* 16 Dec. 1926: 21.

4. "Famous Celtics Far in Lead in Basketball Race," *Philadelphia Inquirer,*

14 Mar. 1927: 18.

5. G. MacKay, "Phillies Trounce Brooklyn Celtics Before Record Breaking Pro Crowd at Arena," *Philadelphia Inquirer,* 5 Jan. 1927: 16.

6. A. Hollander, and A. Sachare, *The Official NBA Basketball Encyclopedia,* New York City, Villard Books, 1989, p. 19.

7. "Rules of Basketball," *Reach Official Basketball Guide, 1922-23,* A. J. Reach Company, Philadelphia, 1922.

8. G. MacKay, "Warriors Sign Keller, Western Star Who Plays Against Hoosier Foes," *Philadelphia Inquirer,* 7 Feb. 1927: 12.

9. "Cunningham and Ely to Start Against Celtics Tonight," *Cleveland Plain Dealer,* 14 Feb. 1927: 16.

10. "Brooklyn Celtics Defeat Cleveland, 24 to 19, at Hall," *Cleveland Plain Dealer,* 15 Feb. 1927: 20.

11. "Celts Barely Top Hoosier Floormen," *Philadelphia Inquirer,* 17 Feb. 1927: 19.

12. "Phillies Fail to Check Celtics Winning Streak," *Philadelphia Inquirer,* 23 Feb. 1927: 22.

13. Ibid.

14. J. Dietrich, "Holman's Tricks Annoy Cage Fans," *Cleveland Plain Dealer,* 20 Feb. 1927: Sports: 2.

15. J. Dietrich, "Cleveland Cagers Defeat Celtics, 31 to 23, at Hall," *Cleveland Plain Dealer,* 26 Feb. 1927: 19.

16. "Celts Get 2 Field Goals Yet Win 20-18 Over Baltimore," *Philadelphia Inquirer,* 1 Mar. 1927: 22.

17. "Volley of Field Goals by Banks Carries Celtics to Win Over Phillies," *Philadelphia Inquirer,* 2 Mar. 1927: 23.

18. J. Dietrich, "Celtics Are Back Tonight; Will They Play Basketball?" *Cleveland Plain Dealer,* 25 Feb. 1927: 20.

19. "Camden Passers Pull Surprise of Basketball Season by Turning Aside Celtics," *Philadelphia Inquirer,* 13 Mar. 1927: 13.

20. "Double Official System to be used in Cage Playoff," *Cleveland Plain Dealer,* 1 Apr. 1927: 19.

21. J. Dietrich, "Kerr Draws Job of Guarding Dehnert in Cage Series," *Cleveland Plain Dealer,* 2 Apr. 1927: 19.

22. A. Hollander and A. Sachare, *The Official NBA Basketball Encyclopedia,* New York City, Villard Books, 1989, p. 26.

23. "Celtics Win First on Foul Tossing," *Philadelphia Inquirer,* 7 Apr. 1927: 26.

24. "Celts Win Third Game, Take Title," *Philadelphia Inquirer,* 10 Apr. 1927: 21.

25. A. Neft and D. Cohen, *Encyclopedia of Sports-Pro Basketball,* 2nd, New York, St. Martin's Press, 1990, p. 13.

26. A. Neft and D. Cohen, *Encyclopedia of Sports-Pro Basketball,* 2nd, New York, St. Martin's Press, 1990, p. 13.

27. R. D. Bole and A. C. Lawrence, *From Peachbaskets to Slamdunks,* Canaan, B & L Publishers, NH, 1987, p. 189.

28. From 1929 to 1936 the Rens, an all African American squad, were undoubtedly the finest team in basketball. Nat Holman acknowledged this in his 1988 interview with Healy cited earlier. In addition, the Rens are the only other post 1920 team (beside the Celtics) to be elected to basketball's Hall of Fame. From 1927 to 1942, the Rens averaged more than 100 victories a season and lost less than 25 games in each of those years.

Chapter 9

1. "Pro Basketball for Garden; Rickard Takes Over Celtics," *New York Times,* 12 May 1927: 33.

2. It is interesting to note that neither the *Times* nor the *Inquirer* covered this game, nor, in the latter's case even mentioned it. It was also not in the ABL schedule published in the 12 Nov. 1927 *New York Times.* Clearly the leagues publicity machine, was sputtering early on.

3. "Celtics Vanquish Philadelphia Five," *New York Times,* 22 Nov. 1927: 34.

4. "Original Celtics Five to Meet Washington," *New York Times,* 22 Nov. 1927: Sports: 10.

5. "Phils' Rally Fails-Celtics Even Count," *Philadelphia Inquirer,* 22 Nov. 1927: 24.

6. The *Inquirer* said Conaty and Passon fouled out; the *New York Times* added Saunders to that list. See "Celtic Five Conquers Washington 48 to 36," *New York Times,* 28 Nov. 1927: 30, and "Washington Thumped by New York Quintet," *Philadelphia Inquirer,* 28 Nov. 1927: 22.

7. "Celtics Are Beaten in Final Minute," *New York Times,* 30 Nov. 1927: 21. S. O. Grauley, "Glasco's Goal in Last Few Seconds of Play Gives Phils' Win over Celtics," *Philadelphia Inquirer,* 30 Nov. 1927: 25.

8. Grauley, ibid.

9. This explanation would fit with the observation of "Honey" Russell the Hall of Famer who played for the champion Cleveland Rosenblums in 1925-26 and was traded to Chicago in mid year of 1926-27. Russell's son noted that "even though Lapchick was a winning College Coach, my father remained a little rankled by the fact that Lapchick in his opinion, had never been a smart ball player as a member of the Original Celtics," J. Russell, *Honey Russell: Between Games, Between Halves,* Dryad Press, Washington, D.C., 1986, p. 188.

10. "Washington Defeats Celtics 36-30," *New York Times,* 5 Dec. 1927: 31.

11. "Celtic Quintet Wins in Washington, 30-25," *New York Times,* 6 Dec.

1927: 35.

12. Celtics Beat Detroit in League Game 30 to 20," *New York Times,* 8 Dec. 1927: 39.

13. "Celtics Defeat Cleveland 21 to 12," *New York Times,* 9 Dec. 1927: 31.

14. "Phils Finish Western Whirl with Win over Chicago; New York Upsets Cleveland," *Philadelphia Inquirer,* 9 Dec. 1927: 21.

15. "Ft. Wayne Sends Celtics Sprawling," *Philadelphia Inquirer,* 13 Dec. 1927: 22. "Celtics Passes Hand Reverse to Hoosiers," *Philadelphia Inquirer,* 14 Dec. 1927: 22. "Celtics Repulse Ft. Wayne, 33-25," *New York Times,* 14 Dec. 1927: 37.

16. Celtics Only Lead Sends Bruins Down," *Philadelphia Inquirer,* 15 Dec. 1927: 22. "Celtics Again Too Clever for Bruins," *Philadelphia Inquirer,* 16 Dec. 1927: 23.

17. "Celtics Win 25 to 19 from Chicago Quint," *New York Times,* 19 Dec. 1927: 19. "Shamrock Bounce on Chicago Quint," *Philadelphia Inquirer,* 19 Dec. 1927: 24. "Celtics Are Victors over Chicago Five," *New York Times,* 20 Dec. 1927: 24. "Celtics Again Send Chicago Bruins Down," *Philadelphia Inquirer,* 20 Dec. 1927: 22.

18. "Cleveland Swamped by Celtic Quintet," *Philadelphia Inquirer,* 24 Dec. 1927: 22.

19. Baumgartner, Stan, "Celtics Stave off Rally of Cleveland Team and Gain Hard Fought Win," *Philadelphia Inquirer,* 27 Dec. 1927: 19.

20. "Celtics Quint Sends Rochester Tumbling," *Philadelphia Inquirer,* 2 Jan. 1928: 11.

21. "Detroit Quits Cage Loop," *Cleveland Plain Dealer,* 3 Jan. 1928: 21. "Detroit Beats Phils Twice, Quits League," *Philadelphia Inquirer,* 3 Jan. 1928: 22.

22. "Holman Stands Out in Celtics Victory," *Philadelphia Inquirer,* 3 Jan. 1928: 22. "Celtics Defeat Rochester 36-26, *New York Times,* 3 Jan. 1928: 20. "Celtics Lose in Hoboken," *New York Times,* 4 Jan. 1928: 21.

23. "Pro Cagers Still Have Rosy View," *Cleveland Plain Dealer,* 4 Jan. 1928: 20.

24. "Celtics Five Takes Eleventh Straight Win," *Philadelphia Inquirer,* 10 Jan. 1928: 18. "Celts Turn Back Ft. Wayne Five," *New York Times,* 10 Jan. 1928: 21.

25. "Celtics Five Hang Up 12th Straight Win," *Philadelphia Inquirer,* 12 Jan. 1928: 19.

26. "Celtics Cop 13th in Row, Beating Bruins," 13 Jan. 1928: 22.

27. "Celts Win 15th Straight, 47-24," *Cleveland Plain Dealer,* 17 Jan. 1928: 20. "Phillies Fall; Celtics Snare 13th Straight," *Philadelphia Inquirer,* 16 Jan. 1928: 22.

28. See for example: *Wages and Hours of Labor in the Motor Vehicle*

Industry 1925, Bulletin 438, May 1927, or *Wages and Hours of Labor in Foundries and Machine Shops,* Bulletin 471, 1927, both Bureau of Labor GPO, Washington, D.C.

29. "Celtics Stopped, 28-18," *New York Times,* 20 Jan. 1928: 17.

30. S. Baumgartner, "Warriors Defeat Celtics and Bring Long Streak of Fifteen to End," *Philadelphia Inquirer,* 20 Jan. 1928: 21.

31. "Celtics Overcome Philadelphia Five," *New York Times,* 17 Jan. 1928: 25.

32. S. Baumgartner, "Warriors Defeat Celtics . . ." op. cit.

33. "Celtics Defeat Brooklyn San Trouble, 41-23," *Cleveland Plain Dealer,* 23 Jan. 1928: 18.

34. "Visitation Bows to Celtic Passers," *Philadelphia Inquirer,* 23 Jan. 1928: 14. The *New York Times* reported 3,500 attendance, a capacity house. "Celtics Over Power Visitation, 41 to 23," *New York Times,* 23 Jan. 1928: 28.

35. The *New York Times* reported six, the *Inquirer* eight. See "Visitations Half Celtic Five, 28-24," *New York Times,* 24 Jan. 1928: 32, and "Visitation Rallies in Second Half to Vanquish Celtics Five," *Philadelphia Inquirer,* 24 Jan. 1928: 18.

36. "Visitation Rallies . . . ," Ibid.

37. S. Baugmgartner, "Rochester and Warriors in Hot Second Place Tilt at Arena Tonight," *Philadelphia Inquirer,* 31 Jan. 1928: 19.

38. "Celtics-Phils Game Tuesday at Arena," *Philadelphia Inquirer,* 5 Feb. 1928: Sports: 5.

39. "Warriors Make Great Second Half Rally, but Bow before Attack of Shamrocks," *Philadelphia Inquirer,* 8 Feb. 1928: 19.

40. "City College Five Beats Catholic U.," *New York Times,* 12 Feb. 1928: Sports 3.

41. "Celtics Conquer Cleveland Quint," *Philadelphia Inquirer,* 13 Feb. 1928: 16.

42. "Phillies Rally but Bow to Shamrocks," *Philadelphia Inquirer,* 15 Feb. 1928: 24.

43. "Cleveland Edges Celts in Final Seconds, 26 to 25," *Cleveland Plain Dealer,* 24 Feb. 1928: 18.

44. "Cleveland No Match for League Leaders," *Philadelphia Inquirer,* 25 Feb. 1928: 18.

45. S. Otis, "Celtics' Visit Proves Honesty of Pro Game," *Cleveland Plain Dealer,* 25 Feb. 1928: 20.

46. "City College Five Defeats NYU, 29-26," *New York Times,* 26 Feb. 1928: Sports 3.

47. "Rochester Hands Shamrocks Surprise," *Philadelphia Inquirer,* 26 Feb. 1928: Sports 5.

48. "Meat Eating Warriors Will Turn Vegetarians in Fray Here Tuesday

Night," *Philadelphia Inquirer,* 11 Mar. 1928: Sports 5.

49. The *New York Times* said 5,000 and the *Inquirer* said both 6,000 and 7,000 in their story. See "Celtic Five Tames Philadelphia 27-21," *New York Times,* 14 Mar. 1928: 23. "Shamrocks Hand Warriors Setback in First Tussle of Playoff Series," *Philadelphia Inquirer,* 14 Mar. 1928: 21.

50. *New York Times,* Ibid.

51. *Philadelphia Inquirer,* Ibid.

52. Ibid.

53. "Celtics Win and Take Eastern Division Title; Fort Wayne Snatches First in West," *Philadelphia Inquirer,* 15 Mar. 1928: 22.

54. Ibid.

55. "Celtics Beat Hoosiers in First of Series, 30 to 21," *Cleveland Plain Dealer,* 22 Mar. 1928: 23. See also "Celtics Win in First from Ft. Wayne," *Philadelphia Inquirer,* 22 Mar. 1928: 22, and "Celtics Win Opener in Title Series, 30-21," *New York Times,* 22 Mar. 1928: 22.

56. "Ft. Wayne Triumphs Over Celtics to Tie Up Title Court Series," *Philadelphia Inquirer,* 23 Mar. 1928: 22. "Fort Wayne Rallies to Defeat Celtics," *New York Times,* 23 Mar. 1928: 18.

57. "Celtics Win 35-18, from Fort Wayne," *New York Times,* 24 Mar. 1928: 14. "Shamrocks Snatch World's Court Series," *Philadelphia Inquirer,* 24 Mar. 1928: 23.

58. S. Otis, "Professional Basketball," *Cleveland Plain Dealer,* 16 Mar. 1928: 20.

59. J. Dietrich, "Slim Chance for Cleveland Cagers in Battle Tonight," *Cleveland Plain Dealer,* 16 Mar. 1928: 21.

Chapter 10

1. This is important to note because even in the 1930s when the Celtics had been reconstructed by Lapchick, they met the best teams on a regular basis, particularly the New York Renaissance. The Rens were consistently avoided, it should be noted, by the Harlem Globetrotters, another team that claimed a degree of world championship status in the 1930s. For fuller details of this, see Susan Rayl's doctoral dissertation, "The New York Renaissance Professional Black Basketball Team, 1923-1950," Penn State University, 1996.

2. H. Lebovitz, "Teams Better Now, Admit Old Celtics," *Cleveland Plain Dealer,* 1 May 1960: 8-c.

3. N. Holman, letter to Harold Ford, Mar. 11, 1970. Holman file, James Naismith Memorial Basketball Hall of Fame.

4. Ibid.

Chapter 11

1. Neft and Cohen, *Encyclopedia of Pro Basketball,* p. 15.

2. Ibid.

3. J. Lapchick, *50 Years of Basketball,* Englewood Cliffs, NJ, Prentice-Hall, 1968, p. 23. Also see League financial records in the American Basketball League file, James Naismith Memorial Basketball Hall of Fame.

4. J. J. O'Brien letter to W. G. Mokray, Dec. 31, 1960. American Basketball League file, James Naismith Memorial Basketball Hall of Fame.

5. J. Murray, "Celtics Beat Renaissance," *Chicago Defender,* 13 Apr. 1929: Part 1: 9. The *New York Times* had two paragraphs and a box score on the game. "Celtic Five Wins in Pro Title Play," 6 Apr. 1929: 10.

6. D. S. Neft, R. T. Johnson, R. M. Cohen, and J. A. Deutsch, *The Sports Encyclopedia: Pro Basketball,* New York, Grosset & Dunlap, 1975, p. 16.

7. J. Healy, interview with Nat Holman, Sept. 12, 1988. Holman file. Naismith Memorial Basketball Hall of Fame.

8. W. Mokray, *Ronald Encyclopedia of Basketball,* Ronald Press, New York, 1963, p. 2-68.

9. J. Healy, interview.

10. J. Healy, Op. cit., p. 6.

11. S. Goldaper, "Nat Holman Is Dead at 98; Led C.C.N.Y. Champions," *New York Times,* 13 Feb. 1995: B7.

12. Quoted in D. Anderson, "Nat Holman Taught Team Basketball," *New York Times,* 14 Feb. 1995: B9.

13. Lapchick letter in Holman file, Naismith Memorial Basketball Hall of Fame.

14. D. Anderson, "Nat Holman Taught Team Basketball," *New York Times,* 14 Feb. 1995: B9.

15. J. Lapchick, *50 Years of Basketball,* Englewood-Cliffs, NJ, Prentice-Hall, 1968, p. 26.

16. Telephone interview with Norton Rose by the author, Feb. 8, 1996.

17. J. Lapchick, *50 Years of Basketball,* Prentice-Hall, Englewood Cliffs, NJ, 1968, p. 25.

18. R. Lapchick, *Five Minutes to Midnight,* Madison Books, Lanham, MD, 1991, p. 181.

19. S. Padwe, *Basketball's Hall of Fame,* Englewood Cliffs, NJ, Prentice-Hall, 1970, p. 88.

20. J. Lapchick, 1966 Hall of Fame Induction Questionnaire in Lapchick File, Naismith Memorial Basketball Hall of Fame, Springfield, MA.

21. H. Lebovitz, "Teams Better Now, Admit Old Celtics," *Cleveland Plain Dealer,* 1 May 1960: 8-c.

22. J. Lapchick, Op. cit., p xiii.

23. These accounts are drawn from newspaper articles, undated and not identifiable as to exact source, mounted in a scrapbook of articles about Dehnert, originally saved by him and mounted by his son-in-law, Edward Reilly. The scrapbook is the property of Mr. Reilly of Cincinnati and is located there.

24. Les Harrison, telephone interview, Oct. 4, 1994.

25. Charles Ward, "Word to the Wise," *unknown*, Feb. 18, 1941. Dutch Dehnert Scrapbook.

26. Don Lee, "Dehnert Recalls Old Days," Dutch Dehnert Scrapbook, n.d., n.p. Dehnert may have been brought to Reading when Beckman was there in 1916-17 though there is no rcord of his playing in a game at that time. In addition, Reading was never in the Pennsylvania State League, rather the Eastern League.

27. "Trouble ahead for Rens," n.d., n.p. Dehnert Scrapbook,

28. A. Zirin, "Detroit Eagles Thrive on Dehnert's Coaching." Dehnert Scrapbook.

29. R. Murphy, "Bob Tales," Mar. 11, 1942, n.p. Dehnert Scrapbook.

30. "Dehnert, Inventor of Pivot Play New Court Mentor at Loughlin," n.d., n.p. Dehnert Scrapbook.

31. Telephone interview with Hal Lebovitz, Dec. 18, 1995.

32. All these comments come from Ed Reilly, Dehnert's son-in-law. Interview with Ed Reilly, Mar. 14, 1997, Cincinnati, OH.

33. Dutch Dehnert file, James Naismith Memorial Basketball Hall of Fame.

34. Letter from Lawrence F. O'Brien to Henry "Dutch" Dehnert, Dec. 22, 1978.

35. B. Reedy, "Beckman Echoes Opinion of Old Pal That Defense Is Gone in Basketball," *Reading Eagle,* 31 Jan. 1942: 10.

36. (n.i.) Hour, "Basketball in Connecticut-Norwalk, Conn," *Reach Official Basketball Guide 1918,* Philadelphia, A. J. Reach Co., p. 55.

37. N. Holman, letter to Lee Williams, Nov. 3, 1972. Holman file, James Naismith Memorial Basketball Hall of Fame.

38. R. Bole, and A. Lawrence, *From Peachbaskets to Slam Dunks,* Canaan, NH, B&L Publishers, 1987.

39. Beckman file, Naismith Memorial Basketball Hall of Fame, Springfield, MA.

40. E. Beckman, letter to Lee Williams, June 17, 1968. Beckman file. James Naismith Memorial Basketball Hall of Fame.

41. J. Lapchick, Op. cit., p. 20.

42. John Beckman, in *Biographical Dictionary of American Sports-Basketball and Other Indoor Sports*, ed. D. Porter, Greenwood Press, New York, 1989.

43. W. Gammon, "Just between Us Fans . . . ," n.d., n.p. Dutch Dehnert

Scrapbook, Cincinnati, OH.

44. B. Brunning, "Celtics Meet Detroit 5 Here," n.d., n.p. Dutch Dehnert Scrapbook, Cincinnati, OH.

45. Dick Triptow, a player on that team chronicles this and other aspects of the Chicago Gears in R. Triptow, *The Dynasty That Never Was,* Lake Bluff, IL, Author, 1997.

46. "Ernie Reich, Celtics Basketball Star Is Dead," *Philadelphia Inquirer,* 25 Feb. 1922: 13.

47. H. Lebovitz, "Teams Better Now, Admit Old Celtics," *Cleveland Plain Dealer,* 1 May 1960: 8-C.

BIBLIOGRAPHIC SOURCES AND REFERENCES

Allen, F. *Only Yesterday.* New York: Bantam Books, 1931.

"Basketball in Connecticut." *The Reach Official Basketball Guide, 1918-19.* Ed. W. Scheffer. Philadelphia: A. J. Reach Co., 1918.

Basloe, F. *I Grew Up with Basketball.* New York: Greenberg Publishers, 1952.

Berman, J. "Beckman, John." *Biographical Dictionary of American Sports: Basketball and Other Indoor Sports.* Ed. D. Porter. New York: Greenwood Press, 1989.

Bole, R., and A. Lawrence. *From Peachbaskets to Slam Dunks.* Canaan, NH: B & L Publishers, 1987.

Bourdieu, P. "Sport and Social Class." *Social Science Information* 17.6 (1978): 819-40.

Bureau of Labor. *Wages and Hours of Labor in Foundries and Machine Shops.* Bulletin 471, Washington, D.C.: Government Printing Office, 1927.

——. *Wages and Hours of Labor in the Motor Vehicle Industry, 1925.* Bulletin 438, Washington, D.C.: Government Printing Office, 1927.

Carter, P. *The Twenties in America.* Arlington Heights, IL: Harlan Davidson, Inc., 1968.

"Champion Newark. N. J. Turner Quintet." *Reach Official Basketball Guide, 1918-19.* Philadelphia: A. J. Reach Co., 1918.

"Controlling Body for "Pro" Basketball Leagues in East." *Reach Official Basketball Guide, 1920-21.* Philadelphia: A. J. Reach Co., 1921.

Curtis, R. "Ansonia, Connecticut State Champions." *Reach Official Basketball Guide, 1919-20.* Philadelphia: A. J. Reach Co., 1919.

Danzig, A., and P. Brandwein. "Editor's Preface." *Sport's Golden Age.* New York: Harper Bros., 1948.

Durso, J. *Madison Square Garden.* New York: Simon and Shuster, 1979.

"Eastern League Season, 1921-22." *Reach Official Basketball Guide, 1922-23.* Philadelphia: A. J. Reach Co., 1922.

Gallico, P. *Farewell to Sport.* New York: Alfred Knopf, 1938.

Gems, G. *Windy City Wars.* Lanham, MD: Scarecrow Press, 1997.

Harker, R. "Bourdieu-Education and Reproduction." *An Introduction to the Work of Pierre Bourdieu.* Ed. R. Harker, C. Mahar, and C. Wilkes. Basinstroke, Hampshire: Macmillan, 1990.

Hepbron, G., ed. *Spalding Official Basketball Guide for 1912-13.* New York: American Sports Publishing, 1912.

Hollander, Z. *The Modern Encyclopedia of Basketball.* Garden City, NY: Dolphin Books, 1979.

Hollander, Z., and A. Sachare. *The Official NBA Basketball Encyclopedia of Pro Basketball.* New York City: Villard Books, 1989.

Holman, N. *Winning Basketball.* New York: Charles Scribner's Sons, 1932.

Hood, C. *722 Miles, the Building of the Subways and How They Tranformed New York.* Baltimore: Johns Hopkins Press, 1993.

Hubbard, F. *Encyclopedia of North American Railroading.* New York: McGraw Hill, 1981.

Isaacs, N. *All the Moves.* 1975. New York: Harper and Row, 1984.

Kierna, J. "Foreword." *Sport's Golden Age.* Ed. A. Danzig and P. Brandwein. New York: Harper Bros., 1948.

Lapchick, J. *50 Years of Basketball.* Englewood Cliffs, NJ: Prentice-Hall, 1968.

Lapchick, R. *Five Minutes to Midnight.* Lanham, MD: Madison Books, 1991.

Levine, P. *From Ellis Island to Ebbets Field.* New York: Oxford University Press, 1992.

Martin, A. *Railroads Triumphant.* New York: Oxford University Press, 1992.

McCaffrey, L. *Textures of Irish America.* Syracuse: Syracuse University Press, 1992.

Meany, T. "Basketball." *Sports Golden Age.* Ed. A. Danzig and P. Brandwein. New York: Harper Bros., 1948.

"Metropolitan Professional League Season." *Reach Official Basketball Guide, 1923-24.* Philadelphia: A. J. Reach Co., 1923.

Miller, K. "Class, Culture and Immigrant Group Identity in the United States." *Immigration Reconsidered.* Ed. V. Yans-McLaughlin. New York: Oxford University Press, 1990.

Mokray, W. *Ronald Encyclopedia of Basketball.* New York: Ronald Press, 1963.

Murray, J. "Professional Basketball Review for 1921-22." *Reach Official Basketball Guide, 1922-23.* Philadelphia: A. J. Reach Co., 1923.

Neft, D., and R. Cohen. *Encyclopedia of Sports-Pro Basketball.* 2nd ed. New York: St. Martin's Press, 1990.

Neft, D., R. Johnson, R. Cohen, and J. Deutsch. *The Sports Encyclopedia: Pro Basketball.* New York: Grosset & Dunlap, 1975.

Noverr, D., and L. Ziewacz. *The Games They Played.* Chicago: Nelson-Hall, 1983.

O'Connor, R. *German-Americans.* Boston: Little & Brown, 1968.

Official Rules of Basketball. Philadelphia: A. J. Reach Co., 1922-23.

Padwe, S. *Basketball's Hall of Fame.* Englewood Cliffs, NJ: Prentice-Hall, 1970.

"Pennsylvania State League." *Reach Official Basketball Guide, 1921-22.* Philadelphia: A. J. Reach Co., 1921.

Perret, G. *America in the Twenties, a History.* New York: Simon and Shuster, 1982.

Peterson, R. *Cages to Jump Shots, Pro Basketball's Early Years.* New York: Oxford University Press, 1990.

Postal, B., J. Silver, and R. Silver. *Encyclopedia of Jews in Sports.* New York: Bloch Publishing Co., 1965.

Radel, A. "South Philadelphia Hebrew Association." *Reach Official Basketball Guide 1925-26.* Philadelphia: A. J. Reach Co., 1925.

———. "South Philadelphia Hebrew Association." *Reach Official Basketball Guide, 1926-27.* Philadelphia: A. J. Reach Co., 1926.

Rader, B. *American Sports.* 3rd ed. Englewood Cliffs, NJ: Prentice Hall, 1996.

Reach Official Basketball Guides. Philadelphia: A. J. Reach Co., 1926.

Rice, G. "The Golden Panorama." *Sport's Golden Age.* Ed. A. Danzig and P. Brandwein. New York: Harper Bros., 1948.

Riess, S. *City Games, the Evolution of American Urban Society and the Rise of Sports.* Urbana, IL: University of Illinois Press, 1989.

Rosenwaike, I. *Population History of New York City.* Syracuse: Syracuse University Press, 1982.

Rosenwald, M. "New York Celtics." *Reach Official Basketball Guide, 1925-26.* Philadelphia: A. J. Reach Co., 1925.

———. "Original Celtics of New York." *Reach Official Basketball Guide, 1924-25,* Philadelphia: A. J.Reach Co., 1924.

Russell, J. *Honey Russell: Between Games, Between Halves.* Washington, D.C.: Dryad Press, 1986.

Scheffer, W. "Bill Scheffer Says." *Reach Official Basketball Guide, 1924-25.* Philadelphia: A. J. Reach Co., 1924.

———. "Review of Basketball in Philadelphia." *Reach Official Basketball Guide, 1926-27.* Philadelphia: A. J. Reach Co., 1926.

Saylor, R. *The Railroads of Pennsylvania.* University Park, PA: Penn State University Press, 1964.

Silverman, B. *The Jewish Athletes Hall of Fame.* New York: Shapolsky Publishing Co., 1989.

Snowman, D. *America Since 1920.* New York: Harper and Row, 1968.

Stolz, L. "New York State Basketball League." *Reach Official Basketball Guide, 1922-23.* Philadelphia: A. J. Reach Co., 1922.

Stover, J."The Death of Ernie Reich." *Reach Official Basketball Guide, 1922-23.* Philadelphia: A. J. Reach Co., 1922.

———. *Life and Decline of the American Railroad.* New York: Oxford University Press, 1970.

Triptow, R. *The Dynasty That Never Was.* Lake Bluff, IL: self-published, 1997.

Vincent, T. *Mudville's Revenge.* New York: Seaview Books, 1981.

Weller, J. *The New Haven Railroad.* New York: Hastings House, 1969.

Newspaper Articles
Anderson, D. "Nat Holman Taught Team Basketball." *New York Times* 14 Feb. 1995: B9.
"Arrange World Series Games." *Wilkes-Barre Record* 9 Apr. 1921: 22.
"Atlantic Basketeers Defeat Jasper Five in Extra Period Fray." *Philadelphia Inquirer* 15 Dec. 1922: 22.
"Atlantic City Stops Camden Five's Rush." *Philadelphia Inquirer* 2 Dec. 1922: 23.
"Atlantics Run Away from Coatesville." *Philadelphia Inquirer* 16 Dec. 1922: 21.
"Bans Scranton Player for Breaking Agreement." *Wilkes-Barre Record* 25 Jan. 1921: 16.
"Basketball Chatter." *Philadelphia Inquirer* 24 Jan. 1921: 11.
"Basketball Flashes." *Philadelphia Inquirer* 14 Feb. 1921: 14.
Baumgartner, S. "Celtics Stave Off Rally of Cleveland Team and Gain Hard Fought Win." *Philadelphia Inquirer* 27 Dec. 1927: 19.
——. "Rochester and Warriors in Hot Second Place Tilt at Arena Tonight." *Philadelphia Inquirer* 31 Jan. 1928: 19.
——. "Warriors Defeat Celtics and Bring Long Streak of Fifteen to End." *Philadelphia Inquirer* 20 Jan. 1928: 21.
"Brooklyn Celtics Defeat Cleveland, 24 to 19 at Hall." *Cleveland Plain Dealer* 15 Feb. 1927: 20.
"Cage Teams to Play Off Tie." *Philadelphia Inquirer* 24 Jan. 1921: 20.
"Camden Beaten in 50-Minute Game." *Philadelphia Inquirer* 13 Mar. 1922: 13.
"Camden Defeated in Last Minute of Play." *Philadelphia Inquirer* 24 Nov. 1920: 18.
"Camden Fails to Stop Reading Five." *Philadelphia Inquirer* 2 Dec. 1920: 16.
"Camden Passers Pull Surprise of Basketball Season by Turning Aside Celtics." *Philadelphia Inquirer* 13 Mar. 1927: 13.
"Camden Rallies and Beats Out Trenton." *Philadelphia Inquirer* 23 Mar. 1922: 16.
"Camden Rallies at Finish and Wins." *Philadelphia Inquirer* 26 Feb. 1921: 16.
"Camden Runs Away from Reading, 45-28." *Philadelphia Inquirer* 20 Feb. 1921: 21.
"Camden's Future at Stake This Week." *Philadelphia Inquirer* 13 Feb. 1922: 13.
"Camden's Speed Too Much for Resorters." *Philadelphia Inquirer* 23 Nov. 1922: 18.
"Celtic Five Conquers Washington 48 to 36." *New York Times* 28 Nov. 1927: 30.
"Celtic Five Trims Philadelphia 27-21." *Philadelphia Inquirer* 14 Mar. 1928: 23.

"Celtic Five Wins in Pro Title Play." *New York Times* 6 Apr. 1929: 10.

"Celtic Quint Wins in Washington." *New York Times* 6 Dec. 1927: 35.

"Celtics Again Send Chicago Bruins Down." *Philadelphia Inquirer* 20 Dec. 1927: 22.

"Celtics Again Too Clever for Bruins." *Philadelphia Inquirer* 16 Dec. 1927: 23.

"Celtics Are Beaten in Final Minute." *New York Times* 30 Nov. 1927: 21.

"Celtics Are Victors Over Chicago Five." *New York Times* 20 Dec. 1927: 24.

"Celtics Beat Detroit in League Game 30 to 20." *New York Times* 8 Dec. 1927: 39.

"Celtics Beat Hoosiers in First of Series, 30 to 21." *Cleveland Plain Dealer* 22 Mar. 1928: 23.

"Celtics Conquer Cleveland Quint." *Philadelphia Inquirer* 13 Feb. 1928: 16.

"Celtics Cop 13th in Row, Beating Bruins." *Philadelphia Inquirer* 13 Jan. 1928: 22.

"Celtics Defeat Brooklyn Sans Trouble, 41-23." *Cleveland Plain Dealer* 23 Jan. 1928: 18.

"Celtics Defeat Cleveland 21 to 12." *New York Times* 9 Dec. 1927: 31.

"Celtics Defeat Rochester 36-26." *New York Times* 3 Jan. 1928: 20.

"Celtics Enter Eastern Basketball League by Purchasing New York Franchise." *Philadelphia Inquirer* 16 Dec. 1921: 19.

"Celtics Even the Score." *Albany Journal* 21 Apr. 1921: 10.

"Celtics Five Hang Up 12th Straight Win." *Philadelphia Inquirer* 12 Jan. 1928: 19.

"Celtics Five Takes Eleventh Straight Win." *Philadelphia Inquirer* 10 Jan. 1928: 18.

"Celtics Grab Final Fray and Cage Title." *Philadelphia Inquirer* 6 Apr. 1922: 19.

"Celtics-Jaspers Game Postponed." *Philadelphia Inquirer* 19 Dec. 1922: 19.

"Celtics Keep Slate All Clean Defeating Coats." *Philadelphia Inquirer* 16 Jan. 1922: 14.

"Celtics Lose in Hoboken." *New York Times* 4 Jan. 1928: 21.

"Celtics Overcome Philadelphia Five." *New York Times* 17 Jan. 1928: 25.

"Celtics Overload Sends Bruins Down." *Philadelphia Inquirer* 15 Dec. 1927: 22.

"Celtics Overpower Visitation, 41-23." *New York Times* 23 Jan. 1928: 28.

"Celtics Passes Hand Reverse to Hoosiers." *Philadelphia Inquirer* 14 Dec. 1927: 22.

"Celtics-Phils Game Tuesday at Arena." *Philadelphia Inquirer* 5 Feb. 1928: Sports: 5.

"Celtics Repulse Ft. Wayne, 33-25." *New York Times* 14 Dec. 1927: 37.

"Celtics Run Away from Wilkes-Barre." *Philadelphia Inquirer* 23 Jan. 1922: 13.

"Celtics Stage Late Rally." *Philadelphia Inquirer* 29 Mar. 1921: 12.

"Celtics Stars Sign with Shore Five." *Philadelphia Inquirer* 29 Nov. 1922: 22.

"Celtics Stopped, 28-18." *New York Times* 20 Jan. 1928: 17.

"Celtics Take Lead Beating Trenton, 22-16." *Philadelphia Inquirer* 11 Mar. 1922: 13.

"Celtics Trim Bears; Then Trim Potters." *Philadelphia Inquirer* 6 Feb. 1922: 14.

"Celtics Unable to Stop Trenton's Rush." *Philadelphia Inquirer* 17 Dec. 1921: 14.

"Celtics Vanquish Philadelphia Five." *New York Times* 27 Nov. 1927: 34.

"Celtics Win and Take Eastern Division Title; Fort Wayne Snatches First in West." *Philadelphia Inquirer* 15 Mar. 1928: 22.

"Celtics Win First on Foul Tossing." *Philadelphia Inquirer* 7 Apr. 1927: 26.

"Celtics Win from Reading 28 to 21." *Philadelphia Inquirer* 3 Jan. 1922: 17.

"Celtics Win in First from Ft. Wayne." *Philadelphia Inquirer* 22 Mar. 1928: 22.

"Celtics Win Opener in Title Series, 30-21." *New York Times* 22 Mar. 1928: 22.

"Celtics Win 25 to 19 from Chicago Quint." *New York Times* 19 Dec. 1927: 19.

"Celtics Win 35-18, from Fort Wayne." *New York Times* 24 Mar. 1928: 14.

"Celtics Win Twice, Camden One Victim." *Philadelphia Inquirer* 20 Feb. 1922: 12.

"Celts Barely Top Hoosier Floormen." *Philadelphia Inquirer* 23 Feb. 1927: 19.

"Celts Get 2 Field Goals Yet Win 20-18 Over Baltimore." *Philadelphia Inquirer* 1 Mar. 1927: 22.

"Celts Trim Potters, Take Eastern Lead." *Philadelphia Inquirer* 27 Feb. 1922: 14.

"Celts Turn Back Ft. Wayne Five." *New York Times* 10 Jan. 1928: 21.

"Celts Win 15th Straight, 47-24." *Cleveland Plain Dealer* 17 Jan. 1928: 20.

"Celts Win Third Game, Take Title." *Philadelphia Inquirer* 10 Apr. 1927: 21.

"City College Five Beats Catholic U." *New York Times* 12 Feb. 1928: Sec. 10: 3.

"City College Five Defeats NYU." *New York Times* 26 Feb. 1928: Sec. 10: 3.

"City to Have Court Entry." *Harrisburg Patriot* 5 Dec. 1942: 17.

Cleveland Cagers Defeat Celtics, 31 to 23, at Hall." *Cleveland Plain Dealer* 26 Feb. 1927: 19.

"Cleveland Edges Celts in Final Seconds, 26 to 25." *Cleveland Plain Dealer* 24 Feb. 1928: 18.

"Cleveland No Match for League Leaders." *Philadelphia Inquirer* 25 Feb. 1928: 18.

"Cleveland Swamped by Celtic Quintet." *Philadelphia Inquirer* 24 Dec. 1927: 18.

"Coates' Swan Song Becomes a Dirge." *Philadelphia Inquirer* 5 Dec. 1922: 19.

"Coatesville Beaten by Reading 31 to 24." *Philadelphia Inquirer* 11 Dec. 1920: 20.

"Coatesville Downs Celtics." *Philadelphia Inquirer* 21 Feb. 1922: 14.

""Cunningham and Ely to Start Against Celtics Tonight." *Cleveland Plain Dealer* 14 Feb. 1927: 16.

"Detroit Beats Phils Twice, Quits League." *Philadelphia Inquirer* 3 Jan. 1928: 22.

Detroit Quits Cage Loop." *Cleveland Plain Dealer* 3 Jan. 1928: 21.

Dietrich, J. "Celtics Are Back Tonight: Will They Play Basketball?" *Cleveland Plain Dealer* 25 Feb. 1927: 20.

——. "Holman's Tricks Annoy Cage Fans." *Cleveland Plain Dealer* 20 Feb. 1927: Sports: 2

——. "Kerr Draws Job of Guarding Dehnert in Cage Series." *Cleveland Plain Dealer* 2 Apr. 1927: 19.

——. "Slim Chance for Cleveland Cagers in Battle Tonight." *Cleveland Plain Dealer* 16 Mar. 1928: 21.

"Double Official System to Be Used in Cage Playoff." *Cleveland Plain Dealer* 1 Apr. 1927: 19.

"Eastern Basketballers Face Crisis at Meeting to Be Held Here Tomorrow." *Philadelphia Inquirer* 16 Jan. 1922: 15.

"Eastern League Disbands." *Philadelphia Inquirer* 2 Apr. 1921: 12.

"Ernie Reich, Celtics Basketball Star Is Dead." *Philadelphia Inquirer* 25 Feb. 1922: 13.

"Famous Celtics Far in Lead in Basketball Race." *Philadelphia Inquirer* 14 Mar. 1927: 18.

"Fisk Red Tops Lose to Celtic Goal Getters." *Philadelphia Inquirer* 20 Dec. 1920: 15.

"Fort Wayne Rallies to Defeat Celtics." *New York Times* 23 Mar. 1928: 18.

"Ft. Wayne Sends Celtics Sprawling." *Philadelphia Inquirer* 13 Dec. 1927: 22.

"Ft. Wayne Triumphs Over Celtics to Tie Up Title Court Series." *Philadelphia Inquirer* 23 Mar. 1928: 22.

"Germantown Has Easy Time of It." *Philadelphia Inquirer* 2 Feb. 1921: 16.

"Germantown Loses at Trenton 26 to 16." *Philadelphia Inquirer* 2 Apr. 1921: 12.

"Germantown Nosed Out by One Point." *Philadelphia Inquirer* 12 Dec. 1920: 22.

"Germantown Rolls Up 35-18 Score." *Philadelphia Inquirer* 1 Dec. 1920: 24.

"Germantown to Play Trenton State Team." *Philadelphia Inquirer* 30 Mar: 1921: 14.

"Germantown Warned." *Philadelphia Inquirer* 1 Apr. 1921: 20.

"Germantown Wins and Ties Camden." *Philadelphia Inquirer* 9 Feb. 1921: 14.

"Germantown Wins Basketball Title." *Philadelphia Inquirer* 27 Mar. 1921: 21.

"Germantown Wins First of Series." *Philadelphia Inquirer* 25 Mar. 1921: 20.

"Germantown Wins from Phils, 25-15." *Philadelphia Inquirer* 30 Jan. 1921: 21.

"Germantown Wins Rough Battle." *Philadelphia Inquirer* 5 Feb. 1921: 21.

"Germantown Wins Strenuous Game from Reading." *Philadelphia Inquirer* 16 Mar. 1921: 16.

Goldaper, S. "Nat Holman Is Dead at 98; Led C.C.N.Y. Champions." *New York Times* 13 Feb. 1995: B7.

Grauley, S. "Arrange Dates for Playoff Tonight." *Philadelphia Inquirer* 27 Mar. 1922: 13.

——. "Camden Half Game Behind Leader." *Philadelphia Inquirer* 6 Mar. 1922: 13.

——. " Camden Must Beat Trenton This Week to Stay in Eastern League Basketball Race." *Philadelphia Inquirer* 26 Dec. 1920: 16.

——. "Celtics at Shore Will Add Punch to Eastern Cage Race." *Philadelphia Inquirer* 22 Nov. 1922: 19.

——. "Celtics Defeat Brooklyn Sans Trouble, 41-23." *Cleveland Plain-Dealer* 23 Jan. 1928: 18.

——. "Celtics Get Eastern League Franchise and Many Players Are Shifted in New Deal." *Philadelphia Inquirer* 17 Dec. 1921: 14.

——. "Celtics Take First Game from Potters." *Philadelphia Inquirer* 1 Apr. 1922: 14.

——. "Celtics Trim Camden in Extra Period and Take Eastern Lead." *Philadelphia Inquirer* 16 Feb. 1922: 14.

——. "Eastern Basketballers Face Crisis at Meeting to Be Held Here Tomorrow." *Philadelphia Inquirer* 16 Jan. 1922: 15.

——. "Eastern Cage Fives Must Cut Expenses." *Philadelphia Inquirer* 18 Dec. 1922: 19.

——. "Eastern League to Play with Six Clubs." *Philadelphia Inquirer* 18 Jan. 1922: 16.

——. "Eastern Title at Stake This Week." *Philadelphia Inquirer* 3 Jan. 1921: 15.

——. "Germantown Five Looks Formidable." *Philadelphia Inquirer* 17 Jan. 1921: 13.

——. "Germantown May Clash with Albany." *Philadelphia Inquirer* 28 Mar. 1921: 13.

——. "Glasco's Goal in Last Few Seconds of Play Gives Phils Win Over Celtics." *Philadelphia Inquirer* 30 Nov. 1927: 25.

——. "New York and Eastern May Meet." *Philadelphia Inquirer* 7 Mar. 1921: 13.

——. "Potters and Celts in Post Cage Frays." *Philadelphia Inquirer* 31 Mar. 1922: 19.

——. "Reinstate Potters; Owner Pays Fine." *Philadelphia Inquirer* 6 Jan. 1922: 16.

——. "To Decide Tie in Second Half Race." *Philadelphia Inquirer* 10 Jan. 1921: 13.

——. "Trenton Threatens to Walk Off Floor." *Philadelphia Inquirer* 28 Feb.

1921: 13.

——. "Two Teams After Eastern Franchises." *Philadelphia Inquirer* 22 Nov. 1920: 16.

——. "Wilkes-Barre Club Defies Commission." *Philadelphia Inquirer* 29 Nov. 1920: 17.

"Haggerty Quits Bears, Schmeelk Is Signed." *Philadelphia Inquirer* 17 Nov. 1922: 23.

"Holman Stands Out in Celtics Victory." *Philadelphia Inquirer* 3 Jan. 1928: 22.

"Hoover May Head U.S. Owned Railroads." *Washington Times* 10 Mar. 1921: 1.

Hour, (n.i.) "Basketball in Connecticut." *Reach Official Basketball Guide 1918.* Philadelphia: A. J. Reach Co., 1918.

"Jaspers Bar Three; Celtics Done at Shore." *Philadelphia Inquirer* 20 Dec. 1922: 22.

Laney, J. "Why Jews Excel in Basketball." *New York Evening Graphic Magazine* 5 Mar 1927: 1.

"League Orders Reading to Play Tonight." *Philadelphia Inquirer* 14 Mar. 1921: 13.

Lebovitz, H. "Teams Better Now, Admit Old Celtics." *Cleveland Plain Dealer* 1 May 1960. Lapchick file, Naismith Memorial Basketball Hall of Fame, Springfield, MA.

"Local Clubs Will Stick Out Season." *Philadelphia Inquirer* 20 Dec. 1920: 15.

MacKay, G. "Expect Record Crowd When Celtics and Quakers Clash Tonight at Arena." *Philadelphia Inquirer* 4 Jan. 1927: 19.

——. "Phillies Trounce Brooklyn Celtics Before Record Breaking Pro Crowd at Arena." *Philadelphia Inquirer* 5 Jan. 1917: 16.

——. "Phils Fail to Stop Celtics and Lose Their Sixth American Court League Tilt." *Philadelphia Inquirer* 16 Dec. 1926: 21.

——. "Warriors Sign Kellert, Western Star Who Plays Against Hoosier Foes." *Philadelphia Inquirer* 7 Feb. 1927: 12.

McDonaghy, M. "New York State Basketball League." *Reach Official Basketball Guide, 1920-21.* Philadelphia: A. J. Reach Co., 1920.

"Meat Eating Warriors Will Turn Vegetarian in Fray Here Tuesday Night." *Philadelphia Inquirer* 11 Mar. 1928: Sports 5.

"Media Team Makes Germantown Hustle." *Philadelphia Inquirer* 1 Apr. 1921: 20.

"More Basketball Leagues Loom Up." *Philadelphia Inquirer* 21 Feb. 1921: 11.

Murray, J. "Celtics Beat Renaissance." *Chicago Defender* 13 Apr. 1929: Part I: 29.

"Nan-Scranton Game Fizzles." *Wilkes-Barre Record* 23 Mar. 1921: 20.

"National Basketball League Awards Four Franchises." *Philadelphia Inquirer* 3 Mar. 1921: 14.

"New Eastern League Arise from Ashes." *Philadelphia Inquirer* 8 Apr. 1921: 16.

"New York Celtics Nose Out Atlantic City Caseys." *Philadelphia Inquirer* 22 Feb. 1922: 15.

"New York Whirlwinds Termed Perfect Cage Combination." *Wilkes Barre Record* 21 Apr. 1921: 18.

"Newark Reported Out of League." *Philadelphia Inquirer* 20 Nov. 1920: 16.

"Original Celtics Five to Meet Washington." *New York Times* 27 Nov. 1927: Sports: 10.

Otis, S. "Celtics Visit Proves Honesty of Pro Game." *Cleveland Plain Dealer* 25 Feb. 1928: 20.

——. "Professional Basketball." *Cleveland Plain Dealer* 16 Mar. 1928: 20.

"Phillies Fail to Check Celtics Winning Streak." *Philadelphia Inquirer* 23 Feb. 1927: 22.

"Phillies Fall; Celtics Snare 13th Straight." *Philadelphia Inquirer* 16 Jan. 1928: 16.

"Phillies Rally but Bow to Shamrocks." *Philadelphia Inquirer* 15 Feb. 1928: 24.

"Phils Finish Western Whirl with Win Over Chicago; New York Upsets Cleveland." *Philadelphia Inquirer* 9 Dec. 1927: 21.

"Phils Lose Close One, Referee Quits." *Philadelphia Inquirer* 20 Feb. 1921: 21.

"Phils' Rally Fails-Celtics Even Count." *Philadelphia Inquirer* 22 Nov. 1927: 24.

"Pittston Wins First Contest." *Wilkes-Barre Record* 26 Jan. 1921: 19.

"Pittston Wins Pennant in First Half of Race." *Wilkes-Barre Record* 5 Feb. 1921: 22.

"Pro Basketball for Garden; Rickard Takes Over Celtics." *New York Times* 12 May 1927: 33.

"Pro Cagers Still Have Rosy View." *Cleveland Plain Dealer* 4 Jan. 1928: 20.

"Reading Defeats Trenton, 26-12." *Philadelphia Inquirer* 13 Feb. 1921: 19.

"Reading Drops First Game to Germantown." *Wilkes-Barre Record* 25 Mar. 1921: 26.

"Reading Loses to Germantown, 23-15." *Philadelphia Inquirer* 12 Jan. 1921: 16.

Reedy, B. "Beckman Echoes Opinion of Old Pal That Defense Is Gone in Basketball." *Reading* (PA) *Eagle* 31 Jan. 1942.

Reich, Ernest B. "Death Notice." *New York Times* 26 Feb. 1922: 26.

——. "Died." *New York Times* 25 Feb. 1922: 13.

"Rochester Hands Shamrocks Surprise." *Philadelphia Inquirer* 26 Feb. 1928: Sports: 5.

"Scranton and Albany Fives to Fight for Championship." *Wilkes-Barre Record* 16 Apr. 1921: 19.

"Scranton Beaten in Opening Game." *Philadelphia Inquirer* 11 Apr. 1921: 12.

"Scranton Defeats Albany Before 1,000 Fans." *Wilkes-Barre Record* 27 Apr. 1921: 17.

"Scranton Gains First Place." *Wilkes-Barre Record* 8 Feb. 1921: 18.

"Scranton Routs Albany and Evens Up Series." *Philadelphia Inquirer* 13 Apr. 1921: 14.

"Scranton to Play Albany Tonight." *Wilkes-Barre Record* 26 Apr. 1921: 15.

"Scranton Wins Championship." *Wilkes-Barre Record* 28 Apr. 1921: 18.

"Scranton Wins First Battle." *Wilkes-Barre Record* 30 Mar. 1921: 19.

"Scranton Wins 1921 Pennant." *Wilkes-Barre Record* 1 Apr. 1921: 22.

"Shamrocks Bounce On Chicago Quintet." *Philadelphia Inquirer* 19 Dec. 1927: 24.

"Shamrocks Hand Warriors Setback in First Tussle of Playoff Series." *Philadelphia Inquirer* 14 Mar. 1928: 21.

"Shamrocks Snatch World's Court Series." *Philadelphia Inquirer* 24 Mar. 1928: 23.

"Skeeters Are Too Fast for Celtics, Winning by 26 to 12." *Philadelphia Inquirer* 16 Mar. 1922: 16.

Smith, J. "Haggerty and Original Picked into Court Hall of Fame." *Reading (PA) Eagle* 17 Jan. 1960.

"State League Cage Notes." *Wilkes-Barre Record* 29 Jan. 1921: 23.

"State League Cage Notes." *Wilkes-Barre Record* 3 Feb. 1921: 19.

"State League Cage Notes." *Wilkes-Barre Record* 8 Feb. 1921: 18.

"State League Grants Franchise to Trenton." *Wilkes-Barre Record* 7 Mar. 1921: 17.

"State League President Announces New Schedule." *Wilkes-Barre Record* 2 Feb. 1921: 18.

"Tigers Rally, Beat Atlantics and Tie Camden for Lead." *Philadelphia Inquirer* 6 Dec. 1922: 23.

"Trenton Admitted to Pennsylvania State League." *Philadelphia Inquirer* 7 Mar. 1921: 12.

"Trenton Beats Coats with Suspended Players." *Philadelphia Inquirer* 3 Jan. 1922: 17.

"Trenton Checks Germantown Rush." *Philadelphia Inquirer* 12 Feb. 1921: 12.

"Trenton Defeats Pittston." *Wilkes-Barre Record* 12 Mar. 1921: 22.

"Trenton Fined $1,000 and Retains Franchise." *Philadelphia Inquirer* 4 Mar. 1921: 16.

"Trenton Regulars, Eastern Leaders, Suspended Because of Refusal to Pay the Celtics." *Philadelphia Inquirer* 2 Jan. 1922: 9.

"Trenton Wins and Takes First Place." *Philadelphia Inquirer* 11 Dec. 1920: 20.

"Trenton Wins Rough Game from Reading." *Philadelphia Inquirer* 15 Mar. 1921: 16.

"Two Teams after Eastern Franchise." *Philadelphia Inquirer* 22 Nov. 1920: 16.

"Visitation Bows to Celtic Passers." *Philadelphia Inquirer* 23 Jan. 1928: 14.
"Visitation Halt Celtic Five, 28-24." *New York Times* 24 Jan. 1928: 32.
"Visitation Rallies in Second Half to Vanquish Celtics Five." *Philadelphia Inquirer* 24 Jan. 1928: 18.
"Volley of Field Goals by Banks Carries Celtics to Win Over Phillies." *Philadelphia Inquirer* 2 Mar. 1927: 16.
"Warriors Make Great Second Half Rally, but Bow Before Attack of Shamrocks." *Philadelphia Inquirer* 8 Feb. 1928: 19.
"Washington Defeats Celtics 36-30." *New York Times* 5 Dec. 1927: 31.
"Washington Thumped by New York Quintet." *Philadelphia Inquirer* 28 Nov. 1927: 22.
"West Chester Loses Final Cage Contest." *Philadelphia Inquirer* 8 Apr. 1921: 16.
"Whirlwinds Beat the Celtics." *Albany Journal* 18 Apr. 1921: 10.
"Will Get $2,000 for 4 Basketball Games." *Philadelphia Inquirer* 31 Jan. 1921: 11.
"With Brown Out, Coats Were Easy." *Philadelphia Inquirer* 10 Jan. 1922: 14.

Archival and Unpublished Material

Barry, P. Obituary. *New York Times* 30 Aug. 1968: 33.
Beckman, J. Letter to L. Williams, June 17, 1968. Beckman File. James Naismith Memorial Basketball Hall of Fame.
Borgmann, B. file, Naismith Memorial Basketball Hall of Fame, Springfield, MA.
Bradley, H. "Dempsey to Open Basketball Duel by Tossing Sphere." Joe Lapchick Scrapbooks. Richard Lapchick Family, Boston, MA. 1927.
Brunning, B. "Celtics Meet Detroit 5 Here." Dutch Dehnert Scrapbook. Edward Reilly, Cincinnati, OH. (n.d.) n.p.
Dehnert, H. file, Naismith Memorail Basketball Hall of Fame, Springfield, MA.
"Dehnert, Inventor of Pivot Play New Court Mentor." Dutch Dehnert Scrapbook. Edward Reilly, Cincinnati, OH. (n.d.) n.p.
Gammon, W. "Just Between Us Fans." Dutch Dehnert Scrapbook. Edward Reilly, Cincinnati, OH. (n.d.) n.p.
Haggerty, G. Scrapbook, Naismith Memorial Basketball Hall of Fame, Springfield, MA.
Healy, J. "Nat Holman, Player and Coach." Holman File. Naismith Memorial Basketball Hall of Fame, Springfield, MA. (n.d.)
Holman, N. "Basketball 50 Years Ago." Holman File. Naismith Memorial Basketball Hall of Fame, Springfield, MA. 1971. (n.p.)
——. Letter to H. Ford, Mar. 11, 1970. Holman File. Naismith Memorial Basketball Hall of Fame, Springfield, MA.

——. Letter to L. Williams, Nov. 3, 1972. Holman File. James Naismith Memorial Basketball Hall of Fame.

Lapchick, J. Hall of Fame Induction Questionnaire, Lapchick File. James Naismith Memorial Basketball Hall of Fame, Springfield, MA. 1966.

Lee, D. "Dehnert Recalls Old Days." Dutch Dehnert Scrapbook. Edward Reilly, Cincinnati, OH. (n.d.) n.p.

Leonard, L." Joe Lapchick and Davey Banks Are 'Mutt and Jeff' of Professional Basketball." Joe Lapchick Scrapbook. Ricard Lapchick, Boston, MA. (n.d.)

Murphy, R. "Bob Tales." Dutch Dehnert Scrapbook, Edward Reilly, Cincinnati, OH. n.p. Mar. 11, 1942.

O'Brien, J. Letter to W. Mokray, Dec. 31, 1960. American Basketball League File. James Naismith Memorial Basketball Hall of Fame.

——. Letter to D. Dehnert, Dec. 22, 1978. Author's possession.

Rayl, S. "The New York Renaissance Professional Black Basketball Team, 1923-50." Doctoral Dissertation. The Pennsylvania State University. 1996.

Sullivan, E. "Ed Sullivan's Sports Whirl." *New York World.* Joe Lapchcik Scrapbooks. Richard Lapchick Family, Boston, MA. 1926.

"Trouble Ahead for Rens." Dutch Dehnert Scrapbook. Edward Reilly, Cincinnati, OH. n.p. (n.d.)

Ward, C. "Word to the Wise." Feb. 18, 1941. Dutch Dehnert Scrapbook. Edward Reilly, Cincinnati, OH.

Williams, J. Letter to E. Hickok, Nov. 4, 1962. Celtics file. Naismith Memorial Basketball Hall of Fame, Springfield, MA.

Zirin, A. "Detroit Eagles Thrive on Denhert's Coaching." Dutch Dehnert Scrapbook. Edward Reilly, Cincinnati, OH. n.p. (n.d.)

Interviews

Harrison, Les, telephone interview, Oct. 4, 1994.

Lapchick, Richard, telephone interview, Feb. 10, 1995.

Lebovitz, Hal, telephone interview, Dec.18, 1995.

Litwack, Harry, Cheltenham, PA, July 27, 1995.

Povich, Shirley, telephone interview, July 16, 1997.

Reilly, Edward, Cincinnati, OH, Mar. 14, 1997.

Rose, Norton, telephone interview, Feb. 8, 1996.

INDEX